MASTERS OF CORRUPTION

MASTERS OF CORRUPTION

HOW THE FEDERAL BUREAUCRACY
SABOTAGED THE TRUMP PRESIDENCY

BY

MARK MOYAR

Encounter BOOKS

New York • London

First American edition published in 2024 by Encounter Books, an activity of Encounter for Culture and Education, Inc., a nonprofit, tax exempt corporation. Encounter Books website address: www.encounterbooks.com

Manufactured in the United States and printed on acid-free paper. The paper used in this publication meets the minimum requirements of ANSI/NISO Z39.48–1992 (R 1997) (*Permanence of Paper*).

FIRST AMERICAN EDITION

LIBRARY OF CONGRESS CATALOGING-IN-PUBLICATION DATA IS AVAILABLE

Information for this title can be found at the Library of Congress website under the following ISBN 978-1-64177-385-0 and LCCN 2024932975.

Waste: The thoughtless or careless expenditure, mismanagement, or abuse of resources to the detriment (or potential detriment) of the U.S. government.

Fraud: The wrongful or criminal deception intended to result in financial or personal gain.

Abuse: Excessive or improper use of a thing, or to use something in a manner contrary to the natural or legal rules for its use.

Posted on the website of the
USAID Office of Inspector General
April 16, 2018

To:

Senator Charles Grassley
Robin Marcato
Father John Anderson
Pete Marocco
Adam Lovinger
Senator Tom Coburn, RIP
Steven A. Luke, RIP
Thomas Drake
David P. Weber
Robert Wright
Darrell Whitman
John R. Crane
Tim Shindelar
Sheila Walsh
Dr. Julian Kassner
Greg Kendall
Teresa Manning
Andrew Bakaj
Mike Zummer
Jason Amerine
David Schaus
Gary Shapley
Joseph Ziegler

And all the people whose
resistance to corruption
remains hidden

Contents

Author's Introduction

When I joined the Trump administration at the start of 2018, I had no intention of writing a book about my experiences as a political appointee. I had previously written six books, but they were all about the experiences of other people, and I had long since concluded that I, like nearly every other writer in recorded history, was primarily an observer of events rather than a participant. From my prior governmental service, moreover, I had learned that most of what takes place in government is as boring to the general reader as the daily routine of a podiatrist's office. As far as books on the U.S. government were concerned, I knew, the public was most interested in the president and the White House, and my job involved no interaction with President Trump and scarcely more with others in the White House. Once I completed my time as a political appointee, I planned to return to writing history.

I came to write this book by several strange twists of fate. Each one highlighted an area of public concern, and as they were linked together in sequence, they formed a story that revealed much of what is wrong with the federal government today. This story illustrated, in particular, how the career federal bureaucracy was able to thwart the political appointees President Donald Trump sent to drain corruption from the federal swamp. Out of the story have emerged numerous lessons for fighting corruption more effectively in the future.

The first twist involved the government's violation of its own rules for censoring the speech of former government employees. The second concerned bureaucratic resistance to White House policies and to the political appointees who were supposed to implement those policies. Third came governmental corruption in the office that I led. Fourth in line was whistleblower retaliation, which involved violations of due process rights and abuses of the security clearance system, among other crimes. Fifth, the inspectors general, who were supposed to protect whistleblowers, conducted a series of sham investigations that protected only the perpetrators of waste, fraud, and abuse.

The sixth twist of fate was witnessing career bureaucrats override a partial remedying of the whistleblower retaliation by reaching across agencies to perpetrate fresh security clearance abuses. Seventh, security bureaucrats who had punished Trump appointees for fabricated offenses took no action against career staff and Biden appointees for very real offenses. Eighth, reporters who had prepared stories exposing the government's misbehavior were squelched by media executives who cared more about promoting their ideological agendas than exposing governmental corruption. Ninth, in the one demonstration of what is good in the government, a senator and his staff provided critical assistance in rectifying all of the foregoing. Tenth, the government refused to turn over documents concerning my case that it was required by executive order to relinquish, and then used every trick in the legal playbook to delay and deflect my ensuing lawsuit.

Of these issues, the federal government's mistreatment of employees who report corruption ranks among the most concerning in the current era, when the continuous ascent of government spending provides ever more opportunities for waste, fraud, and abuse. In writing this book, I seek to draw attention to the plights of countless other Americans who have been harmed in reprisal for reporting governmental graft. These individuals are typically called whistleblowers, but that label doesn't do them full justice. Terms like "people of conscience" and "truth tellers" are more suitable. Most were not trying to become heroes or celebrities, but thought they were fulfilling the duties outlined in their job descriptions by pointing out corrupt practices. Given the prevalence of the term *whistleblower* in popular culture and congressional legislation, however, it will be used in this book to describe individuals who report corruption.

The successes of a small number of high-profile whistleblowers conceals the reality that most whistleblowers never obtain the justice they are due. As Tom Devine, a leading whistleblower advocate, has written, "The majority of whistleblowers suffer in obscurity, frustrated by burned career bridges and vindication they were never able to obtain." It is my hope that shining a light on the problem will stimulate reforms that will better protect individuals who take the moral and ethical course of action, and encourage people and institutions to support those individuals.

The events described herein also show the need to rein in what critics have called the "administrative state," the conglomeration of federal executive agencies whose bureaucrats frequently usurp the authorities of the chief executive, the legislature, and the judiciary. Bureaucrats who exceed the limits of their authorities are nothing new, even if they are much more numerous and are protected by more complex doctrines and institutional forces than in the past. Since the dawn of human government, bureaucrats have been driven to encroach on the authorities of other government officials and institutions by one of two motives. The first is their belief that they are more enlightened than those officials and institutions. The second is the desire to advance their personal interests or those of their families, tribes, or the bureaucratic class more generally.

Both of these motives proliferated in the heads of career government officials during the Trump era. The presumption of moral and mental superiority was the more pronounced of the two, owing to the contempt most bureaucrats felt for Trump's policies and persona. Naked self-interest would overtake it in the Biden era, because the bureaucratic class counted Biden as a member of the club of the enlightened.

Employees of the administrative state sought to sabotage me and other political appointees in the Trump administration for both of these reasons. My status as a senior Trump appointee in an agency where nearly the entire workforce had voted against Trump in the 2016 election made it easier for my bureaucratic adversaries to gain the cooperation of other bureaucrats. Had

I been an appointee in a Democratic administration, or had I been one of the Trump appointees who showed little desire to implement conservative policies, some of the officials in question might have refrained from participating in the assault on my security clearance, and hence I might have kept my job. I should add, though, that the administrative state frequently torpedoes employees of all ideological stripes who report corruption. In addition, it sometimes finds accomplices among self-serving Republican political appointees, as it did in my case.

The administrative state also succeeded in bringing me down by employing dubious tactics that circumvented the protections afforded to federal employees. Security bureaucrats and lawyers decided they could make up rules and issue legal judgments without regard for the Constitution or the powers it conferred on Congress and the judicial branch. They ran roughshod over the free speech protections of the First Amendment, the search-and-seizure provisions of the Fourth Amendment, the due process clause of the Fifth Amendment, and the confrontation clause of the Sixth Amendment, along with federal whistleblower protection laws and court rulings on publication rights.

The inspector general system is supposed to be the main bulwark against federal corruption and whistleblower retaliation. When I sought help from the inspectors general at the U.S. Agency for International Development and Department of Defense, however, they conducted bogus "investigations" generating no evidence and clearing the government of any wrongdoing. Media reporting subsequently forced the USAID inspector general to reopen the case, but the second investigation proved nearly as atrocious as the first.

I have since learned that great numbers of current and former government employees have experienced similar problems with the inspectors general at their agencies, during both Republican and Democratic administrations. The leaders of an Office of Inspector General are supposed to be vigilant guardians of ethical governance, but they have failed to meet that standard with alarming frequency. Few of the victims of inspector general misconduct have been able to get their stories into the public eye—another reason why I decided to write this book. The fatal flaws of the inspector general system revealed by my case and others need to be corrected, and soon.

I also decided to write this book because I believe Americans don't talk enough to each other about ethics in government. My experiences and research have convinced me that corruption and other unethical behavior are more prevalent in the federal government than most people realize. Plenty of capable and dedicated individuals join the government and perform services that benefit the American people, and they need to be protected from the bad actors. If they are not, they will become demoralized, refrain from reporting criminal activity, and eventually quit, as some of the people touched by this scandal did. Detoxifying the government requires more than administrative actions—it requires an ethical culture, which is especially difficult to engender in a nation where many of the elites adhere to secularism and multiculturalism.

The conversations recounted in this book are based on my recollection unless otherwise indicated. In most cases, I wrote down the content of these conversations shortly after they took place. Owing to the imprecision of the human memory, the words in my notes may differ slightly from those that were spoken, but I am confident that the substance of the conversations has been accurately recorded.

In this book, I have changed or omitted the names of many of the story's participants, to protect their privacy and to spare them from acts of retribution by the people who visited retribution on me. I have used the actual names of certain government officials who were complicit in illegal or unethical acts, for the purpose of informing Americans on matters of public interest, and also for the purpose of deterring skepticism about whether the incredible events described herein really happened. As this story will demonstrate, government officials frequently abuse their power in the belief that they can escape punishment, a belief encouraged by the refusal of numerous inspectors general and other authorities to punish the bureaucrats they are supposed to be overseeing. One of the few ways to combat this culture is to shine light on the perpetrators. The American people and their elected representatives are more likely to demand corrective action if specific culprits have been identified, and government officials are less likely to become culprits if they run a serious risk of public exposure.

The United States, steeped in traditions of self-government and civic participation, expects its citizens to sound the tocsin when they learn the government is violating the public trust. The Constitution safeguards the right to publish criticisms of government officials, even for matters that do not rise to the level of waste, fraud, and abuse. As the U.S. Supreme Court unanimously affirmed in the landmark case *New York Times v. Sullivan* of 1964, the First Amendment protects such speech, so long as the critic does not recklessly disregard the truth. In their ruling, the justices put great weight on what they termed "a profound national commitment to the principle that debate on public issues should be uninhibited, robust, and wide-open, and that it may well include vehement, caustic, and sometimes unpleasantly sharp attacks on government and public officials."

Prologue

On the morning of July 9, 2019, I put on a business suit for the first time in nearly four weeks. I'd been summoned to the Ronald Reagan Building and International Trade Center to answer questions from special investigator Jack Thompson (not his real name), who was investigating the allegation that I had divulged classified information in a book published two years earlier. For eighteen months, I had driven to the Reagan Building every day at 6:30 a.m. and returned home roughly thirteen hours later, but I hadn't been there since the USAID Office of Security had abruptly and unexpectedly suspended my clearance and placed me on administrative leave.

I arrived in the lobby of the Reagan Building shortly before 11 a.m. My federal ID card had been confiscated the day I was placed on administrative leave, so I couldn't pass through the turnstiles separating the agency's headquarters from the rest of the Reagan Building. For this reason, Thompson had arranged for us to meet in a basement office that was just outside the headquarters complex. To reach this office, though, I had to walk past the rear entrance to USAID, the primary orifice where employees entered and exited the headquarters. I dreaded the possibility of running into friends or acquaintances, since there would be no time to explain my mysterious disappearance from work. To my relief, I didn't see anyone I knew. Thompson was waiting for me near the entrance, and after introducing himself he took me to the basement.

The room was small and blank, without windows or artwork, its walls so thin that muffled voices could be heard from the room next door. It possessed none of the gravitas of the interrogation rooms in Hollywood movies where detectives grilled suspects about their relationships with mafia dons or murdered heiresses. It was more like a place where bureaucrats grilled other bureaucrats about their tardiness in making mortgage payments or their protracted viewing of pornography on government-owned computers.

Thompson sat down in a chair behind a cheap white table, and I occupied a chair on the other side. He was a balding, grizzled man at the upper end of middle age who, he told me, had served in the Army prior to working in the USAID Office of Security. He could have passed for an investigator in a military court-martial.

Looking me straight in the eye, Thompson spoke with the relaxed confidence of a man who had been through this type of meeting a thousand times. An unnamed individual at U.S. Special Operations Command, he explained, had alleged that I had published classified information in my book *Oppose Any Foe: The Rise of America's Special Operations Forces*. Thompson was gathering all the relevant information for a report he would hand to his superiors, who would then render judgment.

I had never been the subject of an investigation in my twenty-five-year career. Not since getting called into the high school principal's office for sneaking off campus at lunchtime had I even been subjected to an interrogation on a disciplinary matter. It was the first time I got to see what it was like to face questioning by a person who could ruin my future.

I was not especially nervous at this moment, because I knew in my heart that I hadn't committed the alleged offense. The agency had told me that I could bring a lawyer with me, but I had not done so, as both I and the lawyers whom I had consulted had thought my defense to be unassailable. Nevertheless, the desolation of the white room and the stern demeanor of the investigator were making me uncomfortable. Recent news stories, moreover, had shaken my confidence in the integrity of federal investigators. As part of the FBI's ill-begotten Crossfire Hurricane probe into alleged collusion between Trump and the Russians, the Justice Department had punished George Papadopoulos and Michael Flynn for very minor discrepancies in statements to investigating officials who intentionally deceived them about the questioning. I had no way of knowing whether Thompson would try to trip me up and catch me on some triviality.

In front of Thompson sat a stack of papers. He shuffled through them as he talked. "Your case," he said, "is a civil case, not a criminal case. That is why you didn't need to have an attorney present."

That was good news. If the government was convinced that I had revealed secrets of vital importance to American national security, then presumably it would have launched a criminal investigation on suspicion of unauthorized disclosure of classified information, a felony offense punishable by up to ten years in prison. Apparently they were considering some lesser charge.

Thompson informed me he was looking into an alleged violation of the non-disclosure agreement I had signed when receiving a Top Secret-Sensitive Compartmented Information (TS-SCI) clearance. He showed me a copy of the non-disclosure form with my signature on it. He said that I was under no obligation to answer any of his questions, though if I did not, then I might undermine my own defense. He was not permitted to record our conversation, but would take notes.

"Dr. Moyar," Thompson said, "do you have any questions before we begin?"

"Have you received any evidence from SOCOM or anywhere else to support the allegation of unauthorized disclosure of classified information?" I asked. SOCOM stands for Special Operations Command, the organization from which the allegation had sprung.

"I have not," Thompson replied, turning his eyes upward from his papers. "Frankly, my supervisor and I are mystified."

That revelation gave me additional hope. "I don't know how you can have an infraction without any substantiating evidence," I remarked. "When your office suspended my clearance last month, Tara Debnam told me that the purpose of the investigation was to gather evidence that would show whether the allegation was accurate."

"The lack of evidence is a glaring hole," Thompson acknowledged. He looked at me sympathetically, though there was no way to know whether it was just a ruse to lure me into greater candor. "All I have received is the email exchange between you and the Defense Department's prepublication review office, which you had provided to the USAID leadership when this first surfaced. My supervisor went to the Pentagon to obtain information from that office, but all they would give him was this same email chain."

This information was also encouraging.

"If I really had spilled damaging secrets," I continued, "the Defense Department would have contacted the Justice Department, which would now be prosecuting me for a felony offense. All of the information in the book on sensitive subjects was already known to the public, and the government had made no objection to any content despite receiving it more than a year before publication."

I paused for Thompson to make notes in his yellow notepad. Then I said, "It's difficult to defend against an allegation in any detail when there is no evidence supporting the allegation."

"Yes."

"All I can do is talk in general terms about why I could not have committed an unauthorized disclosure of classified information."

"Then let's start there."

In the preceding weeks, I'd spent scores of hours writing down all the facts of the case and assembling the building blocks of my defense. I began with the strongest foundation stones.

"I wrote the book after I left government, using only information already in the public domain," I recounted. "I'd spent much of my career conducting and reviewing open-source research within the federal government. The First Amendment, I knew, entitles former government employees to cite open-source materials in their publications."

"I know the value of open-source research," Thompson interjected.

I explained that I submitted the manuscript for prepublication review on April 10, 2016, more than a year before the publication date. The Department of Defense guidance stated that prepublication review could take up to sixty working days, but at the end of the sixty working days I had received nothing back, so I sent emails to the prepublication review office requesting prompt completion of the review. The Defense Department repeatedly responded that it was busy with other matters and hadn't completed the review yet. After several more months of back and forth, the head of the office informed me they could not prohibit me from publishing the book before the review was done, but that I could be held liable if I published classified information. Seven months in, I notified the office I would go ahead with publication if the government provided no specific objections.

"Dr. Moyar, you could have kept waiting," Thompson said.

What appeared to be a new skepticism on his part caused my nerves to pulse, but I was prepared for the question. I explained that the non-disclosure I'd signed gave the government only thirty working days to respond to a prepublication review request. The Defense Department, with its "30 to 60" working days, had doubled the time limit, but I had given them their desired sixty working days, then seven months, and ultimately an entire year.

"At one place in the email chain," said Thompson, "you asked if the government thought that its right of prepublication review would expire at some point in time." He smiled as if amused by the temerity.

"Yes, I did. They refused to answer. This official was arguing that the government could take as long as it wanted. By this logic, the government could simply withhold judgment until the day I died. That's not the kind of country we live in."

Thompson nodded. "It does look like you had gone out of your way to give the government time to respond," he said.

I nodded back, and added that the only other realistic options left to me at that point were to sue the government for failing to do its job or proceeding with publication. I opted for the latter, for several reasons. First, I believed I was already entitled to publish the manuscript, because all the material was in the public domain. Second, the government had failed to respond in a reasonable time frame. Third, if government officials truly believed that material in the manuscript would damage national security, they would be obliged to notify me or the publisher promptly, as otherwise they'd be responsible for failing to avert the damage caused by publication.

I added that Leon Panetta, Barack Obama's Secretary of Defense and CIA Director, had faced the same problem two years earlier. He had chosen the same option—sending the manuscript to his publisher and informing the government that he planned to proceed with publication.

"I remember that case," Thompson said. "It is similar."

"Panetta's decision to move forward with publication forced the government to approve his manuscript," I said. "In my case, it didn't cause the government to take any action. I didn't hear back from the Defense Department during the remaining five months leading up to publication, and I didn't hear anything from the government about the book for two years after publication."

"It seems strange that they would leave it alone for two years and then come after you," Thompson remarked.

"Yes," I replied. "It is even stranger that they would provide no supporting evidence to USAID after accusing me of a felony offense. And it doesn't seem like a coincidence that the complaint was sent to USAID on the very same day that another investigation against me began. In my twenty-five-year career, I have never before been the subject of an investigation, and then I become the subject of two investigations on the same day."

"I wasn't aware of a second investigation," Thompson said.

Here was another interesting revelation. Within USAID, two

groups were investigating me, and neither knew what the other was doing.

The other investigation, I explained, had begun with a complaint that someone else at USAID had made against me. A man had shown up at my office on May 21 with orders to replace my hard drive. Having just received a new computer, I had inquired with agency authorities about the taking of the hard drive, and was eventually told by an agency lawyer that I was under investigation by the USAID Office of Employee and Labor Relations, in what seemed to the lawyer to have been an attempt by someone at USAID to retaliate against me.

"Was there anything incriminating on the hard drive, Dr. Moyar?" Thompson asked sternly.

"No."

"Did you attempt to destroy any electronic records upon learning of this investigation?" Thompson asked.

"No."

Thompson paused for a moment, looked down, then looked me squarely in the eye. "Dr. Moyar, why do you think people are making the allegations against you?"

"They are trying to retaliate against me."

"Why are they trying to retaliate against you?"

"Because I held them accountable for misconduct and poor performance."

His face brightened, as if some of the fog had just lifted from the road in front of him. "I'm aware that it is difficult to hold people accountable in the federal government," he said, leaning back in his chair. In his previous jobs, he had reported subordinates for wrongdoing, and some of them had filed complaints against him. He added, with a grin, that he had survived the slings and arrows.

I told him what I had reported about several of my subordinates, one person at a time. When I got to the fourth individual, Thompson commented, "I can see why people might want to retaliate against you."

I noted that several of these individuals had connections at

SOCOM, and I suspected they had used those connections to initiate the complaint of unauthorized disclosure of classified information.

As the meeting ended, Thompson remarked, "Dr. Moyar, I appreciate your cooperativeness and your candor. We often get people who are uncooperative and unpleasant. In writing my report, I will take your cooperation into consideration."

It was a positive note at the end of what had been a generally encouraging interview. I was especially heartened by the knowledge that USAID still had no evidence in support of the accusation. If there were no supporting evidence, then surely I could not be found guilty.

On the drive back home, I called my wife, Kelli, the love of my life. I told her about the absence of supporting evidence. The nightmare of the past month, it appeared, would soon be over, and I could go back to work.

It was the first of many overestimations of the government's rationality and integrity in handling my case.

Chapter 1

Foundations

My earliest memory of politics was the U.S. presidential election of 1980. At my elementary school in Shaker Heights, Ohio, a mock election enabled aspiring citizens to practice the art of vote casting, and I eagerly cast mine for Jimmy Carter. When the results of the student voting were announced over the classroom loudspeaker, I was delighted to learn that Jimmy Carter had won in a landslide. He was followed in a distant second by John B. Anderson. In third place was someone whose name I had never heard before, Ronald Reagan.

My friends and I were stunned when we heard the outcome of the real election. Reagan won forty-four of fifty states, including our own state of Ohio, along with nearly 51 percent of the popular vote to Carter's 41 percent. Who, we wondered, were all these people voting for Ronald Reagan?

The Shaker Heights of my boyhood was populated mainly by highly educated liberals who commuted to the city of Cleveland. The routes from Shaker Heights to downtown Cleveland were lined with neglected houses, abandoned businesses, burned-out storefronts, and flashing police lights, which was why in my youth I embraced the view of so many in Shaker Heights that the government needed to spend more on programs to fight poverty. At least some of the adults of Shaker Heights knew then what I did not yet know, that the government had already spent massive sums on welfare, housing, education, and health in

Cleveland and other blighted cities. Presumably they believed that the spending hadn't been large enough, since they continued to vote for liberal Democrats like Jimmy Carter who wanted to spend even more.

Few, if any, residents of Shaker Heights had read the serious right-wing criticisms of the anti-poverty spending boom. Scholars like Thomas Sowell, Charles Murray, and Glenn Loury were explaining how liberal programs had inadvertently perpetuated poverty and crime by discouraging work and marriage. Ronald Reagan would soon use their ideas in shaping government policy. But neither the publications read by people in Shaker Heights, such as the *New York Times* and *Newsweek*, nor the handful of television channels available at the time paid attention to the likes of Sowell, Murray, and Loury.

I won't bore you with the details of my upbringing, except for a few parts that have relevance to the political upheaval and corruption to come. My views on politics and morality began moving from left to right during the summer before my junior year in high school as a result of reading the novels of Fyodor Dostoyevsky. I was fascinated by the struggles of Dostoyevsky's protagonists against the evil within themselves and the paramount role of God in those struggles. His depiction of the malign influences of abstract and atheistic reasoning chillingly foreshadowed the murderous regimes of twentieth-century communism and fascism, as well as the less violent nanny states of the twenty-first century.

Although I had learned Christian teachings in Sunday school, it wasn't until reading the great Russian's novels that I fully appreciated the perils of ignoring the evil in our own hearts and putting man before God. Nor had I fathomed how faith in God helped men strive for the good and love one another, whereas denial of God led men to yield to their darkest impulses. Evil had convinced political leaders that their greatness allowed them to take the place of God, wielding unconstrained authority to achieve heaven on earth—a delusion that had repeatedly led to tyranny and wanton violence. Countries that had provided lasting freedom and security to their people, including the United States, had recognized man's sinful nature and constrained government to limit the damage that fallible government officials could inflict. To fortify government leaders as well as private citizens in their struggles against evil, they had marshaled the powers of religion and nationalism.

Out of these contemplations emerged another truth I had only dimly understood from daily existence—that individuals are not helpless victims of circumstance, in perpetual need of assistance from the state, but instead are beings of free will who have considerable control over their own fates. A person's environment did impose constraints, but even in environments grimmer than any in twentieth-century America individuals could be found who triumphed by choosing love and morality and industry, as well as individuals who met disaster by pursuing selfishness and nihilism and sloth. If humans possessed this freedom, then they could also be held responsible for their actions—a truth that had always been central to the objections of the political Right to the collectivism and statism of the Left.

My conversion to conservatism was largely complete by the time I arrived at Harvard as a freshman in the fall of 1989. A sizable minority of my undergraduate peers held conservative political views, and a smaller minority was brave enough—or foolhardy enough, depending on whom you asked—to express these views openly. I became a part of the latter group, joining the Harvard Republican Club and writing regularly in the *Harvard Salient*, a conservative student newspaper. Our group generally respected political and cultural traditions and thus didn't qualify as a band of rebels as far as the general society was concerned, but our contempt for Harvard's conventional wisdom gave us an aura of rebellion. It took a rebel's independent thinking, suspicion of authority, and high risk tolerance to flout the opinions of the professors and graduate students who issued grades.

Students on the Right came under attack whenever we ventured our opinions on political controversies. It was annoying and sometimes dispiriting, but it also gave us a crucial advantage.

To protect ourselves from abject humiliation, we learned to anticipate the ambushes, and to strengthen our arguments accordingly. Students on the Left, by contrast, did not face comparable aggression, and thus were less inclined to refine their thinking.

Showing your political colors was especially perilous for those interested in careers in academia or journalism, for it was well known that the major institutions in these fields avoided hiring conservatives. America's conservative colleges and media outlets of the early 1990s lacked the influence and resources they would possess in later times, and thus Harvard students didn't even think of them as possible career destinations. Most of us looked forward to spending our careers in fields like business or law or medicine, where our opportunities would not be circumscribed by imperious intellectuals of the Left. Some had political aspirations, but the general consensus held that it was best to make money first and then run for Congress or become a political appointee.

Prior to my arrival at Harvard, multiculturalism had wiped away all requirements for students to take courses on American history and Western Civilization. Secularism had chased God and religion from the curriculum with such thoroughness that a visitor from another planet would never have guessed that Harvard had been an institution of Christian learning for the greater part of its existence. Students still had to take "core" courses in history and philosophy, but they could meet these requirements with classes on niche topics, leaving the students without a common body of knowledge to inform discussions or engender solidarity. In the absence of knowledge about the United States, its European roots, or Christianity, students could form whatever opinions about those subjects suited their prejudices.

In the course of writing this book, I tried locating the Harvard course catalog from the period of my attendance, but the online holdings of the Harvard registrar did not go back that far. I then turned to the most recent course catalog to see what was on offer. The niche courses that satisfied the core requirements were even narrower and more political than in my time. Among them were Black Radicalism, East Asian Cinema, Ethics of Climate Change, American Food: A Global History, Global Feminisms, Race in a Polarized America, Gender and Science, and How to Build a Habitable Planet.

Fortunately for my generation of Harvard undergraduates, the Harvard course catalog of thirty years ago contained a much greater number of broad courses than the catalog of today. The senior faculty was at that time was comprised of scholars of the Silent Generation, a group whose respect for community, tradition, and hard work set them apart from the self-absorbed generation that came next, the Baby Boom. They had a greater interest than the Boomers in the general education of the undergraduate student body, along with a greater tolerance for political ideas that differed from their own.

My favorite core course was Moral Reasoning 13, Realism and Moralism, which was taught by Harvey Mansfield. One of only a few Harvard professors who openly admitted to conservative political beliefs, Mansfield was by far the campus's most outspoken right winger. By this time, three decades into his six-decade career, he had already stamped his influence on thousands of Harvard students.

As the instructor for Realism and Moralism, and also as faculty adviser of the *Harvard Salient*, Mansfield brandished Aristotle in forceful rebuttals of the Left's prevailing moral code. When questions of traditional morality arose—such as whether it was moral to steal or commit adultery—leftist professors and students pronounced that such offenses were not necessarily immoral, because morality was relative and it was usually manipulated by the powerful to their own benefit. What society considered moral merely reflected the prejudices of wealthy white males, who stood to lose more from those alleged crimes than did impoverished racial minorities or unhappy feminist wives. When, however, it came to moral issues of real concern to these same individuals—for instance, whether employers could discriminate based on sexual orientation, or whether women could have abortions—moral relativism went out the window and moral absolutism reigned supreme.

To employ both moral relativism and moral absolutism in this manner, Mansfield observed, was irrational as well as hypocritical. Relativism deprived morality of authority, while absolutism deprived morality of reason. Aristotle had produced an alternative moral framework that avoided these pitfalls, Mansfield explained. Right and wrong existed in an absolute sense, but what was right and wrong in a given situation depended on context and thus had to be identified through reason, not through reference to simple formulas. It was the same type of reasoning Christians would subsequently use to fulfill Christ's injunction to treat others as they would wish to be treated. I would return to this moral framework again and again in decades to come, when confronting moral decisions more momentous than those facing a college student.

During my senior year, a number of professors and graduate students encouraged me to apply to Ph.D. programs in history. By that time, however, it was clear not only that my conservative political views would hurt my job prospects in academia, but also that a career in a history department dominated by leftists would be less than pleasant. I decided, instead, to pursue a career in business.

I went to work in management consulting, one of the most popular fields for newly minted Ivy League graduates. Had I gone on to business school and then continued with consulting, investment banking, or the like, I could have amassed a small fortune and retired by forty, as a number of my college peers would do. Yet I found corporate work tedious and unfulfilling, and began to question whether I could stomach it every day for another fifteen or twenty years. (At the time, age forty seemed not only far away, but also really old.) In addition, as someone more moderate on economics than on politics and culture, I was put off by the excesses of some of the corporate elites, such as their zeal for shifting jobs from the United States to low-wage countries and their willingness to use anti-competitive practices to crush small businesses. I was soon contemplating an early exit from this career path.

At the end of 1997, I published my first book, which had been built upon my undergraduate thesis on counterinsurgency during the Vietnam War. The positive reception the book received from Vietnam veterans led me to seek a contract for a book on the broad history of the war, which I obtained several months later. Here was an opportunity to change how Americans thought about the most momentous event in recent American history, to show that while American politicians had made terrible mistakes, the war had not been the criminal enterprise depicted by the Left, but instead had been, as Ronald Reagan had once put it, a noble cause. As I would often tell people in explaining why I dedicated so many years of my life to studying the Vietnam War, a nation cannot maintain its moral vitality if its history shows its people to be scoundrels and villains.

At the dawn of the new millennium, I traveled to England with Kelli and our two-year-old daughter so that I could begin work on a Ph.D. at Cambridge University. An academic career would give me time to produce histories of the Vietnam War and other seminal events. It could also lead to a job at a top research university. Although these universities were short on conservative professors, they at least had a few, like Harvey Mansfield, and they might be open to hiring me as a token conservative to show they had a modicum of respect for the diversity they were always touting. If that didn't work out, a doctoral degree would enable me to work at the colleges and universities run by the U.S. military, which generally hired professors without subjecting them to ideological filtration.

I completed my Ph.D. in the middle of 2003. The Bush School of Government and Public Service at Texas A&M University then offered me a year-long postdoctoral fellowship. It came as a pleasant surprise that at least one major university was willing to offer me a foot in the door. And where better than a school named after a conservative president? We headed to Texas.

Chapter 2

Crumbling Towers of Ivory

Future generations seeking to understand the rise of Donald Trump will first have to understand the ideological climate at America's elite institutions in the early twenty-first century. It was during this period that the stoics of the Silent Generation retired and handed the keys over to the activists of the Baby Boom Generation. The Boomers, in their evolution from college students denouncing the American "system" to high-salaried elites controlling that same system, had become more refined and subtle in their conduct, but they had not lost their supreme confidence in their own goodness and intelligence.

As Yale deans and *New York Times* editors, the Boomers exhibited pretensions to omniscience no different from those of the Boomer students chronicled four decades earlier by professors like the University of Michigan's Stephen J. Tonsor. "Every professor has in the past several years encountered, in what he thought a rather sober discussion of an academic question a sudden denunciation by a student member of his audience," Tonsor had written in 1969. "The student does not challenge the professor's method or even question his data but simply rejects his position as immoral, as fascist or racist or as simply irrelevant. There is no debate or discussion, no attempt to identify the question or purposefully expose the issue. It is assumed that absolute right prevails on one side and that moral obtuseness, Marxian false consciousness, or plain wrong-doing characterizes the other side."

At universities, media conglomerates, tech giants, and other repositories of elite culture, the Boomers of the early twenty-first century hurled their time-tested epithets at dissenters and used the smears as pretexts for depriving them of employment. Opponents of illegal immigration and sanctuary cities were racists and fascists. Opponents of high taxes and lifetime welfare were racists and exploiters. Proponents of traditional definitions of marriage and gender were hate-filled homophobes. Americans who favored using the U.S. military to protect American national interests abroad constituted fascists and militarists.

During my first months at the Bush School of Government, I often joined my new colleagues for brown-bag lunch gatherings in the faculty lounge. They made no attempt to disguise their political opinions during these discussions, since they assumed I was a person of the Left like all the other academics they knew. The large majority of them, it turned out, did not care for George H. W. Bush, or for any other Republicans. They ranged from liberal to left on the spectrum, though none were open admirers of Stalin or Mao—those people were more likely to be found in departments of sociology, history, or English.

Some professors vented frustrations over the school's affiliation with the nation's 41st president. It gave the impression, they complained, that the institution was conservative. This misperception was said to be especially damaging when it penetrated the minds of the professors at other universities whose votes determined the school's all-important *U.S. News & World Report* ranking. The Bush name had the further disadvantage, in the opinions of the professors, of attracting conservative students.

After I had been at the Bush School for a few months, several of the professors learned that I held conservative political views. They had unearthed this dark fact from my first book, which I'd written at a time when I hadn't expected to pursue an academic career and hence had unhesitatingly expressed support for conservative interpretations of the Vietnam War. As I would soon learn, the discoverers concluded that hiring me would show their academic peers that the school named after a Bush was indeed a hotbed of the dreaded Right. And they worried that a conservative professor and his dangerous ideas would attract a following among moderate and conservative students.

When the Bush School conducted a search for a tenure-track historian in early 2004, I became one of three finalists. The faculty had been asked to rank the finalists, which normally would have meant ranking them first, second, and third. Three of the Bush School's professors, however, declared that I was an "unacceptable candidate." Their votes ensured that I would not receive the position.

I was later told that the three professors had justified their blackballing of me by claiming that I was "overtly political." I'd been quiet on political subjects since arriving at Texas A&M, so I never figured out how they had come to that conclusion. Perhaps they had dredged up articles I had written for the *Harvard Salient* a decade earlier. In any case, expressing political views was not a disqualifier in academia for most people, because most academics professed the opinions of the Left. Only when political expression diverged from that orthodoxy did it demonstrate an unacceptable bias.

This double standard had very recently reared its head with the rise of the Historians Against the War. During my time at Texas A&M, more than 2,600 academic historians signed onto this group's public mission statement, which was "overtly political" by any definition. "We oppose the expansion of United States empire and the doctrine of pre-emptive war that have led to the occupation of Iraq," declared the Historians Against the War in their mission statement. "We deplore the secrecy, deception, and distortion of history involved in the administration's conduct of a war that violates international law, intensifies attacks on civil liberties, and reaches toward domination of the Middle East and its resources." None of those historians suffered any adverse career consequences for their political activism.

My job prospects weren't helped by the fact that I was a white male or that I studied military history—those attributes were also listed as undesirables in the unofficial academic hiring guide. But neither one was as undesirable as ideological non-conformity. Colleges and universities were still hiring white males, military historians, and even white male military historians, so long as they espoused the politics of the Left. A white male historian of the Vietnam War could obtain an Ivy League professorship by writing about the stupidity of Americans who wanted to save Vietnam from Communism, the heroic resistance of Ho Chi Minh to American neo-imperialism, or the toxic masculinity of American soldiers. The only attribute that consistently disqualified the seemingly well-qualified was conservatism. (For an illustrative example, compare Fredrik Logevall's book *Choosing War*, which led to tenured professorships at Cornell and Harvard, with my book on the same subject matter, *Triumph Forsaken*.)

Over the next few years, I would apply for over two hundred academic professorships. My academic degrees, publications, and recommendation letters, when measured against official standards, should have caused the interviews to gush from the academic job spigot. But instead there came only a trickle. As had occurred at the Bush School, the faculty who scrutinized my application looked for signs of ideological predisposition, and found it in my written works. At a handful of the universities that did interview me, I advanced to the final round of interviewing on campus, owing to the inclusion of a few open-minded people on the search committee, but when it came time for a department-wide vote, the forces of the Left invariably congealed to vote in someone else. Of the more than two hundred civilian institutions where I applied, only one extended a job offer, and it did so only after three other people had turned it down because of the low salary and high teaching load.

At Texas Tech University, for instance, I reached the final round with the support of one of the few Vietnam veterans who taught in an academic history department. Like Texas A&M,

Texas Tech was sometimes labeled a "conservative" university, but its history department was packed with liberals and leftists like the rest. Advice on how to torpedo me evidently traveled from Texas A&M to Texas Tech, for fifteen of the department's twenty faculty sank my candidacy by declaring me "unacceptable." In an email exchange that later surfaced through the Texas Open Records Act, one history professor informed another that "[Moyar] has been given the litmus test" and he "very clearly has failed." The second professor replied, "It seems to me that you are correct in your analysis."

At Duke University, where my name did not even make it onto the preliminary interview list, controversy over the history department's hiring practices erupted during the search thanks to the campus's conservative newspaper. The paper's enterprising students had published voter registration statistics showing that Democrats outnumbered Republicans 32 to 0 in the Duke history department. Duke administrators and faculty responded to the revelation by claiming that their hiring wasn't biased—there was just a lack of qualified conservative applicants. Professor Robert Brandon declared, "We try to hire the best, smartest people available. If, as John Stuart Mill said, stupid people are generally conservative, then there are lots of conservatives we will never hire."

The history department chair, John Thompson, tried to explain away the 32–0 disparity by saying that "the interesting thing about the United States is that the political spectrum is very narrow" in comparison with places like Canada. Therefore, political affiliation in the United States "becomes relatively trivial." In other words, America's liberals really weren't very different from its conservatives, and thus couldn't possibly hold their views against them.

Only one Duke professor, Michael Munger of the political science department, challenged the party line. According to Munger, Duke faculty sneered in private that "asking history to hire a conservative is exactly like asking biology to hire a Creationist."

Perhaps the most telling, and certainly the most momentous, act of ideological discrimination took place at the University of

Iowa. According to public voter records, the University of Iowa history department had 27 registered Democrats and 0 registered Republicans when I applied. The University of Iowa happened to be one of the first American universities to amend its non-discrimination statement to include the categories of "associational preference" and "creed." In its hiring manual, the university stipulated that search committees had to "assess ways the applicants will bring rich experiences and diverse backgrounds and ideology to the university community."

Discrimination based on associational preference and creed was painfully obvious at the University of Iowa. A recent Associated Press article about the university had stated, "Some conservative students said they cloak their political leanings to appeal to professors. . . . Conservatives say the abundance of Democratic professors affects course offerings, reading selections and class discussions, shaping impressionable minds. . . . Some conservative students complain their political views are not just absent, but criticized when professors show political cartoons mocking President Bush or allow Republican bashing."

By the time I received the University of Iowa's rejection letter, I had become so appalled by the political corruption of academia that I explored the possibility of suing the university for violating its own non-discrimination statement. But when I spoke with legal experts, they warned me that a lawsuit would be a long and time-consuming process, and the university might be able to wiggle its way out through protracted litigation and dishonest excuse-making. I decided to forgo the legal route.

My case did, however, spark the interest of another conservative academic who had been shunned by the University of Iowa, Teresa Manning (Wagner). She sued the university in January 2009 for ideological discrimination. Sure enough, the university denied wrongdoing, fabricated excuses for rejecting her application, and dragged the court proceedings out for years. Wagner's lawsuit went through a mistrial and several appeals, the last of them in 2018. Although she had plenty of compelling evidence in her favor, she didn't get a penny out of the university.

In the interest of promoting change, I wrote several articles about the politicization of academic hiring. Although most conservative Americans found the politicization of higher education objectionable, few considered it a major issue at the time, evidently believing that the poisonous effects of faculty radicalization would remain confined to the campus. They would have cause to regret their indifference in the years ahead, when the doctrines of the academic Left took hold far beyond faculty clubs and student social justice centers.

Another group that should have cared more than it did was the faculty of the moderate Left. Although some liberal professors did not share the obsession of their radical colleagues with excluding different viewpoints, very few of them would lift a finger to help conservatives get faculty appointments. They were paralyzed by disdain for conservatives, fear of retribution by the totalitarians of the far Left, or both. They would later rue their inaction in the face of radical intolerance, when that intolerance was redirected toward them. "Until the conservatives were gone," one liberal academic told Megan McArdle of the *Washington Post* in 2021, "I hadn't realized how much they were serving as our human shields."

By 2016, the intolerance of the Baby Boomers had killed the spirit of reasoned debate that had once animated American higher education and politics. It had driven talented conservatives out of the institutions where they could have become the next Harvey Mansfields and Thomas Sowells and Henry Kissingers, deep thinkers who could inform and inspire politicians along with the general public. By embedding close-mindedness and condescension in the nation's most influential academic and media institutions, the Boomers had chiseled resentments into the hearts of moderates and conservatives and encouraged the political Right to counterattack with the same types of close-mindedness and condescension. Through their belittling of patriotism and religion, their obsessions with race and gender, and their open embrace of illegal immigration, the Boomer elite had driven the white middle and working classes into a corner, the corner where Donald Trump was to find and mobilize them.

Chapter 3

The Military

In the spring of 2004, I landed a professorship in the one segment of American academia where conservatives were still accepted, the military segment. Hired by the U.S. Marine Corps University in Quantico, Virginia, I began teaching its student body of mid-career national security professionals that summer. The institution's faculty was politically diverse, with a balanced mixture of conservatives and liberals, an island of open inquiry in the sea of politicized academia.

The Marine Corps University opened my eyes to the many virtues of the Marine Corps. Whereas other armed services emphasized cash bonuses or college tuition in their pitches to potential recruits, the Marines focused on battle, weapons, and self-less sacrifice. Hence they attracted individuals who liked to toil and fight, and who were not especially preoccupied with their own safety or interests. They were precisely the type of people required to vanquish fanatical Japanese foes on Pacific islands or cunning Taliban guerrillas in Afghanistan. The Marines' indomitability and directness suited them, in addition, for confronting paper-pushing staff officers and bureaucrats who let personal or bureaucratic interests interfere with the larger cause, a virtue I would not fully appreciate until much later. The Marine Corps didn't have as many toxic leaders as other services, even if it had enough to cause trouble and drive some service members out of the military.

The Marines also gave me a new appreciation for the power of positive thinking. Prior to my time at Quantico, I'd had a penchant for negativity—about immediate events, people, and sometimes even life itself. You can easily get away with being angry or sullen when you're a college student or a junior employee in a commercial enterprise. The same is not true when you're a Marine whose responsibilities determine whether people live or die. The Marines didn't let difficulties or setbacks get them down, but instead approached even the most daunting tasks with a confidence that they would prevail by dint of skill, resolve, and solidarity. The Marine students applied that same attitude when living in the comfort of the United States, and I learned to follow their example. Positive thinking gave me a sense of inner peace and contentment that had previously been unknown, and added a thick layer to the mental armor that is needed to protect the soul from trauma.

The Marines taught me about the many facets of leadership that my education at Harvard and Cambridge hadn't covered. From students who had just returned from combat tours in Iraq and Afghanistan, I learned about the nuts and bolts of tactical leadership, as well as the importance of ethical leadership. Of particular significance to later events, I came to understand that Marine officers bore responsibility for the conduct of their troops, no matter where or when. One could question whether it was fair to punish a lieutenant after one of his privates neglected to salute another officer—that private, after all, bore responsibility for his own behavior. Yet there was no question that this culture of accountability ensured that Marines misbehaved less often than college students or corporate administrators or government bureaucrats. In 2007, with the protracted wars of Iraq and Afghanistan continuing to maim and kill, I set aside work on my multivolume Vietnam War history to write a book on leadership in counterinsurgency.

I might have remained at Quantico for the rest of my career had it not been for the chance intervention of a corruption scandal. Beginning in 2007, I held the Kim T. Adamson Chair of

Insurgency and Terrorism, whose endowment had been placed in a certificate of deposit at the venerable Stanford Financial Group. On February 17, 2009, federal authorities raided the Stanford Financial Group's offices and seized its assets, based on information showing that the firm's chief executive had been inflating investor returns in a pyramid scheme. The funds for the Adamson Chair, along with everything else on the firm's books, were frozen while a receivership began the protracted process of sorting out what money was left and who owned it. Bereft of funds, the Adamson Chair could no longer be filled. I had to find a new job.

I left Quantico in 2010 to join a defense startup that was doing exciting counterinsurgency work for the U.S. military in Afghanistan and elsewhere. Barack Obama was president then, and his foreign policy struck me as a combination of liberal naïveté and Machiavellian narcissism, but it didn't stop me from working for the military. America was at war, and I was an American before I was a Republican. Projects in Afghanistan brought me into contact with U.S. military leaders at all echelons. Discussing counterinsurgency with American troops and their Afghan counterparts at military bases and villages wasn't something the average American scholar wanted to do, but for me the trips into rural Afghanistan were some of the most captivating and satisfying moments of my career. I believed I was helping Americans and Afghans prevail over their enemies, and prized the friendships formed with other patriotic Americans.

My time in Afghanistan gave me my first direct exposure to governmental corruption. The rampancy of corruption within Afghanistan's government had been widely publicized in Western media, so that part didn't come as a surprise. What shocked me was the corruption on the American side. During visits to Afghan bases and training centers, I found that many of the American contractors who were supposed to be training and advising the Afghans were either absent, incompetent, or both. U.S. government officials who were supposed to be overseeing the contractors were also missing in action. The granting and renewal of large U.S. government contracts were fraught with abuses, including the exchange of sex for contracts.

The draconian slashing of the U.S. defense budget stemming from the Budget Control Act of 2011 was to cut short my time as a defense consultant. While much of the fat in the Defense Department found ways to survive the cuts, some of the research I had been performing fell victim to bean counters who decided it was preferable to slash well-paid consultants than to prune out unproductive employees. In the spring of 2013, I took a job at the Joint Special Operations University in Tampa, Florida, and moved the family there during that summer.

The Joint Special Operations University was at that time a school for short-term training, not a real university. I decided to join because Admiral William McRaven, the SOCOM commander, was planning to turn it into a robust educational institution, comparable to the Marine Corps University and other military universities. Whereas most of the military was reeling from the cuts to the defense budget, McRaven and SOCOM were rolling in cash because of their success in eliminating Osama Bin Laden in May 2011. SOCOM was the place to be.

Like every other part of the Defense Department I'd encountered, the Joint Special Operations University and its SOCOM parent were staffed with all sorts of people. Many were conscientious Americans, who would readily have given their lives to protect the United States and their fellow Americans. Others exuded toxicity and corruption. The latter category included my boss. I had been forewarned about him before taking the job, but had also been told that my time under his rule would be short, as sweeping changes to the institution were on the horizon.

The attributes of toxic leaders have changed little since the time of Nebuchadnezzar. Toxic leaders are far more concerned with their own power and success than with the good of the organization and its people. When subordinates succeed, toxic leaders claim credit for their work; when subordinates fail, toxic leaders blame the subordinates. Toxic leaders surround themselves with flatterers and sycophants and shun constructive criticism.

They kiss up to those above them in the organizational hierarchy, while kicking down at those below. In leading, they prefer coercion and intimidation to encouragement and inspiration.

In the past, I had worked for individuals with significant flaws, but only one of them had come close to the foregoing description, and he did not check every box. I had questioned whether any human could really check all these boxes, let alone someone selected to serve in a leadership position. Perhaps the toxic leaders described in books were caricatures, their bad traits exaggerated and their good traits ignored.

My time in Tampa quickly disabused me of that notion. Toxic leaders could really be as bad as the above description made them sound. My boss's antics and incompetence gave the staff a never-ending supply of topics for conversation, which we bandied about with a mixture of humor, astonishment, and horror. Working for a toxic leader spelled pain and frustration, and caused me for the first time to gripe regularly about work problems at the dinner table. But it also taught me lessons I could apply if and when I held a leadership position in the future.

First and foremost, the experience instilled in me a conviction that senior leaders must take all possible measures to keep toxic individuals out of supervisory positions. If toxic people make it into those positions, the best solution is to remove them as quickly as possible, to spare their subordinates and to provide a mental jolt that might awaken the "removees" to the poison in their souls. The organization can ill afford to keep such people in managerial roles while hoping and praying for them to become less toxic, because the destructive practices are likely to continue for some time even if there is progress toward detoxification.

This experience, which went on much longer than anticipated, also heightened my interest in leading, as opposed to researching and teaching as I'd done for most of my career. According to personality tests I'd taken, I wasn't the type of individual who was driven by nature to lead, as in the manner of Napoleon or Patton. Instead, I was the type who was willing to let others lead but would assume a leadership role if the alternative was to be led by a numbskull.

During my time in Tampa, the U.S. Special Operations Joint Task Force in Afghanistan invited me to lead a study group on the Afghan Local Police, a 30,000-man paramilitary organization supported by American special operations forces. Like most experts, I was delighted to hear that my expertise was desired, and leapt at the opportunity to provide it. A variety of individuals, from a variety of organizations, sought to join the team, and several were imposed on me by the toxic boss. The Special Operations Joint Task Force assigned a few superb U.S. military officers to the group.

As I was preparing to travel to Afghanistan, a former government official whom I shall call the VIP learned of the project from a senior military official and asked if he and a think-tank associate of his could join our group. I'd heard that the VIP was knowledgeable about Afghanistan and had friends in the upper levels of the American government—the sorts of friends who might help our cause if he joined the team, and who might present difficulties if I refused his offer. After meeting with the VIP and his colleague and receiving assurances that they would be team players, I agreed to let them on the team. They were not able to travel at the same time as the rest of us, but would arrive two weeks later.

The first two weeks of the Afghan Local Police project ranked among the most exciting and productive moments of my career. Flying by helicopter, cargo plane, and tilt-rotor Osprey, our team climbed over high mountains and cruised through lush river valleys to provincial capitals and military bases. Special operations troops ferried us in armored vehicles to remote villages of mud-wall houses, where the Afghan Local Police were the only entities protecting the population against the Taliban.

We met with U.S. Army Special Forces, Navy SEALs, and Marine Special Operators in high-tech tactical operations centers, where we could chat for hours over inexhaustible quantities of Gatorade and energy drinks. These Americans were public servants of the highest order, people whom I would have been glad to count as the closest of personal friends. At Afghan government facilities and military outposts, we candidly exchanged thoughts with governors and police chiefs and tribal elders.

Then the VIP and his associate arrived. The presence of such a VIP had implications that I had not considered when agreeing to his participation. Whatever our team did, wherever we went, the U.S. government took extra measures to ensure his safety and respect his status. I had the feeling that some of the military staff were less than thrilled by the need to divert so many assets to the transportation and protection of the VIP. Still, the special treatment would not have been unduly disruptive had the VIP and his associate been team players.

The VIP was very intelligent and knowledgeable. He also was imperious and cocksure, making no effort to conceal his certainty that he had a better grasp of the situation than people who had served in the country more recently than he. The VIP had, in addition, a penchant for speaking down to people whom he deemed insufficiently knowledgeable about the topic of discussion.

Shortly after he and his associate arrived, we met with a U.S. embassy official in the airy garden across from the Kabul headquarters of the International Security Assistance Force. The official was relatively new to the country, and he answered questions with the official pablum one typically heard from embassy staff whose knowledge amounted only to repeating things other officials had told them. I was willing to cut him some slack, as I knew that presenting the official line was part of his job description, and that security precautions prevented most civilian officials from venturing into the countryside. The VIP, however, lit into him like an irascible high school teacher dressing down a mediocre student for failing to grasp the nuances of *The Scarlet Letter*. His associate followed his lead, piling on with biting questions and commentary.

The gratuitous insults made me wince. I tried to interrupt the verbal beating at several points, but the VIP and his associate jumped back into the fray as though they were professional

wrestlers pushing past the referee to resume the elbow smash-
es and piledrivers. The thought of cutting them off entirely occurred to me, but I was paralyzed by respect for the VIP's status.
Shutting him down in the middle of a conversation might cause
him to turn on me and complain to higher authorities who, as
he had already made clear to me, were his old buddies. And so
the beating continued.

During the next two weeks, the VIP and his associate would
administer similar drubbings to several other individuals,
though usually not in my presence. I also learned that the VIP
was telling people that he was the real leader of the project. I
didn't let him hijack the project, but I didn't confront him about
these problems, either—for the same reasons I'd allowed him to
abuse the embassy official in the garden.

The non-confrontational approach did succeed in preventing conflict from hindering completion of our work. At the end
of the project, after incorporating input from all the members
of the team, I delivered the team's final report to the top U.S.
military leaders in the country. Then most of the other team
members and I returned to the United States, while the military
members stayed on to put the ideas into action.

In the weeks and months that followed, rumblings of discontent began to filter in. The conduct of the VIP and his
associate had irritated American personnel at multiple locations, and some of the irritation reportedly had spilled over
onto me because I had been the team leader. Although my
years with the Marines had taught me that military organizations generally hold leaders responsible for the actions of
subordinates, I had banked on the principle that leaders of
short civilian projects can't be expected to prevent employees
from getting into mischief. And I'd succumbed to the wishful
thought, more common on the civilian side of government
than in the military, that managers can weather problems by
ignoring them.

Now it was clear to me that military leaders expected others
who worked in their world to keep their teams in line, no matter

who the team members were. While some leaders in the military community still got away with underperforming or misbehaving subordinates, those leaders were derided by people of integrity—the people whom I respected and whose respect I wanted. By avoiding confrontation, I had averted conflict in the short run, but had allowed problems to grow unchecked in the longer run. Beset by guilt, I vowed that if I were given leadership responsibilities in the future, I would act swiftly and decisively to nip bad behavior in the bud.

The Joint Special Operations University also gave me my first glimpses into the world of inspectors general. The United States Congress had begun creating inspectors general in the 1970s to combat waste, fraud, and abuse, and by the early twenty-first century they had grown in number to 74. In theory, the inspectors general were independent of the agencies they were charged with policing. In practice, they often were not.

I did not have any direct contact with the SOCOM inspector general. It was common knowledge, however, that staff and contractors were repeatedly lodging complaints with the inspector general about waste, fraud, and abuse, mainly involving inappropriate collusion between contractors and government employees. The inspector general repeatedly conducted investigations at the Joint Special Operations University in response to complaints that university leaders had awarded contracts to friends and issued full payment for work that had been incomplete or substandard. Contracting companies often filed protests alleging that their rivals had won contracts by unlawfully obtaining information from friends on the government side. Solid evidence often supported the allegations of wrongdoing, yet the inspector general never seemed to punish anyone. That fact gave rise to speculation that the inspector general's office was in the pocket of senior management.

During my second year in Tampa, chance again intruded to shift the course of my career. In the aftermath of the Bin Laden raid, SOCOM had been showered with so much praise that Admiral McRaven concluded he was no longer bound by the government's usual rules. He began ignoring members of Congress and their staffers when they asked for information about SOCOM's activities. At first, he had gotten away with it, but executive branch officials can't indefinitely stiff-arm the branch of government that funds them. Congress retaliated in 2014, depriving McRaven of authority and funding for several of his signature initiatives, one of which was the transformation of the Joint Special Operations University into a real academic institution. My dreams of helping build the university from the ground floor went up in smoke.

I told Kelli and the kids that I could stay on at the university if they wished to remain in Tampa, but would also be willing to go back to Virginia if that was what they preferred. Having borne the greatest burdens of relocation, they deserved the final say. They all voted for a return to Virginia, so we left Tampa in the middle of 2015.

Chapter 4

Subversion of the First Amendment by Unelected Bureaucrats

Upon our family's return to Virginia, I signed on with a Washington think tank called the Foreign Policy Initiative. I spent my first year writing a book on the history of special operations forces, which was to be published under the title *Oppose Any Foe: The Rise of America's Special Operations Forces*. From my experiences in Tampa, I had concluded that such a book was badly needed for the education of America's special operators. The fallacious allegation that was used to fire me from the Trump administration during the summer of 2019 had its origins in the writing of this history.

Like my previous five books, *Oppose Any Foe* was a scholarly history, intended to benefit U.S. national security professionals and the general public. It was neither a tell-all memoir nor an exposé that purported to reveal state secrets. I wrote it in the conviction that special operations forces and the leaders who deployed them needed more insights and less hype than they had been getting from other books. While lauding the heroism of numerous special operators, the book also provided cautionary tales of toxic and corrupt leaders, of whom the special operations community had a considerable number.

As I wrote the manuscript, I included operational details only if they had already been published by someone else, and I footnoted all my sources. I could have included details from my time with the government that hadn't been published before, but they were not essential to the story of special operations forces, and seeking permission to publish such information could lead to delays and headaches as government reviewers sought to determine whether any of it was classified.

In the book's conclusion, I noted that special operations forces needed to keep certain information secret in order to maintain the upper hand against the nation's enemies, but they also needed to resist the temptation to hide information for reasons unrelated to mission accomplishment. Toxic leaders in the special operations community had shown a tendency to withhold information about unethical and criminal conduct in order to spare themselves or their friends, which demoralized the victims and witnesses, emboldened bad elements, and led to larger scandals if and when Congress and the media learned of the cover-ups. Unnecessary secretiveness, I added, impeded the study and public conversation that promoted excellence in a profession. Published books, articles, documents, and speeches were the main tools of the special operations forces in finding solutions to contemporary problems. Classified studies were few in number and difficult to access.

Like other former government employees who had possessed high-level security clearances, I had been required to sign a non-disclosure agreement that gave the government the opportunity to check my writing for classified information prior to publication. Because my manuscript was based solely on publicly available information, prepublication review by the government should not have been necessary. Previous authors with clearances who had relied solely on public information had often published their books without submitting them for review.

When I was completing the manuscript in the spring of 2016, however, the Department of Defense was unusually skittish about prepublication review, owing to the recent appearance of a few high-profile books that divulged secret information. Chief among these books was *No Easy Day* by Matt Bissonette, a veteran of the Bin Laden raid. My book was nothing like that one—it wasn't based on classified information I'd obtained as a government employee, or any other sensitive information that wasn't already known to the public.

When I contacted the SOCOM Public Affairs office near the end of my research to request interviews with SOCOM leaders, the head of the office, Colonel Thomas Davis, gave me an unsolicited lecture on the necessity of prepublication review, after saying that he wouldn't make the leaders available because "I don't think it is in our best interest to provide any additional information." Colonel Davis informed me, "If you signed a non-disclosure statement, at any time in your career, you are obligated to send in your manuscript thru [*sic*] the DOD security review process. . . . In the [non-disclosure agreement] you signed, one of the consequences of not doing so is: 'I hereby assign to the United States Government all royalties, remunerations, and emoluments that have resulted, will result or may result from any disclosure, publication, or revelation of classified information not consistent with the terms of this Agreement.' Which I am sure you would want to avoid."

To be on the safe side, I mailed the manuscript to the Defense Office of Prepublication and Security Review (DOPSR) on April 10, 2016. A notice of receipt came back a few days later along with a message that this office intended to complete the review between June 22 and July 13, 2016. The latter date was sixty working days away, the maximum number of days the Defense Department asked authors to allow for prepublication review.

The sixty working days came and went without any further response from the prepublication review office. I then began sending emails to find out what was going on. After receiving no reply to the first messages, I eventually was told that the government was still working on the review and could not say when it would be finished. When I contacted Colonel Davis at SOCOM, he said he would look into it, but nothing came of whatever effort he made. A Congressman contacted the Pentagon on my behalf to urge them to complete the review, but his attempt did not produce results, either.

As the delay grew longer, I researched the legal underpinnings of prepublication review. The most important court case was *United States v. Marchetti*, which the CIA had brought against Victor Marchetti in 1972 for publishing classified information he'd obtained as a CIA employee. In the final opinion, the Fourth Circuit Court of Appeals ruled that the government was permitted to prohibit publication of classified information by former federal employees who had signed non-disclosure agreements, but with some important caveats. The court asserted that Marchetti's non-disclosure agreement covered only "classified information obtained by him during the course of his employment which is not already in the public domain." If information were in the public domain, then the defendant "should have as much right as anyone else to republish it." The judges of the Fourth Circuit recognized the obvious truth that republishing information already in the public domain would not cause damage to the nation's security.

The judicial and executive branches had abided by these guidelines ever since. The Department of Justice codified them in the clearest of terms in federal regulation 28 CFR 17.18. Governmental authority to censor materials via prepublication review, the regulation stated, did not apply "to any materials that exclusively contain information lawfully obtained at a time when the author has no employment, contract, or other relationship with the United States Government or that contain information exclusively acquired outside the scope of employment." The Defense Office of Prepublication and Security Review, in its own submission guidelines, stated that it would take no action on submissions when the "material is already in the public domain."

In *United States v. Marchetti*, the Fourth Circuit also asserted that the First Amendment offered certain rights and protections to individuals who had signed non-disclosure agreements, including the right to timely prepublication review. The government had an obligation to "act promptly to approve or disapprove any material which may be submitted to it," the court stipulated. "Undue delay would impair the reasonableness of the restraint, and that reasonableness is to be maintained if the restraint is to be enforced. We should think that, in all events, the maximum period for responding after the submission of material for approval should not exceed thirty days."

The requirement for a reply within a short, fixed time frame conformed to the standard set by the U.S. Supreme Court seven years earlier in *Freedman v. Maryland*. In that case, the nation's highest court had ruled 9–0 that First Amendment considerations required that a government censor had to reach a decision "within a specified brief period." Both the Fourth Circuit and the Supreme Court had been wise enough to know that affording long or indefinite review periods to censors was an invitation to abuse.

The non-disclosure agreement I'd signed had turned the court's thirty calendar days into thirty working days. The government, it stated, would "make a response to me within a reasonable time, not to exceed 30 working days from date of receipt." I distinctly remember being told, at a security briefing shortly after my arrival at the Joint Special Operations University, that "by accepting a clearance with access to Sensitive Compartmented Information, you are agreeing for the rest of your life to allow the government thirty working days to review material you intend to publish." The speaker had said nothing of a discretionary government right to extend that time period, nor had she spoken a word about clearance holders needing to sue if the government failed to meet its own deadline.

Not until I went to submit the manuscript did I see that the Defense Department was telling authors to "allow 30-60 working days" for prepublication review. The sixty working day period came out to eighty-four calendar days, nearly triple the standard established by *United States v. Marchetti*. The Pentagon had not explained to employees, the courts, Congress, or taxpayers why or by what authority it had stretched out the review period.

The Defense Department sought to give itself additional wiggle room by asserting in Department of Defense Instruction 5230.29 that "Manuscripts and books will be submitted to DOPSR at least 30 working days before the date needed," but "more time may be needed if DOPSR determines that the material is complex or requires review by agencies outside of the DoD." The Department didn't provide any explanation or justification for this proclamation, either. The most logical and reasonable explanation one could infer was that the complexity and external reviewing necessitated the department's self-granted extension from the thirty working days in the non-disclosure agreement to sixty working days.

Someone with a special affection for big government might have been willing to accept as reasonable the Defense Department's extension of the court's thirty calendar days to eighty-four calendar days. I didn't fit into that category, but as a man of moderation I was willing to cut the government a bit of slack and wait some extra days. More days and weeks went by.

On August 30, one hundred thirty-three days after DOPSR had received the manuscript, I emailed the head of the office, Darrell Walker. "I am now in a very difficult position," I wrote, "for I have contractual obligations with a publisher that will be breached should the review last much longer." The delay in reviewing the manuscript, I noted, would "set an unfortunate precedent for others who wish to share their knowledge and insights with the public and other communities beyond the Department of Defense." I asked Walker whether there was a maximum number of days in which DOPSR was obliged to review the manuscript, or whether it reserved the right to take as long as it wanted.

On September 8, Walker sent me a response. "Review obligations are not fulfilled until our review is complete and the author so notified," he wrote. In other words, he did believe the Defense Department could take as long as it wanted.

Walker went on to say that "we cannot prohibit you from publishing prior to us completing our review," but "I would

be negligent if I did not warn you that if you were to publish your manuscript and it contained classified or otherwise
release-prohibited information, you could be the subject of an
Unauthorized Disclosure inquiry with potentially personal or
pecuniary liabilities." The statement that "we cannot prohibit
you from publishing prior to us completing our review" caught
my attention as much as the threat, because it suggested that
the government lacked a valid basis for blocking publication
through a civil action.

Completion of the manuscript review, Walker continued, depended on the actions of the Defense Department offices that
were reviewing the manuscript, and he could not compel them
to act in a specified time period. "Although we routinely check
on overdue cases such as this one is now," he stated, "we have
no control over the offices to which we task the reviews and our
review requests are additional work often unrelated to their primary duties." Matters were becoming clearer. If individuals in
the offices tasked with the reviews didn't like how their offices
were depicted in the manuscript, or if they simply didn't think
that manuscript review was important, they could sit on the
manuscript as long as they wanted. They just had to send Walker and his staff emails now and then saying they were busy with
activities that they, in their unimpeachable bureaucratic judgment, considered more important.

By all appearances, Walker and others at the Defense Department had convinced themselves that the opinions of unelected
career bureaucrats superseded the First Amendment, Supreme
Court rulings, and federal regulations. Such bureaucratic over-
reach was emblematic of a broader usurpation of judicial and
legislative authorities by federal executive branch agencies. So
massive and pernicious had this power grabbing become that a
cottage industry had grown up in opposition, and with it deri-
sive nicknames for the federal bureaucracy like "the administrative state" and "the fourth branch of government."

As described by Columbia University law professor Philip
Hamburger, one of the leading deriders, the expansion of federal

agency power during the twentieth century represented the triumph of Woodrow Wilson's vision for the executive branch, in which rules and laws were created by "a self-perpetuating bureaucratic class," whose members "were never even picked by elected politicians" and were largely "appointed by other administrators." The powers and perils of the administrative state had grown in parallel with the federal budget, which had climbed during the century from 3 percent to 17 percent of GDP, and the federal bureaucracy, which went from 400,000 to 8 million employees.

This expansion also transformed federal employees into a large voting bloc, one that politicians courted with promises of pay raises and further enlargement of the bureaucracy. The Democratic Party's preference for big-government liberalism made it the more attractive home for federal employees, with the exception of those in the Defense Department, the one part of government that Republicans liked more than Democrats. The more a president sought to trim federal agencies or pursue other policies unpopular with the majority of the federal workforce, the greater the resistance he encountered from the career bureaucracy.

Woodrow Wilson had been confident that vast authorities could be entrusted to the bureaucrats because of their expertise and impartiality. Public faith in the federal bureaucracy, however, was never that high, and as the federal government grew, both Democrats and Republicans were strengthened in their convictions that bureaucrats were using the bureaucracy to abet political factions and special interest groups. After the Second World War, presidents, legislators, and judges took turns imposing constraints on the administrative state. The bureaucrats, however, devised effective methods for circumventing some of the constraints and persuading authorities to lift others.

To enhance my understanding of the legal issues and options, I contacted Mark Zaid, a lawyer who specialized in prepublication review. He told me that at this point my best option for getting the book published was a lawsuit. He also noted that the threat of a lawsuit might rouse the bureaucracy to action. I decided to start with the threat because it was the less extreme option and would not prevent me from taking the other option later.

On September 30, day number 164, I emailed Walker again. "Next week, the review period for my manuscript will surpass 120 working days, twice the maximum duration of 60 working days specified in your office's policy," I stated. "Please be advised that if the review has not been completed by the end of next week, I intend to undertake legal action as the sole remaining means of recourse."

A response did not arrive until October 7. It read, "I regret to inform you that we will not be able to meet your requested review completion date of October 6, 2016. We have been informed by the command with cognizance over the subject of your manuscript that it is still being actively worked/reviewed by subject matter experts for whom such reviews are an additional duty. Temporary duty supporting real-world, time-sensitive missions must be a priority for those assigned to review these documents and such duties have hindered a more timely review of your document. Recognizing the problem, the command has recently hired an individual, currently being trained, to assist in the review process."

I'd been around government long enough to know that except at times of extraordinary crisis, there are always people in a sprawling bureaucracy with time on their hands. By the fall of 2016, the wars in Afghanistan and Iraq had receded and the military bureaucracy had returned to the 8 a.m. to 4:30 p.m. routine of peacetime. Having worked at SOCOM for two years, I knew for a fact that it had hundreds of underemployed staff. And an employee with special operations experience did not need much training to check footnotes, which was all that was really required in my case.

Other authors had experienced delays in prepublication review, but the authors I knew who had sent manuscripts to the Defense Department during this period had not encountered delays this long. Increasingly I had the feeling that someone at SOCOM was deliberately stalling the review of my book. The manuscript could have gained the attention of an official who thought its insufficiently flattering description of their program or unit could lead to a loss of prestige or funding.

Among academics who wrote about military affairs, I was considered one of the most pro-military. This disposition was one of the main reasons why I had irked the Left, which since Vietnam had generally despised the U.S. military. At the same time, I was staunchly pro-truth, believing that the American military and the American people were best served by sober analysis of the facts, rather than the cherry-picking of facts, whether to glorify or malign.

Over the years, I'd learned that some SOCOM leaders welcomed the straight truth about special operations forces, because they knew the importance of learning from mistakes and shining light on unethical conduct, yet others only liked publications that candy-coated the flaws or left them out altogether. My manuscript generally depicted the special operations forces in a positive light—a reviewer in *Publishers Weekly* would later write, "Moyar admires these elite units," citing an "enthusiastic, warts-and-all approach." But my book couldn't satisfy those who wanted not just admiration, but adulation.

Considering that the delay involved the government, though, I couldn't rule out sheer incompetence as the cause. Nor could I rule out sheer stupidity. My time at the Joint Special Operations had shown me that even the world of special operations had a good share of stupid thinking.

Now I began giving serious consideration to a lawsuit. Several previous authors had sued the government for delays in prepublication review, and some had prevailed, but at exorbitant costs in time and money. In 2002, former FBI agent Robert Wright had sued the FBI for attempting to obstruct publication of a book critical of FBI counterterrorism operations, and the litigation had dragged on for seven years. Although District Judge Gladys Kessler ultimately ruled in favor of the plaintiff, the protracted litigation resulted in huge legal bills and deprived the book of its timeliness. By the time of the judge's ruling, Wright's subject matter had become so dated that he never published the book.

In her decision, Judge Kessler lambasted the FBI for its obstructionism. "This is a sad and discouraging tale," she wrote, "about the determined efforts of the FBI to censor various portions of a 500-page manuscript, written by a former long-time FBI agent, severely criticizing the FBI's conduct of the investigation of a money laundering scheme. . . . In its efforts to suppress this information, the FBI repeatedly changed its position, presented formalistic objections to release of various portions of the documents in question, admitted finally that much of the material it sought to suppress was in fact in the public domain and had been all along, and now concedes that several of the reasons it originally offered for censorship no longer have any validity."

The Defense Department's actions up to this point had given little reason for believing that it would be less inclined to string me out than the FBI had been with Robert Wright. With its bottomless pit of in-house lawyers, the government often drew out legal proceedings until attorney fees exhausted the personal savings of private citizens. A multi-year lawsuit would also damage the commercial viability of my book, as it had done for Wright's.

The Department of Justice, in regulation 28 CFR 17.18, had provided authors another option for resolving such disputes. Individuals who were dissatisfied with the government's prepublication review, the regulation stated, could notify the government they intended to proceed with publication of the submitted text, provided they allowed the government 30 working days to "file a civil action seeking a court order prohibiting disclosure." This option put the onus for seeking judicial review on the government, where it properly belonged.

I decided to take this route. In an email dated October 25, I informed Walker that I would not be suing, because "legal action at this juncture would not be a good use of either my resources or those of the government, given the lack of release-prohibited information in the manuscript." The government, I stated, could have until November 10 to request changes. By November 10, the government would have had 145 working days and 205 calendar days to review the manuscript, more than twice the amount it had set as the maximum time required, and more than six times what the judicial branch had specified as the maximum.

The book's scheduled publication date was more than five months after November 10, giving the government plenty of time to file a civil action. If, in fact, Defense Department officials had genuine concerns about the manuscript, they would be obligated to transmit those concerns to me directly or via court action before publication, in order to prevent a harmful disclosure. Otherwise, they could themselves be held culpable for sitting on their hands while secrets spilled out.

In past cases, government officials had intervened rapidly when they believed a manuscript contained prohibited information. Once the Defense Intelligence Agency received an advance copy of Anthony Shaffer's *Operation Dark Heart* in July 2010, it took just eight days to warn the author that his book contained classified information. When the Department of Defense received an advance copy of Matt Bissonette's book *No Easy Day* in August 2012, Defense Department General Counsel Jeh Johnson immediately sent Bissonnette and his publisher a letter threatening legal action. After former CIA Director Leon Panetta circulated the copyedited manuscript of his book *Worthy Fights* in August 2014 in the face of unresponsiveness from the CIA Prepublication Review Board, the board promptly completed its review and notified Panetta of its findings.

Walker responded on November 1. "While we respect your right and desire to publish," he stated, "we cannot give DoD clearance until all reviews, and especially critical ones, have been received. We have been in contact with a key component reviewing your manuscript and are still waiting for that input to enable us to consolidate and evaluate all review comments."

Walker's message of November 1 was the last I ever heard from DOPSR. November 10 came and went without a word from his office or anyone else at the Department of Defense. I informed the publisher that the government had sent me no objections to any material in the book after seven months of review, and that I was prepared to proceed with publication. The editorial and marketing processes at Basic Books kicked into gear.

Between November 2016 and April 2017, and for a long time afterward, I heard nothing from the government about the book. The government didn't file a civil action to block publication. None of the U.S. government officials who had received copies of the manuscript through the prepublication review process ever contacted me to warn that its contents would harm America's national security.

Basic Books published *Oppose Any Foe* on April 25, 2017. That same day, the *New York Times* printed an op-ed I had written based on material from the book. I also appeared that day on *Morning Joe* on MSNBC to discuss the book with Joe Scarborough and Mika Brzezinski. These details are significant because they cast great doubt on later claims from SOCOM that the command didn't know the book was published until the following year. Other op-eds, media appearances, and reviews were to follow. Dozens of reviews of the book appeared, including several in Defense Department and CIA publications, none of which said that the book divulged government secrets. As the weeks turned into months and the months into years, no one from the Department of Defense registered a protest or initiated disciplinary proceedings.

Chapter 5

The Election of Donald Trump

During the second half of 2016, as the wrangling over prepublication review played out and the election season heated up, I created a new program on military and diplomatic history at the Foreign Policy Initiative. The neoconservative thinkers Bill Kristol and Robert Kagan had founded the Foreign Policy Initiative in 2009, with funding from Paul Singer, a billionaire who had made his fortune running a New York hedge fund. Whereas many of the organization's foreign policy experts shared the neoconservatism of Kristol and Kagan, I aligned with traditional conservatives like Edmund Burke, Alexander Hamilton, and Russell Kirk, so I differed with colleagues on policy issues like immigration and nation building. But we had more in common with each other than we did with the Obama administration, which we all criticized for its diminution of the U.S. military, its feckless handling of allies and overseas commitments, its efforts to cozy up to longstanding enemies, and its Pollyannaish confidence that diplomatic dialogue and unilateral concessions could persuade adversaries to stop their objectionable activities.

Early in the presidential primary, Kristol, Kagan, and other neoconservatives became some of the fiercest critics of Donald Trump's candidacy. They decried Trump for his bravado, personal vendettas, and adulteration of facts. They blasted him, in addition, for pandering to populism with crude and outlandish rhetoric.

I didn't pay much attention to Trump at first, because I was sure he stood no chance against his Republican rivals, an impressive set of politicians with polished manners and decades of political experience. From the early moments of the Republican primary, I favored Marco Rubio. Like most people in Washington, I thought the charismatic young Senator from Florida stood a much better chance in the general election than the uncouth, aging billionaire from New York.

In March 2016, 122 Republican foreign policy specialists signed an anti-Trump petition produced by Eliot Cohen and Bryan McGrath. "As committed and loyal Republicans, we are unable to support a Party ticket with Mr. Trump at its head," the petition stated. "We commit ourselves to working energetically to prevent the election of someone so utterly unfitted to the office." A second petition, circulated a few months later, attracted the signatures of fifty Republican national security figures. These petitions were the founding documents for what became known as the "Never Trump" movement. The predominance of national security experts in the movement furthered suspicions in the Trump camp that the whole Republican national security establishment opposed Trump and his agenda.

No one came to me to pressure me into signing, but some of my friends experienced such pressure. McGrath employed public shaming to push Republicans into the anti-Trump crusade. In July, the website War on the Rocks published a letter McGrath had written to an unnamed Republican after that individual expressed interest in supporting Trump. "It never escaped my notice that you were not among the 120 or so signers of the 'Open Letter on Donald Trump from GOP National Security Leaders' back in March," McGrath stated in this new public letter. Recalling an earlier encounter in which the recipient had spoken of supporting a Trump administration, McGrath wrote, "Had I more grace and poise the last time we met, I would have looked you in the eye and told you that you were making a grave error. I would have told you that when the dust settles, there will be an accounting, and those who sacrificed principle will bear the 'Scarlet T.' If Trump loses, the long-term consequences to your reputation won't quickly wash away. There will be a lingering stench. If he wins, your reputation will suffer even more as you will be a willing accomplice in what happens next. And if he does even half of what he has promised to the shape of American power, it will be disastrous for this country and the world."

McGrath's letter stimulated a good deal of bickering and backbiting among the Republican foreign policy community. Many were repulsed by its smug finger wagging and its bitter threats, which sounded more like something out of Hillary Clinton's mouth than the pronouncements of a serious conservative. Critics warned that the country would suffer if every Republican foreign policy expert ruled out serving in a Trump administration by publicly trashing Trump.

A surprisingly large fraction of the petition signers and their supporters failed to grasp that signing a virulently anti-Trump petition would preclude employment in a Trump administration. After the election, some of them would publicly express outrage that Trump didn't want their services. Starry-eyed youths who hadn't been in the real world long enough to comprehend its ways might have been forgiven for thinking that their signatures should not disqualify them. Less understandable was that McGrath himself, a retired naval officer, would expect a leader to hire someone who had publicly reviled him as "utterly unfitted to the office" and had villainized not only his supporters but those on the fence.

I didn't sign the petitions. Like many other conservatives who had backed a Republican other than Trump at the start of the primary, I was willing to support Trump once the other leading candidates had departed the scene. I was well aware of his character flaws, but saw them as no worse than those of his Democratic opponent, Hillary Clinton. When the mainstream media trotted out new evidence of Trump's foibles, such as his demeaning personal attacks, his payouts to mistresses, and the Billy Bush tape,

Republicans were disappointed and discouraged, but we were also disgusted by the media's silence about comparable stains on the resumé of Clinton, from the Whitewater and Benghazi scandals to the corrupt funding of the Clinton Foundation to the routing of classified information through an unauthorized private email server.

Many of the Democrats now howling about Trump's lack of character and integrity had claimed that character and integrity weren't important during the 1992 campaign after it had come to light that Bill Clinton had cynically manipulated the draft system to evade service in Vietnam. They had made the same argument several years later when opposing the impeachment of Clinton following the appearance of a sullied blue dress that proved he'd lied about an affair with a White House intern. The continued praise of Democrats for Bill Clinton decades later did further injury to the notion that America needed to be governed by the sort of person you'd want marrying your daughter.

When Democrats took to the airwaves to denounce Trump for outrageous or erroneous statements, it reminded Republicans of how often Democrats had trotted out their own absurdities and falsehoods. And it wasn't just the Clintons. Barack Obama and his lieutenants had misrepresented, concealed, or destroyed information on a myriad of scandals, including the bungled gunrunning of Operation Fast and Furious; the murders of four Americans in Benghazi; the targeting of conservative organizations by the IRS; the abandonment of Iraq to ISIS maniacs; the leaking of details on the Bin Laden raid to sycophantic journalists and film producers; the payola schemes that funneled Chinese and Ukrainian money into the pockets of Hunter Biden; the Justice Department's surveillance of journalists; the CIA's hacking of Senate computers; Obama's smearing of police officers in Massachusetts, Missouri, and Maryland with false allegations of racism and excessive force; James Clapper's lying to Congress about the collection of private phone call data; Eric Holder's prosecution of whistleblower Thomas Drake; and Ben Rhodes's hoodwinking of the media about the Iran nuclear deal.

Most Americans, it seemed, preferred morally upright politicians to morally degenerate ones, but were resigned to the fact that neither party generally elected the likes of Ned Flanders to high office. Hence, they were also resigned to the fact that voters would, of necessity, focus on the policy positions of candidates more than their moral characteristics.

As far as policy was concerned, Trump leaned toward the cultural and populist wings of the conservative movement, which prioritized national culture and the livelihoods of the American middle and working classes over issues of greater concern to many establishment conservatives, such as free trade, low tax rates for high earners, and the importation of cheap labor. Trump's vows to revive manufacturing through better trade negotiations promised better-paying jobs for Americans who had been left behind by corporate outsourcing. Trump's proposed crackdown on illegal immigration could drive up the wages of working-class Americans, as well as curb the threats to the nation's culture and politics posed by swelling enclaves of unassimilated immigrants.

In Washington, conservatives were divided over the advisability of moving the Republican Party in a more populist direction. I was sympathetic to the view that the party needed to cast off establishment conservative dogmas about trade, immigration, and labor if it wanted to conserve what was best about America and sustain a coalition capable of defeating the Democrats. Establishment conservatives like Jeb Bush and John Kasich who had resisted these accommodations during the Republican primary seemed to generate little enthusiasm outside the Beltway, reinforcing the impression that the conservative establishment was as out of touch with the American people as the liberal establishment was.

Most conservatives, from establishment icons to hard-core populists, shared Trump's view that the nation needed to take a tougher stance against China. Trump's vows to drain corruption from the federal swamp pleased everyone on the Right, aside from the few who were deeply entrenched in government-subsidized institutions. Profligate government spending had made federal bureaucracies and their private-sector partners too large, too powerful, too self-serving, and too inefficient. Trump's independence from the Washington establishment offered at least a glimmer of hope that he would be more vigorous than past politicians who had failed to deliver on promises to cut the fat from bloated bureaucracies and close the revolving doors between the public and private sectors.

Candidate Trump also impressed Republicans with his unflappability in the face of media attacks. Whereas fear of criticism by liberal journalists and pundits often paralyzed establishment Republicans, the opinions of media figures bounced off Trump as impotently as the opinions of doctors who thought he should replace the hamburgers and candy bars in his diet with chickpea lettuce wraps and seaweed pudding. When the media took swings at Trump, he swung back, and without any concern about butchering liberal sacred cows that other Republicans dreaded to touch. The sheer impertinence of Trump and the ire he aroused among the media appealed to Americans who were fed up with the haughty lecturing of liberal newscasters, talk-show hosts, and entertainers.

The top establishment Republicans of recent times—George W. Bush, John McCain, and Mitt Romney, among others—had been more genteel than Trump, and more accommodating toward the liberal establishment. They had also lost repeatedly to that same liberal establishment on matters of central importance, such as immigration, welfare, federal spending, and marriage. Having seen respectable and agreeable politicians fail time and again, most Republicans were willing to take their chances on a boor.

On the day of the presidential election, November 8, 2016, I was in Cambridge, Massachusetts, for an event hosted by the U.S. Agency for International Development. No one had told me why I had been invited to one of the agency's events for the first time, but I surmised that some forward-thinking employee had pegged me as a prospective Republican appointee at USAID, and wanted to build a bridge just in case Donald Trump won the election. Nine months earlier I had published a book on international development.

At the time of the invitation, though, a Trump victory had seemed a long shot, and it still did on November 8. The number crunchers at the *New York Times* declared on the morning of election day that Clinton had an 85 percent chance of winning. CNN put the figure at 91 percent. Some pundits asserted that it was closer to 95 or 99 percent.

Clinton's big lead in the polls generated a sense of expectation and excitement that day among the USAID employees and contractors who had gathered in Cambridge. These groups had long tended to lean left; I wouldn't have been surprised had someone said I was the only Trump voter in the group of several hundred. As a relative newcomer to the field of international development, though, I didn't know any of the attendees, so I couldn't be sure that there weren't any closet conservatives in the room.

The outcome of the election that night took me and nearly every other American by surprise. Democrats, it turned out, had lost the votes of the white working class by lecturing them about "white privilege" and advocating citizenship for illegal immigrants while promoting trade deals that shifted jobs from the United States to China and Mexico. Voters in the lower and middle income brackets had watched their incomes plummet on Obama's watch while the oligarchs of Facebook, Amazon, the Clinton Foundation, Harvard, and Goldman Sachs had multiplied their wealth.

When I showed up the next morning for the final day of the USAID event, the room was filled with an aura of shock and despair, as if Pearl Harbor had just been bombed. Little was spoken about the election result. The first moderator to speak made a brief reference to "getting through a new era," but from then on the speakers focused on the originally scheduled topics. I was impressed by this show of professionalism, which contrasted with the conspicuous lamentations at a number of colleges, newsrooms, film sets, municipal offices, and other bastions of liberalism.

Chapter 6

The Trump Administration Is Formed

Trump's victory had been so unexpected that few members of his campaign or the Republican National Committee had thought much about how thousands of politically appointed positions would be filled. During the campaign, Trump had assigned responsibility for transition planning to New Jersey Governor Chris Christie, but Christie's planning had received little attention prior to election day because no one had expected Trump to win. After Trump notched his improbable victory, he and others looked at Christie's plans and concluded that Christie wanted to fill too many positions with establishment figures who hadn't supported Trump. Three days after the election, the president-elect took transition planning away from Christie and installed a new transition staff.

The new administration needed to find several thousand Republicans who had not repudiated Trump and would be willing to work as political appointees inside the federal bureaucracy. A large segment of the Republican Party harbored concerns that Trump's inexperience in government, his over-the-top tweets, and his sometimes impulsive behavior would create serious problems for the administration and those who served in it. Yet those concerns also made a powerful argument for serving in the administration. The government needed good people to ensure that an unusual president steered the ship in the right direction and stayed clear of icebergs. The American people had elected an anti-establishment candidate out of a valid dissatisfaction with the establishments of both political parties, and establishment Republicans could help address the sources of that dissatisfaction by joining the administration, which to most of us seemed a more productive route than scribbling editorials about Trump's faults or the good old days of the George W. Bush administration.

Even Democrats and Never Trump Republicans agreed that Americans need have no qualms about serving as political appointees in a Trump administration. They told me and many others that we'd be doing the country a favor by joining the administration, and assured us that working for Trump after the election did not carry the stigma of vocally supporting Trump before the election. The Washington establishment and the mainstream media applauded when people with close ties to the Republican establishment decided to join Trump's administration, such as Nikki Haley, Rex Tillerson, John Kelly, Steve Mnuchin, James Mattis, and Gary Cohn. (The establishment's approval was to dissipate in the years to come, and it would disappear entirely by the end of Trump's term. In 2020, establishmentarians of both parties would regularly claim that Trump appointees wore the dreaded "Scarlet T" for having "enabled" Trump's purported racism, xenophobia, misogyny, authoritarianism, disinformation, etc.)

The White House Presidential Personnel Office (PPO) was responsible for filling the roughly 4,000 politically appointed positions in the new administration, which ranged from administrative assistants to cabinet secretaries. The office had been a black box in the past, and it remained so now. No one seemed to know how or why the office made decisions, and any attempt to extract information from them was futile.

Although I had previously published articles supporting partisan causes and policies, I hadn't engaged directly in partisan political activity. Like many Americans, I was wary of partisan politics because of the excesses of politicians, such as the routine breaking of campaign promises, the subordination of public interests to personal and partisan interests, and the pursuit of ideological agendas without regard for facts. Non-partisanship had an appealing aura of independence and dignity.

What had led me toward active partisanship was the reality that partisans wielded much greater power over the country than the non-partisans. Partisans decided how much money the government took from citizens, and how much it gave to able-bodied adults who didn't have jobs. They decided how easily immigrants could enter the country illegally, and how easily immigrants could stay illegally. They set trade policies that could create or destroy entire industries. If you wanted to have a say in such matters, you needed to become a partisan.

Most important, from my perspective at the time, was the power of partisans over the national defense. My time in the defense world had given me a front-row seat to the partisan use, and abuse, of military force in Iraq and Afghanistan. America's founders had made the military a non-partisan institution, subordinate to the president, and it had remained so ever since, which was one of the reasons why so many Americans admired it. The founders had also wanted the presidency to be non-partisan, but that dream lasted only to the end of George Washington's career. Ever since, the presidency had been a partisan institution, with the result that the non-partisan military was required to carry out the wishes of partisans.

Some presidents had been far too willing to put personal and partisan concerns before national security in times of war. Barack Obama's concern for his own political fortunes, along with his partisan ideology, had led him into a series of disastrous decisions in Iraq, Afghanistan, Libya, Yemen, Syria, and Somalia. Most disturbing to me had been Obama's early and public setting of withdrawal dates for the American troops he had sent to Afghanistan. This policy, which was motivated in part by a desire to campaign on troop withdrawals during the next election, had emboldened Afghan enemies and demoralized Afghan friends, at considerable cost in American lives.

Friends who had worked in the George W. Bush administration told me that if I wanted to work for the new administration, I should send my resumé to anyone I knew who possessed influence in the Trump camp, and those people would then recommend me to PPO or to agency leaders who could weigh in with PPO. I duly contacted a variety of individuals who had ties to the Trump transition, including several who were already working for the transition team. They promised to put in a good word. One of them said that my name was already appearing on lists of potential Defense Department appointees. But weeks went by without a peep from PPO.

Only many months later would I learn that some of the people I'd asked for support were seen as rivals by powerful agency heads, including the heads of the foremost national security agencies—Secretary of State Rex Tillerson and Secretary of Defense James Mattis. Trump had selected Tillerson and Mattis based on their big personalities and big reputations, without dissecting their political views. Both men, it turned out, were less conservative and more establishmentarian than Trump, and thus they were suspicious not only of preexisting rivals but also of peers and potential subordinates whom they viewed as too conservative or too sympathetic to Trump's populism. So the endorsements I received were as helpful to me as a recommendation letter from Julius Caesar would have been for a position on the personal staff of Brutus.

Jockeying between factions of the Republican Party also impeded prospective appointees. The populist faction of Steve Bannon, the libertarian faction of Rand Paul, the traditional conservative faction of Mike Pence, the neoconservative faction of John Bolton, and the Chamber of Commerce faction of Steve Mnuchin all had people they wanted to place in jobs, and they often blocked candidates from other factions when they could, especially those who opposed them on key issues. If you had worked for an organization that supported robust military spending, a libertarian potentate might knock you off the candidate list. If you had written an article advocating tariffs on Chinese goods, the Chamber of Commerce guys might cross you off.

The transition apparatus was further hindered by disorganization. Newly arrived staff, along with some other persons of influence, hurriedly sifted through mounds of unfamiliar resumés to fill unfamiliar appointee jobs. Some of the jobs were given to highly qualified individuals, but others went to people whose only qualifications were their connections to the sifters.

Thousands of political appointee slots would remain unfilled for months to come. Trump deliberately prevented the filling of some positions, on the principle that it would help limit the size of the government. "You look at some of these agencies, how massive they are, and it's totally unnecessary," Trump explained in October 2017. "They have hundreds of thousands of people." What Trump didn't comprehend was that several thousand appointees were needed in the bureaucratic trenches to ensure that the millions of career bureaucrats followed his instructions, and not the instructions of Barack Obama, Rachel Maddow, or the high panjandrums of the career bureaucracy.

When my initial efforts to gain the attention of the Trump transition team bore no fruit, I turned to the next most popular tactic for those seeking a presidential appointment—writing an op-ed. For the topic, I settled on the advantages America could reap by replacing the feckless internationalist foreign policy of Obama with a strong nationalist one. Tracing the history of American presidents since 1945, the op-ed argued that the United States had been most successful in achieving its foreign policy objectives when the president had stricken fear in America's enemies by projecting toughness and unpredictability, and had fared worst when the president had bent over backwards to avoid frightening other countries.

To my surprise, the New York Times agreed to publish the op-ed. It appeared in the paper on December 9, 2016, beneath the title "The World Fears Trump's America. That's a Good Thing."

It drew praise from Trump supporters, curiosity and concern from foreigners, and condemnation from liberals.

As events would have it, writing an op-ed in support of the president-elect hurt my chances for landing a top job in the administration. In another indicator of the disarray of the early Trump period, some of the people in charge of selecting political appointees purposefully rejected candidates deemed to be supportive of Trump. Most notable in this regard were leaders at the Department of Defense, where I would have been the most obvious fit.

The Defense Department's political appointments were controlled by Secretary of Defense Mattis and his chief of staff, Kevin Sweeney. As press reports would reveal, Mattis and Sweeney wanted to hire only individuals whom they considered "apolitical," based on the notion that national security was nonpartisan and hence should not be managed by political partisans. One Pentagon insider explained to Sydney J. Freedberg Jr. of *Breaking Defense*, "Mattis just doesn't want people who he perceives as being political—which is ridiculous because we're talking about political appointees."

Even more startling was the belief of Mattis and Sweeney that a number of establishment Democrats qualified as apolitical, but no Trump-supporting Republicans did. Mattis tried to fill the position of deputy secretary of defense—the number two position in a workforce of nearly three million employees—with Michèle Flournoy, a partisan Democrat who had served in the Clinton and Obama administrations. The buzz generated by Flournoy's pending nomination, however, provoked an outcry from Republicans in Congress and the White House, and eventually Flournoy withdrew from consideration.

Mattis did succeed in bringing a purportedly apolitical confidante, Sally Donnelly, into a senior Pentagon position. Donnelly would become a bête noire for Republicans when evidence surfaced of her efforts to help Amazon Web Services obtain the Pentagon's $10 billion JEDI contract. Prior to joining the Trump administration, Donnelly had run a consulting firm whose clients included Amazon and Ashton Carter, Obama's Secretary of Defense. She had sold her company in 2017 without disclosing that the buying entity was controlled by André Pienaar, the boyfriend and future husband of the Amazon Web Services official responsible for winning the JEDI contract. Congressional Republicans have spent years documenting the improprieties of Donnelly's assistance to Amazon Web Services during her time at the Pentagon.

Friends of mine who interviewed for political appointments at Defense during the first year of the Trump administration told me that Sweeney and other interviewers gushed with favorable comments about Trump to draw out whatever enthusiasm the interviewee might have about Trump, then offered jobs only to interviewees who lacked enthusiasm. White House officials fumed that nearly all the candidates they had proposed as Defense appointees were getting shot down. Even swamp-dwelling Republicans who had tepidly endorsed Trump—on the sensible assumption that presidential appointees were supposed to support the president—were not making it through. The near absence of Republicans from the nation's largest federal agency during Trump's first months astonished a political class accustomed to the filling of most political positions with individuals from the party that held the White House.

In March 2017, Senators Tom Cotton and Ted Cruz contacted the Pentagon to voice concern about the lack of Republicans selected for political appointments in the Department of Defense. Mattis invited the staff of the senators to the Pentagon to view a list of potential appointees. Upon their arrival, however, Sweeney showed them only a heavily redacted list. According to a report in *Politico*, Sweeney "spent the meeting barking at the staffers before storming out."

Sweeney's performance drove Capitol Hill Republicans to take their discontent to the press. "We've waited eight years for this, to be able to fill these posts with Republicans," a Republican congressional staffer told Eli Stokols and Eliana Johnson of *Politico*. "It should go without saying that a Republican administration is expected to staff federal agencies with Republicans."

Mattis's defenders, as reported by Stokols and Johnson, claimed that "the White House has put Mattis in a nearly impossible position given that a large swath of the Republican foreign-policy establishment was openly critical of Trump during the campaign. Some say that has left Mattis with little choice but to turn to Democrats and to those without a political background to fill senior posts." I wanted to punch my computer screen when I read those sentences. I knew plenty of qualified Republicans who had not denounced Trump and yet were simply being ignored. Mattis and Sweeney knew them, too.

Mattis's aversion to partisan politics was understandable, in light of his recent experiences with the Obama administration. Obama had assembled a hyper-partisan national security team that included the likes of Hillary Clinton, Susan Rice, Ben Rhodes, and Dennis McDonough. His secretaries of defense had filled the Pentagon's political posts with liberals who supported Obama's social engineering initiatives as well as his national security policies. The former included putting women in infantry units, permitting homosexuals to serve openly in the military, and funding sex change operations for military personnel. Time and again, Obama and his appointees had made decisions on military matters for partisan ends, and disregarded contrary advice from the military professionals. Obama had withdrawn troops from Iraq and Afghanistan more rapidly than Mattis and the rest of the generals had desired, leading to the birth of ISIS and the resurgence of the Taliban.

Mattis was, nevertheless, wading into perilous waters in seeking "apolitical" individuals to serve as political appointees. Washington contains a certain number of people who truly have no partisan preferences, but they are disinclined to take jobs as political appointees, because they generally don't wish to be perceived as partisan or to foreclose opportunities to serve in an administration of the opposing party. Others in Washington profess no partisan preferences, but harbor them nonetheless. The career bureaucracy mass produces such individuals, hiring liberals to implement the government's policies while forbidding them from displaying partisanship openly. When appointing hundreds of ostensibly "apolitical" people, as Mattis and Sweeney were doing, it would be all but impossible to tell where all of these individuals stood politically, and how their political views would affect their behavior on the job.

Attempting to keep partisan politics out of personnel decisions presumed that national security was an apolitical enterprise, but it was not, and never had been. Trump had won the election for the Republicans by promising significant changes to the defense policies of the incumbent Democratic administration, many of which reflected ideological differences between the Republican and Democratic Parties. Obama had cut the defense budget, based on the liberal premise that military spending needlessly provoked foreign countries and detracted from domestic programs. He had intervened in the Libyan civil war for reasons of human rights rather than U.S. national interests, based upon an ideological view of American power. He had overturned the U.S. military's longstanding policies on female and LGBT service, matters of profound ideological controversy. Changing the nation's policies in these sorts of areas required political appointees who wanted to change them. Without supportive appointees, the inertia, self-interest, and the hidden ideological agendas of career bureaucrats would strangle change in its crib.

During the early months of 2017, I spent more time networking with people who might be able to help me get into the administration. I knew many of the Republican foreign policy experts in Washington's think tanks, but the widespread hostility to Trump within their ranks had not only destroyed their chances for serving in the administration, but had also damaged mine. Their denunciations had caused Trump and his inner circle to turn their backs on the think-tank community and focus hiring efforts elsewhere. The Presidential Personnel Office concentrated much of its attention on Capitol Hill, where thousands of smart and energetic Republicans worked in congressional offices. Another important recruiting ground was the Republican

National Committee, which had close ties to Trump's first chief of staff, Reince Priebus. I knew a few staffers at these places, but I didn't know enough powerful individuals to gain a leg up.

My books and other academic qualifications counted for much less in the Trump administration than they would have in previous administrations, and not just because so many of the think-tank wonks had thumbed their noses at Trump. Democratic administrations always drew heavily upon the academic world in staffing the senior management of federal agencies, and Republican administrations had formerly pulled in distinguished academics as well. Henry Kissinger had entered the Nixon administration as national security adviser at the same age that I entered the Trump administration, with a similar academic pedigree.

Unlike Kissinger, however, the conservative foreign policy thinkers of the twenty-first century didn't have professorships or research centers at Ivy League universities to link them to the governing elite and the media. Most didn't even have jobs at Clemson, Appalachian State, or Spokane Junior College. The country's best conservative minds had, for the most part, pursued careers in business or law or medicine, while the few who had obtained doctorates and spent decades in deep study had been relegated to think tanks or peripheral academic institutions from which they struggled to be heard.

Conservative scholars were isolated further from the Republican Party by disdain for educational elitism among its leaders, a disdain borne of the liberal establishment's unalloyed contempt for the Right. Matthew Whittaker, a University of Iowa graduate who served in the Trump administration as acting attorney general, expressed the widespread Republican frustration with Washington's collegiate elitism in his memoir *Above the Law*. "The first thing coastal elites want to know about you is where you went to school," Whittaker observed. "They perk up if your answer includes an Ivy League school or handful of others, like Stanford, Chicago, Duke, Georgetown, William & Mary, or the University of Virginia." Americans "who went to a state college or an agricultural school," he continued, "are no-bodies to the coastal elite."

I would sometimes hear such sentiments directly from people who were unaware of my academic credentials. Evidently they presumed that someone who was working for the Trump administration and had spent much of his career teaching at military universities and traipsing around conflict zones couldn't possibly be a Harvard graduate. Admission to Harvard, some of them explained to me in the tone of a sage lecturing a novice, automatically guaranteed cushy employment at a hedge fund, tech giant, or Ivy League university.

Trump himself had graduated from the University of Pennsylvania, and he wasn't averse to hiring people with fancy degrees, but neither did he value elite education as much as his predecessors. From Trump's selections, one could discern a commendable eye for talent and achievement, as well as a regrettable eye for appearance and bluster. The federal agency heads selected by Trump included several graduates of the elite universities, but more common were those with degrees from institutions like Central Washington University (James Mattis), Calvin College (Betsy DeVos), the University of Massachusetts—Boston (John Kelly), East Carolina University (Linda McMahon), Huntingdon College (Jeff Sessions), Hampshire College (David Shulkin), the University of Wisconsin–Eau Claire (Mark Green), Texas A&M University (Rick Perry), the University of Oregon (Ryan Zinke), Wheaton College (Dan Coats), and the University of Georgia (Sonny Perdue).

It was certainly true that leadership ability was not necessarily correlated with educational prestige. That fact, together with lingering resentments over past snubs by Ivy Leaguers, led many of the hiring authorities to discount the value of elite education. In the eyes of some Republican officials, indeed, a degree from a top university was suspect because it was associated with liberal establishment hauteur.

The backlash against educational snootiness had considerable benefits as far as the United States was concerned. Elite institutions really were breeding grounds for liberal snobs who often governed less effectively and ethically than other Americans. Their faculties had been taken over by leftists who pushed radical ideologies that did great harm to the public. For conservative job seekers with prestigious diplomas, however, the backlash was not helpful.

During my initial flailing in the world of presidential personnel, I continued to run my program at the Foreign Policy Initiative. Shortly after the election, however, Paul Singer decided to pull the think tank's plug. Because my program had its own funding, I was able to move it to another think tank, the Center for Strategic and International Studies. A bipartisan institution, it counted some prominent Republicans among its experts, and they were generous in assisting me. A large number of the center's Democrats were still grieving their dashed hopes for service in a Hillary Clinton administration, but they generally were civil and open-minded—quite different from so many of the people I had encountered in the academic world. Having interacted with conservative colleagues on a daily basis for decades, they didn't suffer from the delusions that ran wild among professors who knew little about conservatives other than what they heard from fellow professors and the media. I was treated especially well by the head of the division where my program was located, Kathleen Hicks, a former deputy undersecretary of defense who was later to become Joe Biden's deputy secretary of defense.

By the summer of 2017, I was beginning to doubt that I would ever go into the administration. My networking efforts did not seem to be helping, with the partial exception of a meeting at the end of the summer with National Security Adviser H. R. McMaster and his deputy, Nadia Schadlow. I had met McMaster years earlier as a result of our mutual interest in the Vietnam War, and had come to know Schadlow through her work at the Smith Richardson Foundation. I decided to bring a couple of copies of *Oppose Any Foe* along. At the end of our meeting, I signed one for McMaster, and asked him whether he could get the other copy to President Trump. Sure, said McMaster. I signed that copy with a personal inscription to the president.

Several weeks later, I received a large envelope in the mail from the White House. It contained a letter on White House letterhead, which read, "Dear Dr. Moyar, Thank you for sending me a copy of your book *Oppose Any Foe*, and thank you for your kind words of support. The history of our Nation's military, including the men and women of our Special Operations Forces, is one of great honor, courage, and sacrifice—values we revere as Americans. As Commander in Chief, I have a deep appreciation for quality scholarship and research about these selfless warriors." At the bottom was the high, angular signature of Donald Trump.

When the storm clouds gathered above me later in the Trump administration, I thought about sharing this letter with the media or people inside the government. A presidential endorsement of the book would have undercut the claim that the book jeopardized the security of the United States. I ended up deciding against it, however, out of concern that it would provoke nasty comments about whether the president had read the book, and would incite the most vicious Trump haters to claim that the president had himself engaged in the spilling of secrets by endorsing the book. Trump's critics frequently deplored his lack of interest in reading, and, as someone who had spent many years reading and writing, I was in no position to disagree. But the critics were mistaken in seeing the problem as unique to Trump—plenty of politicians, not least of them the esteemed President Franklin Roosevelt, had been no more inclined than Trump to pick up a book.

In the fall, I received an invitation to speak on a panel at the USAID Innovation Week. The topic of the panel was the use of development programs in support of counterinsurgency, a topic I had addressed in books, articles, and reports. The panel was lightly attended, which may have been because of the early morning start time, or because of disinterest in the topic or the presenters, but it did catch the attention of Mark Green, the

USAID administrator. A few days after the event, I received an email from Green, whom I'd met the previous year when he had served as the moderator for a book talk I had given on Capitol Hill. He asked me to send him my *curriculum vitae*. I did so, and soon thereafter the agency invited me to interview for a political appointee job.

Bill Steiger, the USAID Chief of Staff, ran the interview process. When I met Steiger in the Ronald Reagan Building for the interview, he was intense and focused, uninterested in small talk. Considering how many issues an agency chief of staff has to address on a given day, I couldn't fault him for getting straight to business.

The agency was short on political appointees, Steiger explained. At the moment, he was trying to bring in good people as quickly as possible and figure out where to put them later. The agency wanted to hire individuals as generic "senior advisors" and determine their specific positions once they had gone through the onboarding process, which took several months. By the time I started work, they would have added more people to the roster and thus would have a better idea of which position I would best occupy in the longer term. Steiger then noted that under the reorganization currently in progress, the agency was going to create a new bureau focused on development in conflict-ridden countries, and I would be a strong candidate for leadership of that bureau, given my background.

I was less than thrilled by the lack of certainty. The new bureau sounded like an excellent opportunity, but I was offered no guarantee that I would get that leadership job once I made it into the agency. I didn't know anything about Steiger, and thus had no idea whether he would really look out for me.

At this stage, however, it was very doubtful that I could get into the administration on more advantageous terms. I had spoken with someone else who had gone through this process recently at USAID, and when he'd demanded a specific job, the agency had decided not to hire him. With the administration almost a year old now, prospective political appointees lacked the bargaining power we would have had at the start, when the administration had been rushing to fill thousands of positions. We were like high school students standing awkwardly by the punch bowl while the prom court pulsated on the dance floor— we weren't going to join the dance by waiting for the most coveted partners to offer their hands. If we wanted to serve as political appointees, we'd need to take whatever hand was offered.

As a patriot, I felt a sense of duty to serve the administration. The administration needed people with my skills and knowledge of international affairs in order to make the best use of the government's massive resources. If I refused the offer, the job was unlikely to be taken by someone with both the necessary capabilities and the necessary commitment to the national interest.

After thinking it over, I told Steiger that I would join USAID on the terms offered. I signed on the dotted line, and the paperwork went into the bureaucratic assembly line.

Chapter 7

Wading into the Swamp

I joined USAID on February 5, 2018. For the first few days of employment, all new staff attended an orientation at a non-descript office building in Arlington, Virginia. Having been through federal orientation programs before, I wasn't surprised to find that some aspects of the orientation were informative and others were so tedious and unnecessary that extra cups of coffee were required to stay awake.

The section of the orientation I remembered best was the "privilege walk." It came as a surprise for a couple of reasons. First, it was unlike anything I had seen in the federal agency where I had worked previously, the Department of Defense. In the world of the Marines and the Special Operations Forces, "suck it up" was the preferred guidance to those who found their circumstances unfair or distressing. Second, the training reflected the ideological preferences of the Obama administration, which had already been out of power for more than a year. Apparently some Democratic hands remained on the cultural steering wheel of the agency.

Each trainee picked an identity out of a hat. Mine was "North American woman of Scandinavian descent." I don't remember the other identities exactly, but they were along the lines of "undocumented migrant worker," "male French development official," "blind woman of African descent," "transgender activist," "male prostitute," and "indigenous woman with unwanted child."

We stood side-by-side in a line, facing the instructor, our identities known only to ourselves. The instructor then read a statement aloud. If the statement applied to us, we took a step backward. If it did not apply, then we took a step forward. The statements went something like this:

"Employers are less likely to offer me a job or pay me normal wages because of my identity."

"I am at a heightened risk for sexual assault."

"People will treat me differently because of gender stereotypes."

"I may face discrimination when applying for government services."

At the end, we revealed our identities. The male French development official was at the front, and I was close behind. Most of the others were far to our rear. During the ensuing group discussion, the instructor and some of the attendees talked about what the exercise had demonstrated about identity, prejudice, and privilege.

I had no objection to the general concept of appreciating adversity based upon identity. In fact, I could relate to it personally, as I had been denied numerous career opportunities because of my identity as a conservative heterosexual white male. Nevertheless, I found the event absurd. If adults were not already aware that they should treat others with dignity and respect, or that some people were born with advantages or disadvantages, a two-hour training session wasn't going to change them. The emphasis on group privilege, moreover, was drawn straight from the identity politics of the American Left, and was plainly intended to justify extending the identity spoils system to the countries where USAID worked. In fact, as I later learned, the "privilege walk" had been created as an ideological indoctrination tool by Erica Sherover-Marcuse, the third wife of radical activist Herbert Marcuse.

It would ultimately take nearly four years for the Trump administration to pull the talons of identity politics and other elements of leftist ideologies from the flesh of federal training programs. In an executive order dated September 22, 2020, the

White House would forbid "race or sex stereotyping or scape-goating in the Federal workforce or in the Uniformed Services." The order provided examples of instructors and instructional materials that were even more outrageous than those of USAID. One Department of Treasury training session had informed trainees that "virtually all White people, regardless of how 'woke' they are, contribute to racism," and it instructed small group leaders to encourage employees to avoid "narratives" that Americans should "be more color-blind" or "let people's skills and personalities be what differentiates them." Training materials for non-minority males at Sandia National Laboratories stated that an emphasis on "rationality over emotionality" was a characteristic of the "white male," and asked those present to "acknowledge" their "privilege" to each other.

With the benefit of hindsight, I now believe that the orientation would have served new employees much better by covering a topic that was missing—the reporting of waste, fraud, and abuse. We did receive "ethics training," but it focused on topics like obtaining permission to attend outside events or complying with limits on gifts from foreign governments. It should have covered the agency's vulnerability to corruption, the obligations of employees to report evidence of corruption, and the USAID leadership's commitment to protection of employees from retaliation when reporting these crimes.

The agency or the Presidential Personnel Office also should have provided an orientation for new political appointees. As the implementers of policies that were unpopular with much of the career staff, the new appointees needed guidance on how to achieve our mission in a dangerous bureaucratic jungle. We needed assurances that the leadership would back us up when the tigers and jaguars bared their fangs. No leaders did anything of the kind for me or the other appointees who joined USAID in 2018. We would have to find our way through the jungle on our own, with only intuition and sporadic advice from other newbies and a few veterans to keep the beasts from devouring us.

Following the new employee orientation, I reported for duty

at the Ronald Reagan Building. I met with Diana Leo, who served as the liaison between the White House Presidential Personnel Office and USAID. It had been three months since my interview. Had they determined which position I would occupy? I asked.

I was surprised when Leo answered, rather brusquely, that they were "still figuring out who would be the chiefs and who would be the indians." So much for the greater clarity that had been promised during the interview. For the time being, she said, I would be the "senior advisor for civilian-military cooperation."

Leo presented me with a document known in bureaucratic parlance as a "position description," which stated my roles and responsibilities. According to this document, I was the senior political appointee responsible for promoting cooperation between USAID and the Department of Defense. In this capacity, I was to work closely and frequently with Administrator Green. Early in his tenure as USAID Administrator, Green had stated that one of his priorities was "elevating civilian-military cooperation."

Other appointees advised me to arrange a meeting with Green once I had gotten my feet on the ground, in order to discuss his vision for civilian-military cooperation. After a week or two on the job, I requested a meeting with Green through the appropriate channels. I kept hearing back that he was too busy. Weeks turned into months without a meeting.

During my six months as senior advisor, and in the year that followed, I was never able to meet individually with Administrator Green, or to engage in a conversation with him about civil-military relations or any other topic. On only a handful of occasions did I even attend a meeting at which he was present, and in those cases I had few, if any, opportunities to open my mouth. I never received an explanation for this lack of contact, but the evidence suggested that it was a combination of Green's disinterest in military affairs, his delegation of most internal agency matters to Steiger, and his ignorance of sound leadership practices.

Other political appointees who had arrived as senior advisers told me they were having the same experience. They had been given position descriptions designating them as valued advisors to the USAID administrator, but then never had a single meeting with him. Some senior advisors were unable to gain any traction in their bureaus and became so frustrated that they transferred to other agencies or quit the government altogether.

I was more fortunate as far as my bureau was concerned. Although the Trump administration had been in the White House for more than one year, I was the first senior political appointee in the agency's sprawling Bureau for Democracy, Conflict, and Humanitarian Assistance (DCHA). The senior career bureaucrats who ran the bureau hid as much information from me as they could, but they couldn't blow me off entirely, inasmuch as I might eventually become their boss.

As a senior advisor, I didn't supervise anyone, which was beneficial in important respects. Supervision of employees requires time—or at least it should—so the absence of supervisory responsibilities gave me more time to learn about the agency and the bureau. But lack of supervisory authority also meant a lower bureaucratic status. In the federal government, the more employees and money a manager oversees, the more status the manager possesses, and hence the more opportunities for promotion and higher pay. It's a major reason why government bureaucrats are constantly trying to enlarge their bureaucracies.

Much of the management of money took place at relatively low levels. At USAID, top officials often complained that they had little influence over the spending of the agency's funds. The money going out the door on any given day had been authorized a year or two ago, when someone else had been in charge. Decisions about money were typically developed at lower levels and submitted for signature by senior officials who often didn't have the time or knowledge to vet them rigorously, or didn't see the proposals until it was too late for major changes.

USAID political appointees did not meet together as often as we should have, but once every month or two Steiger convened everyone in the large conference room adjoining the office of the administrator, and he used the meetings to drive home a few key themes, of which the top one was locating and controlling money. The career staff, he said, had devised ingenious schemes for hiding money from political appointees, which enabled them to steer money to their preferred projects and to their friends who worked for contractors, non-profit organizations, and multinational organizations. "If you're not finding the money," Steiger proclaimed on one occasion, "then you're not doing the job we hired you for." As a result of his entreaties, I paid as much attention to the money as I could, though I couldn't do very much at first because my initial job left me outside the bureaucratic loop on budgetary and spending matters.

Mark Green believed that the agency's habitual reliance on a handful of large implementing organizations had bred complacency and corruption. To break this cycle, he directed senior staff to find ways to fund contractors and NGOs that the agency had not funded before. Iraq, where USAID was stepping up assistance to the Christian and Yazidi minorities, provided the first test bed. In early 2018, the Middle East Bureau held a conference for prospective partners in Washington, attended by over three hundred organizations, many of them just the kinds of implementers Green wanted as new partners. A large number of these organizations submitted compelling proposals.

When the USAID bureaucracy went through its award process, however, it ended up awarding nearly all of the work to the same large organizations that always won the contracts. Green and other agency leaders were furious. The outcome appeared to validate suspicions that contracting decisions were swayed by personal connections between the USAID officials making the awards and their friends at the mega-contractors.

Some of those connections had their origins in the previous administration. Between 2013 and 2015, the Obama administration had implanted some of its political appointees in career jobs at USAID and other federal agencies, a process commonly called "burrowing in." If Obama appointees had moved into a career job more than one year before the 2016 election, the Trump administration could not fire them. Some of the implants held very senior positions, from which they could continue influencing policy and contracting after their party had left the White House. The most spectacular case at USAID was Angelique Crumbly. Obama had appointed Crumbly as assistant administrator for the Bureau for Management in 2013, and she then had converted to a career position later in Obama's second term. She became the acting head of that bureau when Obama left office, and remained in that position for the majority of the Trump administration, which gave her extraordinary influence over the spending of the agency's money.

Other Obama appointees stayed involved in the agency's affairs and contracts after January 2017 by taking jobs in other sectors of the aid-industrial complex. Much like the military-industrial complex described by President Dwight Eisenhower in his farewell address, the aid-industrial complex was a massive conglomeration of public and private institutions that excelled at promoting the growth of their industry and the incomes of their executives and shareholders. Swamp creatures rotated frequently among the four cornerstones of the aid-industrial complex—federal agencies, Congress, contractors, and lobbying firms—along with various and sundry aid institutes, think tanks, and non-profits.

During the 2008 presidential race, Barack Obama had vowed to close the "revolving door" of "people going from industry to agency, back to industry." Once he moved into the White House, Obama imposed rules prohibiting the revolving—but then granted numerous loopholes that kept the door spinning at a dizzying speed. In one of the most egregious cases, Google exchanged employees with the federal government, national political campaigns, and Congress 258 times during the Obama administration, according to the Google Transparency Project. The Obama White House bestowed political appointments on thirty-one Google employees, and twenty-two officials left the Obama White House to work for Google.

At the end of Obama's presidency, many of his top USAID appointees headed straight through the revolving door into the legislative, contracting, and lobbying arms of the aid industry.

Susan Markham, who had been the agency's supervisory gender coordinator, landed a job at the gender-equality advisory firm Smash Strategies. From that position, Markham helped craft the Women's Entrepreneurship and Economic Empowerment Act of 2019, whose text sounded as though it had been lifted straight from the USAID gender policy documents of the Obama era. Most significantly, the act required the head of USAID to ensure that "gender equality and female empowerment are integrated throughout the Agency's program cycle and related processes." This provision enabled career bureaucrats to hire new gender advisors to scrutinize everything the agency did through a radical feminist lens. (The act ended up passing thanks to some Republican votes, because most Republican congressional staffers didn't know or care enough to object.)

Nancy Lindborg, who had headed the Bureau for Democracy, Conflict, and Humanitarian Assistance during the Obama years, became the head of the U.S. Institute of Peace. Funded generously by Congress, the U.S. Institute of Peace implemented aid programs, conducted research, and beseeched members of Congress for more money. Its headquarters building, a glass palace near the State Department in Foggy Bottom, had originally been projected to cost taxpayers $100 million but ended up costing $186 million by the time of its completion in 2016. After taking over the Institute, Lindborg hired a bevy of other former Obama appointees to help her run the organization and spend its $38 million annual budget. Despite its public funding and its ostensible non-partisanship, the Institute hired far fewer Republicans than Democrats on Lindborg's watch.

Lindborg maintained close ties with senior career officials at USAID and elsewhere and used those relationships to influence policy and congressional funding. She and her lieutenants succeeded in injecting Obama-era thinking into some of the most pressing policy debates of the Trump administration. Senior Trump administration officials told me, for instance, that they were distraught at the Institute of Peace's sway over American negotiations with the Taliban.

Another act of collusion between Obama administration veterans and career staff, which I witnessed up close, was the Stabilization Assistance Review. In the early days of the Trump administration, when political appointees had been few in number, career officials from the Defense Department, the State Department, and USAID had come together to form the Stabilization Assistance Review working group. The group aimed to write a report on U.S. stabilization operations overseas and use it to gain influence over American policy, operations, and funding. A senior Trump appointee who ought to have had a major role in this endeavor told me that the working group tried strenuously, and often effectively, to hide their work from political appointees.

After conducting a series of interviews, the group wrote their report and leveraged their bureaucratic connections to secure the signatures of senior officials. The report itself was rather anodyne, leaning heavily on conventional wisdom and statements of the obvious. The U.S. government was enjoined, for instance, to "develop and evaluate political strategies based on evidence and rigorous analysis," and to "promote a fair, purposeful division of labor with national partners and international donors."

The working group organized a conference at George Washington University to celebrate the publication of its report. By the time of the event, the Trump administration had been in office for a year and a half, and yet no Trump appointees were invited to speak, only career government officials, government contractors, and former Obama appointees who now worked as contractors, think-tank experts, or professors. Steam poured out the ears of USAID appointees when we belatedly learned of the slanted event.

Chapter 8

Career Bureaucrats

In premodern China, a class of bureaucrats known as the mandarins stood near the apex of the Confucian social hierarchy, just below the emperor, and well above merchants, artisans, entertainers, and soldiers. Prominent families prepared their children for the rigorous mandarin entrance exams as zealously as the overbearing parents of today prepare their children for the SAT. The best mandarin was a man of unquestioned integrity and scholarly learning, commanding a respect bordering on reverence.

The bureaucrats of the United States have never enjoyed anything resembling the status of the mandarins. In parts of Washington, D.C., and in nearly every other place in the United States, the word bureaucrat conjures up negative adjectives like stodgy, pedantic, conformist, and lazy. This stereotype, like most others, contains grains of truth but fails to capture the complexities and aberrations of reality.

Unlike American soldiers, American bureaucrats are not the subjects of innumerable books and films. These public servants live in the shadows, seldom in the view of the taxpayers who fund them. In the interest of familiarizing the public with its employees, as well as continuing this story, I will endeavor to describe in all candor the bureaucrats I encountered at USAID.

Some of the bureaucrats I met did qualify as stodgy. Plenty of others, however, were highly animated. The senior career staff, in particular, had no lack of lively, engaging talkers. Their voices, hand gestures, and body language convinced the person in the opposite chair that they were sincere and knew what they were talking about, even if neither was true. Such skills are useful in any organization, and can be particularly helpful to an organization that often has to sell itself to skeptics in Congress and the White House.

The preeminence of talkers, however, also came with a large downside. People who are good at talking generally like to have meetings where they can talk, and during all the time they are meeting and talking, they are not doing. The amount of time spent chatting in meetings helped account for the agency's glacial pace in completing tasks and projects.

The excellent style of the talkers, moreover, often exceeded the substance of the words emanating from their mouths. Their eloquence could be so overwhelming that listeners didn't bother to question them on substantive matters. The lack of scrutiny in turn heightened the talkers' confidence, making them even more persuasive and less inclined to deepen their own knowledge. It also emboldened those who were tempted to spread falsehoods.

Some of the talkers studiously refused to put anything in writing. I suspected they knew that without their oral eloquence, the flaws in their thinking would stand out. When on occasion I saw them forced to put something in writing, the results called to mind the B- papers I had graded when teaching college students. The verbiage and buzzwords were so profuse as to obscure any bits of worthwhile content. Fluffy, overgrown sentences sprouted, with such text as, "The maximization of our investment in the region and our utilization of all the development tools will demonstrate to the development community and civil society that we are a leading voice in all development sectors," or "We need to consult with all relevant stakeholders, including but not limited to NGOs, multinational organizations, bilateral donors, and civil society organizations, to ensure that we take an inclusive approach to the problem," or "By following the principles of resilience, we will protect the rights of the most vulnerable, marginalized, and neglected populations, which will allow us to optimally fulfill U.S. foreign policy objectives."

I tended to put things in writing. I had spent much of my career in academic environments where writing was paramount, and where speaking was valued far less—so much less that most academic presentations could put even insomniacs to sleep. During my years with the military, I had discovered the power of the spoken word, and hence had worked on improving my speaking skills, to the extent that was possible for someone lacking the natural oratorical talent of a Marco Rubio or even a Pete Buttigieg.

During meetings, I made my points quickly and concisely. When I was leading the meeting, I expected others to speak in the same way. When a talker was leading the meeting, I had to sit back and listen to others take the meeting down interminable and mind-numbing rabbit holes. No amount of coughing or rolling of the eyes seemed capable of bringing such prattling to an end.

I was drawn to the career staff who wrote effectively and who talked for a purpose other than hearing the sounds of their own voices. The writers tended to be more contemplative. Contemplation was critical to the success of USAID, given the political, cultural, and economic complexities of the environments where the agency spent its money. Contemplation, however, could also be taken to excess, becoming an impediment to action.

USAID was an operational organization. Its main purpose was to design and fund development and humanitarian operations for implementation by for-profit and non-profit contractors. The agency's staff quipped that when it came to overseas activities, the Defense Department and USAID were America's operational organizations, while the State Department was its observational organization. But whereas Defense had a natural penchant for action, USAID had a natural penchant for deliberation.

In one instance, I informed staff that I had orders from the political leadership to help them develop a new approach to a longstanding problem, and that it had to be completed in a matter of weeks. They replied that they needed many more months to gather information and study the issues. Being new to the subject matter, I wasn't initially sure what to make of these protests, but soon I learned that the issues had already been studied and debated for several years. I had to drive home the truth that we couldn't afford to postpone action until we reached the point where we had obtained and pondered every last bit of information, because we would never reach that point.

When it came to work ethic, an unfortunate number of the career bureaucrats did conform to the stereotype. They spent much of their time—two or more days per week—out of the office. Ostensibly they were "teleworking," putting in a full day's work at home. But supervisors confided to me that some of these employees were slow to complete tasks outside the office. Some didn't answer phone calls or emails, either at home or in the office. To elicit any action, the boss might have to go to their cubicle and hope to find them there.

When supervisors attempted to get people to show up for work, or otherwise tried to hold staff accountable, the accused employee often responded by filing an Equal Employment Opportunity (EEO) complaint if he or she belonged to one of the groups protected against discrimination by EEO laws. The practice had become so widespread that USAID had ended the filing of EEO complaints against supervisors and mandated that all complaints be filed against the agency itself, via its Office of Civil Rights and Diversity. That change at least relieved some of the burden and anxiety from supervisors.

The misuse of EEO complaints wasn't the only reason to question the need for a large and expensive diversity apparatus. The existence of a different system of justice for women, minorities, and other protected groups created unhealthy perceptions and realities of preferential treatment, which could be justified only by the existence of high levels of discrimination. But the levels of discrimination were much lower now than they had been when the federal government created this two-track system. My position in the agency didn't make me privy to all allegations

of biased conduct, and one can seldom know for sure whether someone is secretly harboring discriminatory intent, but I
saw enough to know that discrimination based on race, sex, or
sexual orientation was not widespread or organizationally de-
bilitating. The supervisors I knew, indeed, were less inclined to
mistreat women and minorities than other employees because
they knew it could lead to indelible branding with the labels of
sexism, racism, or homophobia, in addition to protracted and
potentially biased EEO investigations. Further evidence of the
infrequency of discrimination could be found in the Equal Employment Opportunity Commission's investigations for the entire federal workforce of three million employees, which in 2019
substantiated fewer than 200 complaints of discrimination.

The agency's minority, female, and LGBT employees still had
plenty of real grievances that deserved investigation and disciplinary action. Most of these grievances, however, resulted not
from discrimination, but from evils that know no boundaries
of identity, like greed, arrogance, lust for power, vindictiveness,
and incompetence. I came to this conclusion after learning of
the numerous cases where heterosexual white males were mistreated for these same reasons—often by the same toxic supervisors as other victims—and the numerous cases where people
in groups protected by EEO were mistreated by individuals from
those same EEO groups.

Now let's get down to what really motivated the bureaucrats.
Most of the career staff at USAID had joined the agency because
they wanted to help the American government provide aid to
impoverished countries. They were as inclined as Marines to
view themselves as altruists, and some shared the view of military personnel that they were selflessly serving the country.
Others believed they were selflessly serving the whole world,
which they preferred to serving a United States that was rife
with the people Hillary Clinton had called the "deplorables"
during the 2016 election, and the people who according to Barack Obama "cling to guns and religion." Few of them, however,
were as zealous in their citizenship of the world as the Marines

were in their citizenship of the United States—they weren't signing up to serve as United Nations peacekeepers in Somalia or Lebanon—which meant that they were more easily tempted to make money through questionable side hustles in the course of saving the world.

Their belief in big-government solutions to poverty and their liberal internationalist outlook landed most of the career bureaucrats on the left side of the political spectrum. The political contributions of USAID employees during the 2016 presidential campaign were not published, but according to *The Hill*, 95 percent of contributions from federal employees as a whole had gone to Hillary Clinton's campaign and just 5 percent to Trump's. USAID employees almost certainly exceeded the 95 percent average, given that USAID was known as one of the more liberal agencies.

A surprisingly large number of career USAID staff were the children of Christian missionaries. In the aid world, Christian missionaries are often the foreigners with the most dirt under their fingernails. Inspired by Christian injunctions to help the poor, they often live in rural villages amid the most humble elements of society. By contrast, most officials from USAID and its implementing arms stay in modern hotels or gated communities when working abroad.

Significant numbers of USAID staff were themselves religious, but kept quiet about their beliefs for fear of antagonizing the numerous militant atheists in the career bureaucracy. The atheists of USAID objected to religion, above all, for its opposition to homosexuality. During the Obama administration, active measures against religion and religious aid organizations had surged at the agency in parallel with the creation of new jobs, programs, and vocabulary to advance LGBT empowerment.

Obama's appointees had told USAID staff that the Establishment Clause of the Constitution prohibited the agency from funding religious organizations. It was a gross misrepresentation of the Constitution. As the Supreme Court had affirmed in the landmark case of *Everson v. Board of Education*, nothing in the Establishment Clause or anywhere else in the Constitution prohibited the government from funding religiously affiliated organizations for social services and other non-religious functions. Furthermore, the Establishment Clause, like the rest of the Constitution, applied only to the sovereign territory of the United States, not to the foreign countries where USAID operated.

During one of my first trips as a USAID appointee, to East Africa, I asked USAID staff about their work with faith-based organizations in countering terrorism. They replied that the Establishment Clause prohibited them from working with faith-based organizations. I mentioned this response in my trip report. When that report found its way to Mark Green, he was appalled, according to others who recounted it to me. Recognizing a misappropriation of the Constitution, Green directed agency lawyers to notify all USAID posts that the Establishment Clause did not, in fact, prohibit aid to faith-based groups.

As is common in bureaucracies, USAID career staff developed a strong affection for their organization and its mission, so strong in some instances that it exceeded healthy bounds. When USAID bumped into the Defense Department, the State Department, or the Department of Health and Human Services, career employees often focused on protecting the agency's "equities," without regard for any broader governmental or societal concerns. Political appointees, being only temporary workers, were less susceptible to this bureaucratic parochialism, although a few also succumbed to it. Once I moved into a management position, I made a point of reminding the staff that they were not citizens of USAID, but of the United States. As federal employees, their first priority was the United States and its government. Their agency and its mission came second, and their own career interests came third.

Despite pronounced differences in political affiliation and worldview, I got along well with most of the career staff, at all organizational levels. Most were committed to their work, as was I, which built mutual respect. And although many disliked Trump, the majority did not actively engage in subversion against the Trump administration and its appointees, and they carried out the orders of the political appointees even if they did not personally agree with the underlying policy.

The agency did, however, contain a sizable subversive element. The subversives impeded or redirected the agency's activities for reasons of ideology, personal financial interests, bureaucratic power, or a combination thereof. Among the most common methods of subversion was the slow roll. Bureaucrats would claim that the orders issued by political appointees required protracted series of reviews, consultations, and approvals, and as time dragged on, they would come up with new excuses as to why they needed still more time. Another common method was mislabeling. When, for example, Trump appointees said that agency programs should promote self-reliance, the subversives would avoid changing programs and instead slap the self-reliance label on Obama-era programs that had nothing to do with self-reliance. This deceit took place in numerous sectors, including climate change, LGBT rights, and women's empowerment.

Like Taliban guerrillas operating in their native villages against American soldiers who had spent most of their lives on the streets of Dallas or the cornfields of Nebraska, the subversives used superior knowledge of the environment to conceal their deeds from political appointees. The political appointees couldn't intercept phone calls, inject bureaucrats with truth serums, or employ other intelligence tools and tricks to unmask the plots. What we could do was identify the affiliations of the known saboteurs and look for patterns. This analysis produced a consensus among the Trump appointees that former Obama appointees who had burrowed into the career bureaucracy accounted for a significant percentage of the wrenches thrown into the gears of the political leadership. The other group that seemed to contain significant numbers of wrench throwers was the membership of the Truman National Security Project.

Founded in 2005, the Truman National Security Project had as its mantra the cultivation of liberal Democrats for national security careers. The organization's board boasted A-list members of the Democratic establishment, including Kamala Harris, Jake Sullivan, Ron Klain, John Podesta, Madeleine Albright, Derek Chollet, and Hunter Biden. Jenna Ben-Yehuda, a former State Department official who became the president of the Truman National Security Project in 2019, explained that the Project differed from other Beltway national security organizations in that "we go beyond thought leadership: we advocate, we build movements, we drive policy, we make change. And we bring an army: Yes, our members staff Secretaries and Senators and sit on the National Security Council." Republican friends of mine, at USAID and elsewhere, lamented that the Truman National Security Project was a more effective assembly line for partisan bureaucrats than anything on the Republican side.

Subversion was particularly rampant at the beginning of an administration, when most political appointee positions were vacant and few orders came down from above. Mark Green's arrival as the agency's head in August 2017 had compelled senior bureaucrats in the various bureaus to interact intermittently with him, but they were able to keep Green's interference to a minimum in the bureaus where he lacked political eyes and ears. By the time of my arrival at the DCHA Bureau, political appointees had been absent for so long that some career staff seemed to have forgotten what it was like to have them in the room.

During meetings I attended, some of them made unguarded remarks about their flaunting of the Trump administration's authority. They spoke about locking in spending in ways that would prevent the agency's politically appointed leaders from reversing it, and about preserving programs that the White House wanted to kill. A few of the most brazen career staff openly derided Trump, his political appointees, or his policies.

The most flagrant act of insubordination I witnessed involved USAID's humanitarian programs in Syria. At a Monday morning meeting of the bureau's senior staff, a senior career official named Rob Jenkins reported that USAID employees had spent the weekend figuring out how to keep these programs hidden because President Trump would try to eliminate them if he learned of their existence. Jenkins did not explicitly approve or disapprove of this behavior, but his words and tone suggested that he was sympathetic to keeping the information away from the White House. He clearly had no intention of complaining to anyone about this subversive activity. Shifting my eyes around the room, I saw that no one seemed to be shocked besides me.

Political appointees are supposed to make sure that the bureaucracy carries out the president's policies, especially controversial policies that may clash with the personal preferences of career bureaucrats. It was my responsibility, as a political appointee, to inform higher authorities if the career staff were trying to set foreign policy. Being new to the business, I first asked another appointee for advice on how to handle the matter. When I recounted the words of Jenkins, his face contorted into an expression of incredulity. "You have to tell Steiger," he said. "You have to tell Steiger."

Steiger had informed the political appointees that they were not to communicate with him via email. Hostile persons and groups, he explained, had repeatedly requested copies of his emails using the Freedom of Information Act, and he didn't want them exploiting his communications for their ill-begotten ends. I therefore typed up a memo for delivery in hard copy.

In the memo, I recorded what Jenkins had said at the meeting, and noted that neither I nor any of the other political appointees in my bureau had taken part in recent meetings on Syria. "Since joining the agency on February 5, I have repeatedly seen career staff attempt to conceal information from me and other political appointees," I wrote. "None of the prior instances, however, involved the large sums of money or the high strategic stakes that are at play in Syria, and in no prior case had I heard career staff state explicitly that people were deliberately attempting to hide information from the president. I was, indeed, surprised to hear someone mention such an intent in my presence. I suspect it can be attributed to the fact that political appointees have been absent from most of these meetings for more than one year, and the fact that the career staff still drive these meetings since they hold all the top positions in DCHA."

When I handed the memo to Steiger, he read it in silence, then put it away in a folder. As far as I know, he never informed the White House or took action against anyone for attempting to deceive the White House. Had he done either, I believe, the heads of Jenkins and other bureau leaders would have rolled. Nor did he ever explain his inaction to me. Based on what was to follow, my best guess is that he feared it would produce an imbroglio that would damage his relationships with the career staff and the White House.

Chapter 9

Trump Appointees in the Administrative State

At USAID, the appointees of the Trump administration were a very different breed from the career staff. They were also very different from the bootlicking fascists whom many on the Left claimed were running the Trump administration, and from the resistance fighters who, by other accounts, filled the ranks of political appointees. Most of the Trump appointees at USAID weren't very different from the appointees of preceding Republican administrations, except that Republican foreign policy elites and think tankers were largely absent.

While Donald Trump dominated the media as no other president ever had, his name was spoken infrequently within the agency, even among political appointees. I never heard appointees criticize Trump in front of others. It wasn't the result of a Gestapo-like intimidation, but rather reflected, more than anything else, the normal organizational tendency to support leadership. The employees of General Motors and the World Bank don't go around bad-mouthing their chief executives, either.

Only in one-to-one conversations did you learn anything about what political appointees really thought of Trump. Opinion ran the gamut from admiration of Trump as the greatest president in history to mild contempt for Trump, but most people fell in between, recognizing Trump's foibles but believing that his policies were generally sound and much better than the Democratic alternatives. We didn't like everything the president said or did, and we didn't base our daily actions on slavish adherence to his tweets, but we didn't try to obstruct or override his policies, either.

At times, Mark Green and the other officials in the USAID front office had to contend with White House decisions that didn't sit well with establishment conservatives, like the withdrawal of U.S. forces from Syria and the gratuitous insulting of American allies. Most USAID appointees, though, were insulated from these crises by upper management. We were generally more worried by the efforts of career staff to continue the policies of the Obama administration than by the disrupter-in-chief's sporadic kicks to the groin of the international order.

The National Security Strategy of December 2017, developed by H. R. McMaster and Nadia Schadlow and approved by Trump, focused on Trump's most sound strategic objectives—competing with China instead of coddling it, increasing spending on national defense, eliciting greater security contributions from allies, and improving enforcement of immigration laws. The National Security Strategy briefly addressed foreign assistance, in terms consistent with the national security principles of mainstream American conservatism. Trump himself viewed most foreign aid as ineffective, a position that had stood outside the mainstream since the late 1940s. He didn't pay much attention to the subject, though, except when it came to cutting the total foreign assistance budget or using the threat of withholding aid to achieve foreign policy objectives.

Mark Green, as a man of the conservative establishment, believed that aid could be a valuable instrument of foreign policy when properly employed, and hence the government should maintain aid expenditures at current levels. He cultivated the people who could prevent the president from gutting foreign aid, particularly Melania and Ivanka Trump and key members of Congress. It wasn't covert resistance; nothing involving Melania or Ivanka could remain hidden from the president. Green's efforts to preserve aid proved successful. Melania and Ivanka delivered White House support for various USAID programs, and a bipartisan congressional majority prevented Trump from slashing the total aid budget.

Green and other top political appointees did not diverge from Trump when it came to the foreign policy interests the agency sought to advance. They aimed the agency's resources at countering China and other priorities articulated in the National Security Strategy, often in the face of complaints from career staff who preferred to keep doing what they'd been doing under Obama. Most appointees were pleased by the redirection of aid toward these foreign policy priorities.

Mark Green's central theme as USAID administrator was what he termed the "journey to self-reliance." In speech after speech, he asserted that USAID should provide assistance that built the economic and political capabilities that would eventually end the need for aid. Green would often make his point with a moving story from his time as Ambassador to Tanzania, in which a Tanzanian woman had told him she was taking American aid this time because she had no choice, but in the future she wanted to be able to feed her family through her own family's labors.

Green sought to export the principles of hard work, individualism, private enterprise, and limited government that American conservatives promoted at home. Like many of the other appointees, he had as much compassion for the poor of foreign countries as liberals did, but believed that conservative prudence was required to translate good intentions into good results. To me and the other political appointees, it was a welcome change from the development policies of the Obama administration and other Democratic administrations in recent memory. Those administrations had viewed the poor as helpless victims of predatory elites, autocratic governments, and unfavorable geography, and hence had advanced aid agendas aimed at redistributing wealth, enlarging the welfare state, and building infrastructure without concern for the unintended consequences, like the undermining of private enterprise and the discouragement of employment. Such "redistributive justice" had been even less successful in poor countries than in the United States.

In terms of their location on the political spectrum, the agency's political appointees ranged from centrist to conservative, with populist and traditionalist conservatives outnumbering neoconservatives and libertarians. Many were unapologetically religious, although not in an in-your-face sort of way. Some were committed to advancing the administration's agenda in the face of stiff bureaucratic resistance, and at least a few of us assumed considerable personal risks in fulfilling that commitment.

Some political appointees had come to USAID solely for personal advancement. This group included a number of individuals who had no experience in international development and had sailed into their jobs early in 2017 on the winds of political connections. By dint of their early arrival and their thirst for power and status, they had wrested possession of plum jobs. Their lack of knowledge made them more vulnerable to manipulation by career staff, and their disinterest in administration policies made them less concerned about being manipulated. Career staff polished apples for these appointees, showered them with praise in front of others, and helped them prepare for the end of the administration by lining up lucrative jobs at development contractors and non-profit organizations. In return, the appointees let the careerists do whatever they pleased. The more senior of these appointees had few qualms about kicking less senior appointees to the curb, or letting career staff do it.

At times, my appreciation of human complexity caused me to question whether these people were really as self-centered and one-dimensional as they seemed. In several cases, I ultimately concluded that the first impression had failed to capture the existence of more noble motives. Yet I could not pull myself away from the conclusion that some of the appointees were self-centered in a rather one-dimensional sort of way. Probably there was goodness in them somewhere, but it wasn't visible, or if it was, I was too transfixed by the evil to notice.

The agency also had appointees who promoted conservative policies but would forsake the policies and the cause and anything else when they believed that their personal interests demanded it. If, for example, they had to choose between a virtuous action that would turn powerful bureaucrats or journalists against them and an ignoble action that would spare them from such tormentors, they would choose the latter every time.

Such individuals received encouragement to shirk their duties from press reports of persecution of political appointees by career bureaucrats. During the latter part of 2017, journalists and congressional Republicans began unearthing the shards of Crossfire Hurricane, an FBI investigation into alleged collusion between the Trump campaign and the Russian government. Peter Strzok, deputy assistant director for counterintelligence at the FBI, had initiated Crossfire Hurricane in July 2016, and had supervised it until the following May, when it was folded into the special counsel probe of Robert Mueller. In December 2017, the media reported that the FBI had pulled Strzok off the Mueller probe because of partisan text messages found on his government-issued cell phone, containing jabs like "Donald Trump is an enormous douche."

The FBI had to fire Strzok in the summer of 2018 after the publication of additional text messages, in which he had vowed to use FBI powers to destroy Trump regardless of what the Crossfire Hurricane investigation actually turned up. In the most notorious of the exchanges, from August 2016, Strzok's subordinate and paramour Lisa Page had teed up a question about the possibility of a Trump victory in the election. "He's not ever going to become president, right? Right?!" Page had texted. Strzok had replied, "No. No he won't. We'll stop it."

A staggering number of additional lawyers assigned to Crossfire Hurricane and the Mueller probe would be implicated in investigative misconduct. Among those on the list of transgressors were Kevin Clinesmith, Andrew McCabe, James Comey, Brian Auten, Sally Yates, Bruce Ohr, James Baker, Rod Rosenstein, Andrew Weissmann, Jeannie Rhee, and Dana Boente.

As FBI lawyers were targeting the very top of the Trump administration, other career bureaucrats fed information to sympathetic journalists and inspectors general to sabotage executives Trump had appointed to head federal agencies. Their efforts forced out several cabinet officials for transgressions less serious than those of Obama cabinet officials who had kept their jobs. They included Ryan Zinke of the Department of the Interior, Patrick Shanahan of the Department of Defense, Tom Price of the Department of Health and Human Services, Scott Pruitt of the Environment Protection Agency, and Alex Acosta of the Department of Labor.

USAID appointees like me who had missed out on the early plum distribution grumbled occasionally about the inadequacies of those who had beaten us to the fruit stand. Most of us, though, knew we weren't the first people in history to believe they'd been given jobs less important than their abilities warranted, so we didn't spend time feeling sorry for ourselves, but instead labored to prove our worthiness for the shrinking number of open leadership jobs. I was more fortunate than many of my peers in this regard, for I received a chance to demonstrate leadership skills after only a few months on the job.

This chance arose from the tumult in the tri-border region of the Sahel, where the West African countries of Niger, Burkina Faso, and Mali come together. At this moment in time, the Islamic State and other violent extremist groups were running loose in the Sahel. An extremist ambush in the Nigerien sector had killed four American Green Berets during October 2017, compelling the U.S. government to reevaluate the entire American presence in the region.

Mark Green had asked several USAID bureaus, including mine, to collaborate on a new program to address the Sahel's dire security problems and humanitarian crisis. The USAID bureaus were having trouble acting in concert, primarily because there had been too much chattering and bickering and not enough action. Steiger put me in charge of bringing the bureaus together and developing a multi-bureau strategy.

In June 2018, I led a group of 25 USAID staff to Niger, and from there traveled on to Mali to meet with the USAID mission staff. I also visited the headquarters of U.S. Africa Command in Stuttgart, Germany, where the USAID senior development advisor and her staff introduced me to Defense Department leaders responsible for the Sahel. It didn't take long to figure out which members of the career staff knew how to get down to business, and which preferred a never-ending series of chatty meetings. Spending most of my time with the former, we quickly pulled together a coherent strategy and an implementation plan. Career staff who had been squabbling with bureaucrats from other bureaus or embassies and dragging their feet got in line once they received clear direction from above. The results made a sufficiently favorable impression on agency leaders that they decided to give me a promotion.

In July 2018, Steiger offered me the position of director of the Office of Civilian-Military Cooperation. Steiger, who unlike Mark Green had a strong interest in civilian-military cooperation, told me he had recommended me to the Presidential Personnel Office for this position because he wanted to get more out of this office. He said that if I did well in that job, then I would be the leading candidate to run the new bureau he had mentioned when I'd interviewed to join the agency. That new bureau now had a name—the Bureau for Conflict Prevention and Stabilization, or CPS for short.

I told Steiger that the Office of Civilian-Military Cooperation aligned well with my expertise, but added that its parent bureau urgently needed a political appointee at the next level up, the level of deputy assistant administrator. The bureau had three positions at that level, and in prior administrations at least one had been held by a political appointee, yet career staff had occupied all three since the end of the Obama presidency. With career staff in those three positions as well as the position of acting bureau head, I said, the agency leadership had little visibility of most of the bureau's activities.

Steiger replied that it would be too hard to get the Presidential Personnel Office to appoint me as a deputy assistant administrator. For that position, they would want someone who had managed $500 million somewhere. That comment caught me off guard. Few, if any, of the politically appointed deputy assistant administrators in other bureaus met that threshold. Trump had been in office for a year and a half; surely the Presidential Personnel Office had to be more concerned at this point with filling key vacancies with the best available candidates, rather than waiting for people who met a criterion that was unrealistic and not especially germane. Steiger also noted that the agency leadership would soon have eyes inside the bureau's leadership circle because a new political appointee was coming over from the National Security Council to serve as acting head, Tim Ziemer.

Steiger clearly didn't want to budge on the deputy assistant secretary position. I could have tried pushing harder, but from my time with the military I'd learned that someone who tried too hard to get a position was liable to get slapped with the career-limiting label of prima donna. I told Steiger I was ready to take on the directorship of the Office of Civilian-Military Cooperation, and thanked him for the opportunity.

Word of the appointment fueled speculation that I was a leading candidate to lead the new bureau. A short time later, a senior agency official advised me to avoid telling anyone I was interested in leading the new bureau, because I wasn't the only person who wanted that job, and if other people knew I was in the running, then I would be in the crosshairs. It wouldn't take long to discover that I was already in someone's crosshairs.

Chapter 10

Fixing a Broken Organization

On July 30, 2018, I officially became the director of the USAID Office of Civilian-Military Cooperation. The director and the majority of the office's other fifty-five employees were located in the USAID headquarters in Washington, with the remainder based at the Department of Defense's geographic combatant commands and the Pentagon. Those at the Defense Department sites included seven foreign service officers who were among the most senior people in the agency.

CMC, as the office was called within the agency, was home to several uniformed military officers. Most of these officers had commanded military units during previous assignments, and most would command again in the future, but for now they served in the humbler role of liaison officer. They accepted their relegation to cubicles with such aplomb that no one would have suspected they had previously led hundreds of people from expansive offices. They knew more about leadership than most people at USAID, and in time I learned to consult them on many of the challenges I confronted.

Word of my appointment leaked out several weeks before my official start date. Several CMC staff members who heard the news contacted me in advance to set up meetings, during which they complained at length about the state of affairs at CMC.

The management practices of my predecessors, I was told, had turned CMC into one of USAID's most dysfunctional offices. The individuals who had led the office prior to my arrival stood accused of bullying, harassment, use of government resources for private gain, and other offenses.

In signing on to work at USAID, I had expected to spend most of my time on issues of development and national security policy. I had done that much as a senior advisor. In this office, however, the personnel and ethical problems were so daunting that they became my primary focus.

Through my research on politics, development, and counterinsurgency, I'd acquired a deep familiarity with corruption and its antidotes. Stopping corruption, I had concluded, requires leaders with strong moral convictions, and those convictions usually have deep cultural and religious roots. In my books, I had lauded leaders in the developing world whose ethical principles had led them to fight governmental corruption, knowing full well that a culture of corruption could spell their doom. I had never imagined that I would one day find myself standing at the same perilous precipice of moral decision, or that U.S. government officials would fight back as viciously as third-world tyrants.

Although corruption was not culturally acceptable in most of the United States, there was enough acceptance at agencies of the U.S. government to make it a recurring problem. The misuse of public authority for private gain was especially common at agencies like USAID that issued big-dollar contracts to private companies and non-profit organizations. USAID shelled out more than $20 billion a year for acquisition and assistance— more than the gross national product of many of the nations that received the aid. From the career staff, I heard numerous stories about shady interactions between USAID officials and the recipients of USAID contracting dollars. Contractors were hauled off in handcuffs from time to time, but USAID employees seldom incurred more than a slap on the wrist.

Although U.S. law required all federal employees to report waste, fraud, and abuse to authorities, USAID employees routinely disregarded this law, either because they feared retaliation by the perpetrators or because they wanted to protect cronies. Occasionally, individuals did report evidence of corrupt behavior, usually to the USAID Office of Employee and Labor Relations or the Office of Inspector General (OIG). The more serious allegations were supposed to be handled by the Office of Inspector General, but various agency officials told me that this office frequently ignored allegations of infractions by senior government officials, a problem common at other agencies as well. In the few instances when USAID employees were disciplined, the punishments tended to be lighter when the perpetrator was a senior career official, belonged to the civil service or foreign service, or was based in Washington. They were more severe when the person was low in rank, lacked union protections, or was based abroad.

In one of the inspector general's semiannual reports, for instance, the very short section on employee misconduct stated that a local national working for USAID in South Africa had been forced to resign after an investigation found that the individual had "made false statements on his time and attendance sheet and medical note." Had the inspectors dug into the time and attendance sheets of unionized employees in the Ronald Reagan Building and applied the same standards, the agency would have had to fire hundreds of people.

On the same page of that report, the USAID inspector general described the vastly different treatment afforded a senior official of the Overseas Private Investment Corporation (OPIC), another federal organization that fell under its remit. "An OIG investigation found that a senior employee of OPIC was married to an employee of a company that won two OPIC contracts valued at $987,000," the report stated. "The senior employee failed to disclose her relationship prior to participating in two OPIC technical evaluation boards, and twice failed to complete a standard conflict of interest disclosure statement." In most American institutions—local governments, school systems, private companies, even universities—an employee who repeatedly lied for the purpose of winning a million dollars in contracts for her husband's company would have been fired immediately, and probably criminally prosecuted as well. Not so in the federal government. Here was the stern punishment meted out for this act of fraud: "OPIC issued the employee an official letter of reprimand in December 2019 which required remedial ethics training."

That's right—remedial ethics training. Such lenience sent a clear signal to other bureaucrats that the risks of corruption were low in comparison with the rewards.

By the time I became office director, I had learned that numerous managers at USAID, on both the political and career sides, routinely shut their eyes to the misdeeds of subordinates, for reasons of self-interest. I didn't want to be that type of manager. My years in the Defense Department had instilled the belief that leaders bore responsibility for the actions of everyone under their authority. Instituting accountability and rewarding good work would buck agency norms, I knew, but I took it as a positive—my example could encourage other managers in the agency to perform basic and essential duties of management. If the Trump administration was really going to drain the swamp, it would need bold executives to dig the first drainage channels.

Within days of assuming the new position, I spoke with my new boss, Tim Ziemer, about the reports I'd received of mismanagement and unethical conduct within CMC. Rob Jenkins technically had authority over my office, but in practice I reported to Ziemer because political appointees were not supposed to report to career staff. Ziemer had retired from the Navy as a rear admiral, and had served as a senior executive for Christian relief organizations. He had also been a political appointee in the Obama administration. To my bewilderment and that of many other Trump appointees, a small number of Obama appointees had managed to obtain jobs as political appointees in the Trump administration. What we heard was that these individuals had friends in high places who had convinced others of influence that the appointees were "apolitical" technocrats.

As I explained the situation to Ziemer, he listened intently and conveyed the impression that he was ready to help me find the best solution. As managers, he remarked, we were obliged to act on complaints unless they were obviously frivolous. He recommended that I seek advice from the agency's human resources office, the laboriously named Office of Human Capital and Talent Management.

I proceeded to meet with Bob Leavitt, the head of that office. I laid out before him the numerous allegations that had already come to my attention. Having previously served in my bureau, Leavitt was already familiar with the cast of characters, and he told me he had been shocked by some of the things they had been able to get away with. Leavitt, in turn, connected me to Frank Walsh, the head of the USAID Office of Employee and Labor Relations, which had the authority to investigate the types of problems that had been reported.

Leavitt and Walsh suggested a management review, conducted jointly by their offices and the Bureau for Management. They cautioned that a management review would ruffle a lot of feathers. Many managers in the agency, they said, avoided badly needed management reviews for this reason.

"People will lose their jobs," Leavitt said to me when we were alone in his office. "Are you sure you are ready to go ahead with this?"

This prediction, more than anything else, impressed the gravity of the situation on me. Losing a job was a serious business, especially in the federal government, where it was customary to keep a job for a lifetime. I wasn't eager for people to lose their jobs. In my younger days, I had experienced a thrill in confronting the wicked and in proving I was right, but experience, religious contemplation, and the study of history had taught me that such self-righteousness was a manifestation of hubris, of man's conceit that he could possess the knowledge and wisdom of God. Zealous pursuit of justice could lead to errors in judgment and new injustices. I couldn't be sure that whoever investigated the allegations would be thorough and fair, though I didn't dwell on that point as much as I would have if I'd known then what I learned later about federal investigations.

Nonetheless, certain employees evidently had engaged in waste, fraud, and abuse, in violation of nearly every ethical code known to man. Having been vested with executive authority, I had taken on obligations to safeguard the integrity of the government, including a legal obligation to the government and a patriotic obligation to the American people, on top of the omnipresent moral obligation to God. If I were to treat the teacher in Indiana, the carpenter in Nevada, the pharmacist in Georgia, and my own staff as I would wish to be treated, then I had to prevent federal bureaucrats from stealing public funds and trampling on other bureaucrats.

I was aware that reporting subordinates for misconduct could provoke retaliation or drag me into an administrative quagmire, but believed that leaders of character should not let such risks stop them. I'd never been one to run from danger or difficulty, and I wasn't going to start now. Prudence, it was true, dictated that the contemplated course of action should not be suicidal, but the odds of catastrophic failure seemed low. Senior agency officials appeared to share my devotion to ethics and accountability. Bill Steiger had implored the political appointees to search for the misuse of money by career bureaucrats so that the agency leadership could set it aright. Bob Leavitt and Frank Walsh had said it was their job to back managers who held employees to federal ethical standards, and they had themselves taken action against subordinates for failing to meet those standards. If anyone tried to retaliate against me, I could surely count on support from these quarters.

I also weighed the practical consequences of inaction. Tolerating employees known to be engaged in corruption probably wouldn't land me in any trouble with the USAID authorities—no one else was getting busted for that offense—but it could diminish my reputation and effectiveness within USAID and the Defense Department. If business were to go on as usual, moreover, employees with records of abusing power would be perpetual drags on the morale of my staff. Thus, inviting external authorities to scrutinize the office was likely to improve the performance of the office and its employees.

This was the Aristotelian moral reasoning, and the Dostoyevskyan theology, that led me to the fateful decision. I told Leavitt I was ready to go ahead with the management review.

After a few more preparatory meetings, I informed the CMC staff that the review would start soon. Before it even began, the person who had served as acting office director for the past eighteen months, Bob Schmidt, decided to jump ship. His lifeboat was a one-year detail to another USAID office. The head of that office, the Office of Security, was John Voorhees, a personal friend of Schmidt whom I had not yet met but who would play a large role in what was to follow. In the federal government, a detail temporarily reassigns an individual to another agency job, with the concurrence of the managers of the giving and receiving offices. As the head of the giving office, I was happy to part with someone who had run the office into the ground.

In the ensuing weeks, two individuals from the Management Bureau and one from the Office of Employee and Labor Relations conducted the management review. Interviewing CMC's current employees and some of its former employees, they ran down lists of questions about mismanagement and misconduct. The CMC staff buzzed with speculation and rumor about who was saying what to the interviewers. A number of individuals—the ones with the most reason to be concerned—tried so strenuously to find out what other people were saying that I and several human resources officials had to issue individual reprimands and warn the entire office that they should cease efforts to find out what others had said.

The review uncovered a wide range of problems. Some were delivered to me in writing, while those of a more sensitive nature were delivered orally. I wrote down a list of the latter, which read as follows:

1.   Unauthorized personnel actions, most notably the creation of a new civil service deputy
2.   Bullying of employees
3.   Allocation of nearly all CMC travel money to two individuals
4.   Maintenance of a small inner circle of favorites that dominates hiring panels and receives most of the perks, such as bonuses and slots at war college courses
5.   Marginalization of senior foreign service officers and elevation of pliant junior foreign service officers
6.   Firing of a staff member for the mistakes of another staff member who was part of the inner circle
7.   Fostering of low employee morale, as reflected in high attrition and low Federal Employee Viewpoint Survey scores
8.   Unprofessional remarks at meetings and events with Defense Department, undermining USAID credibility
9.   Lack of strategic vision
10. Conflicts of interest

During and after the management review, I received additional information directly from USAID and Defense Department staff about waste, fraud, and abuse involving employees in my office. Forwarding this material to the review team and other relevant offices would increase the likelihood the agency would hold the perpetrators accountable. It would also increase the likelihood those perpetrators would learn details of my involvement in the management review, whether through legal action or through improper transmission of information among friendly bureaucrats. That thought gave me pause. If someone found a way to get back at me, they could damage not only me but the family that depended on me. But withholding evidence of criminality and misconduct would be irresponsible and cowardly, so I didn't hesitate long before handing over all of the information to the appropriate authorities.

The review team and the authorities had said they would do their best to protect the identities of sources. Later, however, I would find out that at least one person learned I had shared incriminating information about him with agency authorities. The bureaucratic corruption I subsequently encountered would lead me to suspect that my identity had been divulged by a friend of the accused inside the agency, though it's also possible the information was revealed during disciplinary proceedings.

The most incriminating evidence concerned Mick Crnkovich. During the preceding eighteen months, when the office had possessed no political appointees, Crnkovich had served as acting deputy director. Schmidt, as someone with a type B personality, had let the type A Crnkovich perform many of the director duties. Several members of the office's staff later told me that when Crnkovich bullied them, he boasted that whatever he did had the backing of Schmidt. It was probably because of Mick's outsized role that everyone in USAID knew the pair as "Mick and Bob," rather than "Bob and Mick." As in "Can you believe what Mick and Bob just did to that poor employee?" Or "Rob Jenkins is relying on Mick and Bob to push around the senior foreign service officers." Or "That office has really gone downhill since Mick and Bob took over."

While working as a full-time GS-15 employee at USAID, Crnkovich was simultaneously serving as the chairman of the board of directors at IMPL. PROJECT, a defense and development contractor. According to federal law, serving on a board of directors in any capacity imputed a financial interest in the organization to an individual, regardless of whether the organization was directly compensating that person. The agency's designated ethics official, John "Jack" Ohlweiler, could have concluded that IMPL's contracting work for USAID made it unethical for a USAID employee to serve as its chairman of the board, but instead he had authorized Crnkovich to serve in both capacities provided that he didn't use his government job to benefit IMPL.

Using his government job to benefit IMPL, however, was exactly what Crnkovich was doing. USAID employees, in and out of CMC, attested that Crnkovich was using government time and government information to pursue government contracts for IMPL. They also stated that Crnkovich had directed select CMC staff to gather information for IMPL's benefit at Defense Department sites. Witnesses inside the Defense Department corroborated this information.

The management review also exposed other concerns about Crnkovich. Various USAID employees reported that Crnkovich was saying he despised Republicans and objected to the conservative direction in which I and other Trump appointees were taking USAID. Although career staff enjoyed considerable freedom of expression during their off-duty lives as private citizens, federal rules prohibited them from badmouthing the president in the workplace. Subsequently it came to light that Crnkovich was one of several career employees in the bureau who belonged to the Truman National Security Project, the Democratic incubator for national security professionals.

Based upon the information about IMPL that surfaced during the management review, the agency asked me if I wanted to reassign Crnkovich to another position temporarily while the matter was investigated in greater detail. I answered in the affirmative. In conformity with standard procedures, Frank Walsh's office offered the agency's Office of Inspector General the opportunity to conduct the investigation, and the inspector general agreed to perform the task. The investigation eventually would gather enough information to force Crnkovich out of the agency.

Just as Crnkovich was leaving CMC, I received an email from someone whom I did not know, Special Agent Lance Timberlake (not his real name). He introduced himself as an investigator in the Office of Security, and said that he was conducting a periodic security clearance review for Bob Schmidt, whose clearance was up for renewal. We set up a time for Timberlake to meet with me in my office.

I had done interviews like this dozens of times before, because I had been the supervisor, instructor, or colleague of numerous individuals who had been required to undergo periodic clearance renewals. During the meetings, the investigator asked a laundry list of questions aimed at determining whether the person could be entrusted with classified information. In more than a decade of these interviews, I had never provided information that called anyone's suitability for a security clearance into serious question.

As Special Agent Timberlake went through his list of questions, he asked if there was anything I knew about Schmidt that would cast doubt on his suitability for a security clearance. I replied that the office management review had revealed some facts that might fit that category. It had identified serious misconduct that had occurred on Schmidt's watch, and at least some of the foul play had been known to him. I gave Timberlake the contact information of the individuals who had conducted the management review so that he could hear from them directly.

When we were done, Timberlake looked troubled. He made a comment to the effect that he had expected just another routine interview. Now, he said, he would have to rethink the whole matter.

I never learned what Timberlake did with the information I had given him, but I do know that it didn't lead to the suspension or revocation of Schmidt's clearance. Schmidt continued working at the USAID Office of Security, where possession of a clearance was a prerequisite. As I would later discover, the job of determining whether the information should affect Schmidt's clearance belonged to the head of the Office of Security, John Voorhees—the same person who had offered Schmidt refuge.

The management review found evidence that another CMC supervisor, Elizabeth Feary, had engaged in abusive conduct toward subordinates, excessive telework, disobedience of a supervisor's orders, and conspiracy to retaliate against individuals who had reported adverse information during the management review. I also learned that the supervisory authorities she held had not been conferred upon her through the proper procedures. With the concurrence of the human resources experts, I relieved her of those supervisory authorities. She lodged complaints with human resources officials, who, I was told, informed her that she was as deserving of censure this time as she had been a decade earlier when she had behaved similarly at another job. She decided to depart CMC for another bureau.

Rumors would soon spread across the agency that I single-handedly went around firing staff after becoming the director of CMC. Those rumors flourished because I kept quiet about the personnel actions, in accordance with the advice of agency lawyers. In truth, I never acted alone, and never could have done so. As a supervisor of career federal employees, I had to consult and coordinate with multiple offices before taking major personnel actions.

A number of senior USAID officials commended me for taking the time and effort to hold employees accountable, and expressed hope that it would motivate other managers to hold their people accountable. Other career staff thanked me for removing managers who were mistreating subordinates, and for detoxifying the work environment. After a protracted period of chronic absenteeism and tardiness at CMC, conscientious staff members welcomed a workplace where everyone came into the office at least four times a week and worked the entire day.

With the departures, I had to fill two supervisory positions immediately, and I would soon have to fill two more that would open up with the normal rotation of personnel. Scouring the agency, I sought people who had strong supervisory and analytical capabilities and were dedicated to the organization's mission. I was able to bring in three rising stars from other parts of the agency, and I promoted another from within the office. Although I gave no special preference to any group, believing it contrary to American principles of meritocracy and individualism, I ended up filling all four of these positions with women, two of whom were African-American.

One of these women, Stephanie (not her real name), came from the Office of Conflict Management and Mitigation. The title of that office ranked high on the charts of agency farces. The office's own toxic leaders had fostered conflicts so bitter that they had driven most of the staff to leave. The Office of Conflict Management and Mitigation had crashed and burned for the same reason as CMC and too many other offices at USAID—the toleration of bad managers by USAID's senior leadership. I asked a few senior officials why the problems at the Office of Conflict Management and Mitigation had been allowed to persist for so long, and was told that "nobody wanted to make a tough decision." Stephanie had stuck it out in the Office of Conflict Management and Mitigation longer than most, and had managed to escape with her reputation and mental well-being intact.

Another was Alexandra (not her real name), whom I had first met in Africa when she was working there as a senior USAID official. We had a common penchant for rapid and decisive action, and a shared impatience for inordinate debate and deliberation. She was boisterous and feisty, spinning from one meeting to the next with a ball of extroverted energy. It was a good complement to my own leadership style, as I was soft-spoken and calm (the uncharitable might have said bland and robotic), making things happen quietly.

The internal promotion went to Courtney (not her real name). I had observed that she had the right talents and skills for the position in question, and my informal polling indicated that other staff had confidence in her ability to take on the supervisory responsibilities. Stepping into the breach immediately, she kept the bureaucratic machinery moving without interruption.

The other person I picked for a leadership position was Jacqueline (not her real name), who came on detail from another office. She had a sterling track record as a manager, in an agency where managerial talent was scarce. She was a foreign service officer, which was a major plus because the job involved supervision of and collaboration with foreign service officers.

As I spent more time speaking with staff and asking questions, I received new evidence of waste, fraud, and abuse within CMC. In one case, after receiving multiple complaints from staff about the poor performance of someone in my office, I was ready to give him only an oral warning, but when I mentioned the complaints during one of my meetings with top human resource officials, I was told that an oral warning carried no weight. They advised me to issue a written warning, noting that this individual had a lengthy history of subpar performance. I also discussed this case with an agency lawyer, who encouraged me to put it in writing because it was the right thing for a supervisor to do, even though many other supervisors in the agency were unwilling to do it. So I issued a written warning.

Several months into my tenure, I learned that my predecessors had detailed a staff member outside the agency without proper authorization, and in violation of agency rules. This employee was largely disconnected from the office, and his main activity appeared to be collecting information for Rob Jenkins, who had set up the arrangement and had been speaking with him nearly every day. After consulting with human resources officials, I nullified the unauthorized action and required the individual to go back to work in the Ronald Reagan Building.

The departures of toxic individuals and the arrival of a new management team greatly diminished tensions in the office. They did not, however, eliminate all problems. Tribal conflicts persisted between the two groups that accounted for most of the agency's staff—the foreign service and the civil service. The USAID headquarters is populated by four tribes: the foreign service, the civil service, the political appointees, and the contractors. The political appointees are supposed to be in charge, but foreign service officers and civil servants often exploit the lack of knowledge among these two groups to manipulate or circumvent them. The foreign service officers view themselves as the intellectual leaders of the agency, since they spend most of their careers at the agency's overseas missions. The civil servants, who reside permanently in Washington, know the headquarters system best and have the best networks inside the Reagan Building. The contractors often rank among the most productive employees, and they are always the most shabbily treated, in both cases because they are the easiest to fire.

Within CMC, some foreign service officers still had chips on their shoulders because of the mistreatment they had suffered under prior civil service management. They complained that their expertise didn't receive due credit among the civil servants. Some civil servants resented the foreign service officers for invoking their overseas experience as proof of their superior command of development issues, and groused that foreign service officers pawned off their work on civil servants. In meetings with individuals and the office as a whole, I had to stress repeatedly that every type of employee brought strengths to the table, and no type had a monopoly on the truth.

Other conflicts were personality-based. Certain individuals were quick to provoke others, and certain individuals were quick to be provoked. Many of the leading lights in the first group were also prominent in the second. A handful of people seemed to play roles in an episode of office drama at least once a month, while others never had any role to play. From time to time, I called someone into my office to say, "I would like to thank you because I never have to deal with drama that involves you."

At USAID, annual performance reviews of staff received exceptionally large amounts of time and attention. The emphasis was especially high during my time at CMC because the performance appraisal system had just been revised. For some members of the staff, the performance appraisal submissions took precedence over their work in the weeks leading up to the deadline. One of my senior employees demanded that the whole office stop what it was doing for an entire month to focus on performance appraisals. I turned the proposal down.

From speaking with various staff members in and out of CMC, I learned that the performance appraisal system worked very differently in practice than it looked on paper. For the most part, employees wrote their own appraisals, including the sections their supervisors were supposed to write. Few supervisors were willing to challenge the statements produced by their subordinates, no matter how excessive they might be in self-adulation. I was informed that if supervisors did try to insert negative comments about the employee, the subordinates were liable to ask another official to write the appraisal instead, or to file a grievance.

As a result, the performance appraisals almost invariably described each employee in glowing terms, and hence the appraisals were not worth the tremendous amount of employee time invested in them. If you really wanted to know how someone was performing, I learned, you spoke with people who had worked with that individual. When conversing face-to-face, the co-workers would provide negative information they'd never put in a written document, knowing that the employee in question might eventually see any document written about them.

Once I figured out how this feedback system worked, I used it liberally. As office director, I had to screen candidates for both regular positions and temporary assignments. I interviewed applicants, but an interview wasn't a good way of telling who might end up destroying your organization. The most toxic individuals can present themselves remarkably well in an interview. I therefore went to my staff and asked them to check with their networks about each candidate.

Very rapidly, usually within twenty-four hours, I would receive multiple reports from people who had worked with the candidate. The comments typically came in pithy and unequivocal form, such as "Robin gets things done without pissing anyone off," or "Everyone hates Bob," or "Buffy is a good GS-12 but should never be given a GS-13 position." Usually, the jury was unanimous in its verdict.

There was one exception to the general rule that written appraisals could not be trusted. The foreign service had a special selection process for its top positions, which were known collectively as the foreign service senior leadership group. The agency sent questionnaires to people who had worked with the individual under consideration, and the responses were aggregated into a binder. The survey respondents were willing to provide candid input because they were not identified by name in the aggregate results and USAID produced only a handful of the binders, which were kept under lock and key and shown only to people with a need to know. My office had seven senior leadership group positions, and several were up for competition during my tenure, so I was among the few who possessed the highly coveted access to the binder.

The contents of the senior leadership group binder were engrossing, at least by the standards of bureaucratic documents. The text mainly consisted of generalizations derived from multiple sources, along the lines of "most respondents rated Pat as one of the best executives in the agency," or "all respondents stated that Chris routinely alienated colleagues through his pompous and self-serving behavior." Anonymous quotes from specific individuals were also included, such as, "one of Sally's former supervisors remarked that she could perform tasks adequately but fell on her face whenever she was assigned a large project."

Decisions on a person's next assignment could be career-altering, even career-ending. I therefore devoted special attention to these decisions. Most of the managerial decisions I had to make were less momentous, but they still made differences in the lives of people I had come to know and respect. In making decisions, I sought whenever possible to show employees that their leadership valued their efforts and looked out for their well-being. My time at CMC brought home to me that each of us, in our daily lives, has opportunities to make moral choices, and there is deep satisfaction to be found in making choices that benefit others—the sort of satisfaction that strengthens our links to our fellow humans and our creator.

Chapter 11

Beyond the Washington Bubble

My second priority as office director, preceded only by fixing personnel and ethical problems, was filling the void of strategic direction. Numerous staff had complained that they didn't know what the office was trying to achieve. They'd simply been told to spend their time working on whatever issues related to civilian-military cooperation interested them, regardless of whether the issues were connected to the objectives of the agency or the administration. It was a surefire way to squander taxpayer-funded labor.

Based on White House and USAID leadership priorities and the work I'd done as senior advisor, I devised a vision, a mission, and objectives for the office. In line with the new National Security Strategy, all three emphasized competition with China, Russia, and Iran. At weekly office-wide meetings, I told the staff to hunt for new opportunities for civilian-military cooperation that aligned with our office's mission and objectives.

Once opportunities took shape, I sought to "build consensus" across the agency. Unlike leaders at the Department of Defense, who sent orders to subordinates who then executed those orders, USAID's leaders first shared ideas with others in the agency and solicited feedback so everyone felt their opinions had been taken into consideration. Career officials, from the top on down, took personal offense if they were not consulted before a final decision was made. If someone caught you not building consensus with them—for instance by learning you had left them off the cc line of an email—you were liable to get called out for it, and hence would be obligated to beg forgiveness and promise to be more inclusive in the future.

For leaders at my level, obtaining support from other USAID officials helped us convince agency leaders to allocate scarce resources to our causes. But the consensus-building process also gave career officials undue influence over decisions that should have been the exclusive preserve of political appointees. In addition, much time was required to meet with so many people and find compromises that pleased everyone, and at the end there was always someone who felt slighted because his or her opinion on some point had been disregarded. It was another of the reasons why USAID took so long to get things done.

To seek opportunities for civilian-military cooperation and to fulfill my managerial duties, I traveled to the Department of Defense commands where my office's senior foreign service officers worked. They included Special Operations Command (SOCOM) and Central Command (CENTCOM) in Tampa, Florida; Southern Command (SOUTHCOM) in Doral, Florida; Africa Command (AFRICOM) and European Command (EUCOM) in Stuttgart, Germany; Indo-Pacific Command (INDOPACOM) in Honolulu, Hawaii; and the Pentagon.

During these visits, I made a point of meeting the heads of the Theater Special Operations Commands, which were attached to each of the Defense Department's geographic commands. The Theater Special Operations Commands oversaw most of the special operations units in the region's countries—the units that often made the best military partners for USAID. In some cases, I learned that USAID staff had not had meaningful contact with these special operations elements for years, so I spent time linking them together and finding opportunities for collaboration that went beyond lip service and photo taking.

When time permitted, I traveled to countries where USAID and Department of Defense personnel were working together to advance America's foreign policy objectives. Past experience had taught me that the only way to find out what was really happening in these countries was to visit them and speak with the people in the thick of the action. They would share much more information with a new acquaintance in person than over the phone or in a video teleconference, including much that they never had time or interest to report within their own chain of command. USAID political appointees who lacked international experience sometimes had difficulty comprehending this point. When I told one senior appointee of my intention to visit a few USAID missions, he scoffed that I could get what I needed by picking up the phone and calling them.

I wasn't required to travel to USAID missions, and no one at USAID would have faulted me for staying in Washington to deal with office management and the agency reorganization. Overseas trips would eat up a week or two at a time, requiring that I spend evenings and weekends back in Washington catching up on office matters. Seeing that my time in government would be limited and that I needed to demonstrate my worthiness for promotion, I readily put in the extra time on evenings and weekends, albeit with a sense of guilt about losing time with Kelli and our three teenagers.

The opportunities for civilian-military cooperation varied greatly from one country to the next. The most difficult challenges, and the most auspicious opportunities, were to be found in countries where both USAID and the Defense Department had large numbers of people, which often meant countries with high levels of internal conflict. For that reason, I traveled to some of the earth's most violent places.

During these trips, I sought to get as close to the scene of conflict as I could, but embassy security officers usually kept me well away from areas considered dangerous. Ever since the death of U.S. Ambassador to Libya Chris Stevens in the Benghazi attack of September 2012, the State Department had been extremely risk-averse. The Department of Defense had a greater tolerance for risk, so whenever possible I sought the military's assistance in getting closer to the fighting. Sometimes they took me to places where none of the embassy civilians were willing or able to go. More could be learned at these locations than any place else, because you could talk to large numbers of people who were witnessing the conflict firsthand, and could glimpse the often-appalling conditions that the local people had to endure.

At one of the first destinations, Mogadishu, the State Department had become so risk averse that American government personnel were forbidden from leaving the grounds of the airport, even though their European counterparts and the representatives of international agencies routinely drove through Mogadishu's streets. The security restrictions and precautions inside the Mogadishu airport compound were more stringent than those I had encountered in Iraq and Afghanistan. For visitors, confinement to the airport was a minor nuisance, preventing us from making brief visits into the country. For the USAID staff, it was a massive impediment to overseeing hundreds of millions of dollars of aid programs.

In each country, I conferred extensively with the senior USAID representative, known as the mission director or country director, and the rest of the USAID staff. The agency's mission civil-military coordinator for the country usually served as the control officer for my trip, responsible for setting up meetings, arranging transportation, and performing other tasks for which they were overqualified, although I never heard them complain about the burdens my visits imposed upon them. I was invited into their homes, and into the homes of other USAID, Defense, and State staff, for dinners that were always congenial and informative.

My travels did not begin until Donald Trump had been in office for well over a year, so I was surprised to find apparitions of Barack Obama lingering at USAID's overseas offices. The walls at some locations were still adorned with posters containing the USAID mission statement from the Obama era, which prioritized the ending of poverty, rather than the Trump-era mission statement, which emphasized promoting self-reliance and supporting American foreign policy. When I was treated to recently created PowerPoint presentations, some showed Obama's mission statement on the opening slide.

From what I could discern, the USAID foreign service officers in these countries offered little overt resistance to the Trump administration. The people who had most fervently despised the Trump administration, I was told, had quit in 2017 and gone to work for the contractors that implemented USAID projects. But while most of the USAID foreign service officers were now going along with the shift in their government's priorities, the programs they were managing were, with only a few exceptions, multi-year programs that had been created during the Obama administration and largely reflected that administration's preferences. Some had been relabeled to assure political appointees and Republican congressmen that the agency was implementing the new administration's policies.

I kept an eye out for mislabeling as well as for outrageous leftism. Prior to joining the administration, in March 2017, I had pointed out exemplary outrages of this sort in a *Wall Street Journal* article. For instance, the agency had touted its "Purple My School" as follows: "Through teachers' facilitation, students discuss issues surrounding homophobia, how to create safe spaces for LGBTI students, and are encouraged to wear, draw, or make something purple." A program to advance transgender rights in Central America had reportedly "helped Guatemala's Election Tribunal update election manuals and provide trainings to electoral officials on how to be sensitive to people whose appearances are not congruent with the birth name on their personal identification card." USAID had spent counterterrorism funds on sponsorship of Somali girls' basketball teams and "community dialogue sessions" that the agency considered to be "essential to the stabilization of regions that have suffered from mistrust, conflict and turmoil for decades."

During my travels as a Trump appointee, I came across a few programs of similar preposterousness that had been rebranded to appease the new administration. In one country, a women's book club that had been started in the Obama era to promote women's empowerment and transgender awareness was now said to be a counterterrorism program because women's voices were powerful instruments in the struggle against violent extremism. Such travesties were, however, the exception rather than the norm. Most of what I saw was more level-headed in design, if not necessarily in ultimate objective. By 2018, agency officials had either modified the most ridiculous programs to avoid the wrath of the Trump administration, or else had obscured them carefully enough to keep Trump appointees from seeing them.

In recognition of the bureaucratic clinging to yesteryear's policies, Chief of Staff Steiger had recently asserted greater control over the agency's field programs. To ensure conformity with the administration's priorities, he'd implemented a review process that mandated political appointee approval of all new programs. But it was as yet unclear whether the career staff could devise methods of bureaucratic jujitsu to bypass this mechanism in a bureaucracy where they knew the tricks of the trade and the appointees didn't.

The Trump administration priority that received the greatest emphasis from Green and Steiger was the countering of China. Every part of the U.S. national security establishment, in fact, had made China its top priority by early 2018. Although some pundits and politicians in the United States were still questioning whether China really was an adversary, nearly all of the American diplomats and military personnel I met during my overseas travels—even card-carrying liberals who in the past had earned the nickname of "Panda Huggers" for sympathizing with China—were alarmed by the growth of threatening Chinese behavior. Their perceptions solidified my conviction that Trump had been right to focus his national security strategy on countering China.

When I traveled to the Philippines in October 2018, I was startled by how much had changed since my last visit to the country, nearly a decade earlier. At the time of that visit, the U.S. embassy had been preoccupied with Islamic terrorism on Mindanao and other Philippine islands. Now it was focused primarily on Chinese activity in the country, which was exploding. The Chinese government was bringing Philippine government officials and military officers to China for training and education. It was bribing members of these same groups, as well as Philippine journalists, to advance its interests. With an aid budget far larger than that of the United States, the Chinese were funding infrastructure projects that would promote China's mercantilist trade practices, and underwriting hotels where their diplomats and businessmen could dine on Peking duck and dim sum and control the wifi, rather than having to stay at a Marriott or Hilton where they would be forced to consume cheeseburgers and Caesar salads and contend with wifi under someone else's control. Until very recently, China hadn't allocated any aid funds to health, education, or jobs for the poor, as Western countries routinely did, but it was starting to move into those sectors, too.

One of the clearest areas of overlap between defense and development in the Philippines, and in many other maritime nations, was "illegal, unreported, and unregulated" (IUU) fishing. The Chinese were the world leaders in this activity. Enormous Chinese trawlers were crisscrossing the oceans and seas to scoop up fish, with no regard for international catch limits or the sovereignty of dozens of America's allies. Once they plundered an area's fish population to the point that it could not regenerate, they moved on to a new expanse.

Illegal fishing was a development issue, as it impinged on efforts to help nations produce food for internal consumption and export. It was a defense issue, because the Chinese navy was surreptitiously abetting the illegal fishing vessels. When I returned to Washington, I told my staff to redirect considerable time and attention toward IUU fishing. I subsequently learned that the National Security Council was thinking along similar lines.

My next trip, in December 2018, took me to Iraq. By this time, ISIS had been stripped of its control of Mosul, Ramadi, and other cities by Iraqi forces, with Iranian and American backing. But the oppression of Iraq's Sunni Muslims by Shiites—the problem that had given rise to ISIS—had not ended. Shiites still dominated the Iraqi government, and neither they nor the Iranian-backed Shiite militias who had rescued the government were willing to treat Sunnis as equal citizens. Millions of displaced Sunnis lived in camps where stories of human rights abuses by Shiite guards ran rampant.

At this juncture, the U.S. embassy was focused first and foremost on the Ninevah Plain, where Iraq's Christian and Yazidi minorities were concentrated. The Trump administration had allocated special support to these areas after learning that the Iraqi leadership had been neglecting them. To oversee the assistance, Vice President Mike Pence had appointed Max Primorac, a USAID political appointee who had joined USAID on the same day as me and had worked with me on a project during our early days as senior advisors. After visiting Baghdad, I traveled to the U.S. consulate in Erbil to spend several days discussing U.S. operations with Max and the military officials responsible for the Ninevah Plain.

From Iraq, I traveled to Saudi Arabia and the United Arab Emirates for meetings on Yemen. Since 2014, pro-Iranian Houthis had occupied the Yemeni capital of Sanaa, compelling American officials assigned to Yemen to work in neighboring Gulf countries. The Saudi and Emirati governments were backing anti-Houthi forces in the ongoing civil war, while USAID and other aid agencies tried to alleviate the suffering of Yemenis caught in the middle. The United Arab Emirates and their Yemeni partners, I learned, were achieving greater success in combating the Houthis than the international media was reporting, but the United States was struggling to articulate and implement policy, casting serious doubt on long-term support from the American Congress and people.

In early 2019, I traveled to Afghanistan, where USAID and the Department of Defense had regularly locked horns for the past seventeen years. The Obama administration had sought to pacify Afghanistan by blanketing it with development programs and deploying a "civilian surge" of more than one thousand U.S. government civilian employees to manage them, but it had been severely handicapped by the refusal of USAID and other civilian agencies to put their personnel in harm's way. Much of the American largesse had been siphoned off by the Taliban, the Afghan government, and development contractors. USAID had since abandoned its efforts to stabilize rural Afghanistan and shifted to economic and social development in the major population centers, where the agency's implementing partners were largely free from Taliban violence. Because of the insecurity of Afghanistan's roads, USAID was now funding programs to transport carpets, gemstones, and other goods to markets by air, a costly workaround that seemed unsustainable over the long term.

I visited the U.S. military headquarters in Kabul, which, although only a short walk from the USAID compound, had rarely been visited by USAID staff in recent years. Accompanied by a handful of USAID staff, I attended a daily command meeting inside a large, windowless room. With dozens of senior military officers packed around tables, the command meeting resembled ones I had attended in Kabul a decade earlier, when the U.S. military presence had been far larger. One officer delivered a weather forecast, and another reported the latest political developments. The bulk of the time was devoted to the operations of American forces and their Afghan partners, with PowerPoint slides identifying the targets and describing the results. Most of the targets were low-level commanders, bomb makers, or ditch diggers, for the insurgent bigwigs were all still living in Pakistan, beyond American reach. Just as it had been a decade earlier.

After we left the meeting, one of the USAID staff remarked, "For the first time since I've been here, I had a real sense of what is actually going on in the country." I did what I could to encourage cooperation between the USAID staff and the military headquarters. But when I departed I had the feeling that the ongoing shrinkage of the American presence would only further encourage the various agencies to focus narrowly on their lanes.

In what would be my final overseas trip as CMC Director, I traveled in April 2019 to Azerbaijan and Georgia. The trip began at the Azerbaijani capital of Baku, which sits on a peninsula surrounded by the cold, deep waters of the Caspian Sea. The city's strikingly modern office buildings, with their curved steel frames and shimmering glass, would have been at home in Paris or Dubai. When, however, we drove north, toward the Russian border, or south, toward the Iranian border, the modern façade of Baku quickly gave way to rustic villages resembling the one in the movie *Borat*.

As the only country bordering both Russia and Iran, Azerbaijan occupied a position of high strategic value. Both USAID and the Defense Department had been directed to "Counter Russian Influence" and "Counter Iranian Influence" across the globe, and U.S. government leaders were using these terms in public speeches, but U.S. agencies were finding it difficult to determine just how to counter these influences. The USAID mission director in Azerbaijan had a keen interest in civilian-military cooperation, so he and I had fruitful conversations with USAID and Defense Department staff about interagency activities that contributed to the countering of Russia and Iran.

From Azerbaijan, I flew to Tbilisi, the Georgian capital. Georgia was a functioning democracy, and suspicious of Russia, but it was also vulnerable to backsliding. Here, too, the USAID mission director was eager to work with Defense Department counterparts, and was already doing so on a number of fronts.

One theme that came up repeatedly at embassies and military commands was the lack of coordination between different elements of USAID. The staff of the Office of Foreign Disaster Assistance (OFDA), the agency's primary arm for humanitarian assistance, were not always in sync with the senior USAID officials. During a conference of USAID mission directors I attended at Maryland's National Harbor, several mission directors stood up to complain that OFDA seemed disconnected from the rest of the agency.

I sent Steiger and Ziemer a proposal for unifying the command of agency personnel under mission directors and senior development advisers. Both liked the proposal and got behind it. Bureaucrats generally do not like surrendering independence, and OFDA staff were no different, but the combined weight of Steiger and Ziemer left them no choice but to go along. As with everything at USAID, though, we had to build consensus through months of meetings and consultations.

At the end, Mark Green signed his name to the unification of authority at missions and Defense commands, under the mantra "One USAID." Instructions went out across the agency to put the concept into practice. I look back on it as one of my most significant accomplishments as a USAID employee.

In the grand scheme of things, it was a pretty small potato. At best, it would permit incremental improvements to USAID operations. Nevertheless, in the world of big government, where the plodding of bureaucratic mammoths is so slow as to be almost imperceptible, achieving anything of substance provides a degree of satisfaction.

Chapter 12

Tribal Warfare

All tribes have leaders. At USAID, the political appointees, foreign service officers, civil servants, and contractors each had their tribal leaders. Most of these leaders held formal positions of authority, in addition to possessing considerable unwritten authority. A select group of senior foreign service officers and civil servants enjoyed so much informal influence that they were likened to mafia godfathers. They had networks of people who supplied them with information, support, and cooperation, in return for jobs, promotions, perks, and protection. When individuals in their networks ran into trouble, say by harassing other people or failing to show up for work, the godfathers bailed them out. Their networks and deep knowledge of the agency's informal operating procedures allowed the bureaucratic dons to run circles around political appointees who sought to reform the agency.

Rob Jenkins enjoyed godfather status in the civil service. Over a period spanning more than two decades, he had accumulated an expansive network of supporters in the Reagan Building, people who would pull the necessary bureaucratic lever at a moment's notice. By obtaining money from hidden bureaucratic crevices, Jenkins had turned several junior employees into his own personal staff—an asset no other agency leader of his rank possessed—and they helped run the network.

Early in my time at USAID, I had submitted a formal request to another bureau to visit one of its overseas missions, and had received word back several weeks later that a senior career official had denied the request. When Jenkins heard about it, he pulled me aside to explain that the agency's informal processes functioned much more quickly and effectively than formal processes like the one I'd used for the request. He could help me navigate the informal channels, he said, so that I didn't experience such unfortunate difficulties in the future.

I accepted his offer, because I lacked other options and figured there could be no harm in availing myself of the hidden networks that made the agency run. Sure enough, the other bureau quickly approved the trip. I proceeded to work with that bureau to organize the trip, and it went off without a hitch. Victory was mine, I thought.

As I was to learn in time, however, political appointees who relied on bureaucrats like Jenkins as their fixers brought harm on themselves and the organization. String pulling was one of the most effective tools career bureaucrats possessed for ingratiating themselves with political appointees. The practice created dependencies, giving the bureaucracy's apparatchiks influence and leverage.

At one point in my tenure, a senior agency official told me, "If you joined forces with Rob Jenkins, the sky would be the limit. You have the political status and strategic ideas to win over the people in the agency who don't like Jenkins, and Jenkins has the network in the bureaucracy to put your ideas into practice." That was probably true. The thought of gaining greater cooperation from the bureaucracy was tempting indeed. Partnering with Jenkins, however, sounded too much like Luke Skywalker teaming up with Darth Vader after hearing "Together we can rule the galaxy!" I knew the dark side well enough to avoid going over.

The departure of Schmidt, Crnkovich, and Feary had removed the most powerful members of Jenkins's network from CMC. It was a blow comparable in magnitude to Tony Soprano's loss of Paulie Gualtieri to the prison system in season four. Other members of Jenkins's network, however, remained in my office. Eventually I learned that a few members of the CMC staff were communicating directly with Jenkins without my knowledge, and that in at least a few cases Jenkins was directing them to disobey my orders. I warned the employees in question that I needed to be kept in the loop, which reduced the problem but did not eliminate it.

On a typical weekday, Jenkins left the Reagan Building at 4 p.m. and headed across Pennsylvania Avenue to the bar at Del Frisco's, a modern, upscale dining establishment framed by high ceilings and walls of wine refrigerators. As a senior USAID official aptly explained it to me, Jenkins held court at Del Frisco's and the courtiers showed up to fawn and flatter. For years, USAID staff members had complained about Jenkins's practice of conducting official business and discussing sensitive national security topics at the bar, but Jenkins was powerful enough that no one shut the court down.

Among the most important of the courtiers at Del Frisco's were Crnkovich and Schmidt. During the eighteen months when these two had run CMC, much of the office's staff had grown dissatisfied with their leadership, but Jenkins had shielded them from the criticism. Matters had come to a head at an office-wide retreat where staff disapproval boiled over. Speculation swirled about a new leader coming in to run CMC. But Jenkins stood up in front of everyone to say that Schmidt and Crnkovich were doing a great job and would continue to run the office until a political appointee arrived. His word settled the matter.

I learned facts like these by talking with the people who had served as CMC Director during the George W. Bush and Obama administrations. I also heard them from other individuals who had worked at CMC in the past. Having long preached the value of history, I thought I should learn as much as possible about the history of the office.

Shortly after I initiated the management review, Jenkins came to my office and upbraided me for authorizing it. I should have checked with him first, he steamed. I didn't tell him that I had intentionally avoided checking with him first because I had reason to believe that he was responsible for many of the problems. Nor did I mention that I'd been leery of him from the moment he talked about concealing agency activities from the White House.

"I also know you have talked with previous office directors," Jenkins said with palpable spite in his voice. "Did you think I wouldn't find out about it? We find things like that out."

I was taken aback. His dismay at my curiosity about the past only made me more curious. "I thought it was common practice to speak with people who have held the job before," I responded. "They gave me some useful advice."

Weeks later, Jenkins would concede tacitly that keeping him away from the review had been appropriate. It happened during a discussion about reassigning Crnkovich during the newly initiated OIG investigation. Jenkins said he wanted to stay out of the reassignment to avoid the appearance of meddling, because eventually people would blame him, as the supervisor of Schmidt and Crnkovich, for all the problems of CMC. Jenkins seemed shaken, ready to back away from CMC completely while the investigation into Crnkovich played out.

That phase soon passed, however, and Jenkins's appetite for meddling in the affairs of CMC returned. He blocked my efforts to obtain additional resources for the office, and poured acid onto my most promising initiatives, relying on his patronage network to do the dirty work for him. Although he went out of his way to conceal his hand, I often learned about his subterfuges because many of the staff in CMC and elsewhere in the bureau were sick of his antics and supported my efforts to clean up the office.

While the management review and the ensuing adverse personnel actions were serious affronts to the Jenkins network, they were not the only reasons Jenkins wanted to prevent me from succeeding. Most significantly, he coveted the leadership of the new Bureau for Conflict Prevention and Stabilization, the position for which I appeared destined. Several senior USAID officials informed me that Jenkins was telling people he had been "born to lead this bureau." Jenkins had been heavily involved in planning for the bureau, and he talked so often about it that many people, at USAID and elsewhere, were referring to it as "the Rob Jenkins Bureau." As a rule, political appointees led bureaus, and I was the senior political appointee in the offices being merged into the bureau. During the protracted period required to staff USAID with political appointees, though, two career staff had managed to secure permanent appointment to the top positions of other bureaus, which stoked Jenkins's hopes for becoming the new bureau's leader.

Jenkins informed agency leaders that he objected to my appointment as head of the CPS bureau. He even told me directly. One day he stormed into my office to declare, in great agitation, that if I were put in charge of the bureau, he would leave the agency. USAID veterans told me that Jenkins had obtained two promotions during the Obama administration by threatening to quit if he did not get his way.

On one occasion, I discovered that Jenkins was leading bureau planning meetings without informing me that the meetings were taking place. I mentioned it to Steiger, who told me that I should be participating in all such meetings. When I relayed that instruction to Jenkins, he replied nastily that he wasn't going to listen to me, that he didn't need me as his minder, and that if Steiger had any instructions for him he would have to deliver them personally.

In the spring of 2019, Jenkins and I were both appointed to the body responsible for forming the new bureau, called the bureau leadership group. The other member was Victoria (not her real name), a foreign service officer who was scheduled to leave Washington for an overseas assignment in June 2019. In communications about the reorganization, agency leaders announced that membership in a bureau leadership group wouldn't necessarily result in appointment to a leadership position in the bureau, but the selections were widely interpreted as indicators of future leadership assignments. With Victoria about to go abroad, Jenkins and I were clearly the leading candidates to head the new bureau.

The other reason why Jenkins wanted me to fail was my support for Trump administration policies that he opposed. Jenkins criticized me and other Trump appointees—sometimes to our faces, more often behind our backs—for aligning aid programs more closely with White House national security priorities like countering China, Russia, and Iran. When we proposed discontinuing humanitarian assistance programs where our enemies were stealing or manipulating the aid, Jenkins declared that the United States could not "politicize" its humanitarian aid. His argument ignored the reality that aid already had been politicized when political actors were stealing it or restricting its distribution, as well as the reality that the United States had a history of withholding aid under such conditions, for instance in Communist countries during the Cold War and in pariah states like Sudan and North Korea after the Cold War.

Another issue that provoked duels between Jenkins and me was what the national security community called "messaging." In the fall of 2018, the Defense and State Departments and the National Security Council were calling for USAID to support local voices in various countries to spread messages about the benefits of democracy and the threats to democracy from malign actors. USAID already had messaging programs in several countries, but there were plentiful opportunities to do more, some of them involving collaboration with the Defense Department. The SOCOM liaison officer in my office had connected me to the head of a new, unclassified SOCOM program in this sphere, and I had begun encouraging others at USAID to speak with this individual about possibilities for working together.

When I broached the agency's participation in messaging with Ziemer, he told me to check with the front office. I contacted Steiger, who said he wanted the agency to become more active in the messaging area. He accepted my offer to help coalesce USAID expertise and to open discussions with other federal agencies.

On November 16, I conveyed Steiger's directive to Ziemer and Jenkins and we discussed the way forward. We agreed to begin discussions that would lead to an action memorandum for Administrator Green. Jenkins promptly mobilized Ami Morgan, a member of his network, to arrange a meeting of bureau experts and managers. That action set me on edge, for Morgan had already stabbed me in the back several times at the behest of Jenkins.

We met in the CMC conference room, one of the largest in USAID headquarters. It had a long table surrounded by chairs, with additional chairs against the walls, as well as several large-screen televisions and secure phones. At the beginning of the meeting, I told the group that Steiger wanted a proposal for increased USAID involvement in messaging, with particular emphasis on countering China, Russia, and Iran. We needed to explore what USAID could produce itself, and what it could do in collaboration with the Department of Defense.

Before I could get into the substance of the matter, Jenkins interjected that he had just come from a meeting with Ziemer. He didn't say who had arranged that meeting, or why no one had told me about it. According to Jenkins, Ziemer had said that we shouldn't spend more staff time on this issue until we had clear guidance from the administrator himself. Jenkins and Morgan then proceeded to question the whole idea of USAID involvement in messaging, in the process demonstrating their ignorance of existing USAID messaging programs. They claimed that by getting involved in messaging, the agency would be sacrificing its interests to those of the Defense Department and straying senselessly from the traditional development sphere.

Meeting surreptitiously with my boss to reopen the conversation on the issue was one of the dirtiest bureaucratic tricks Jenkins could have played. Even dirtier was showing up at a meeting designed to implement Steiger's guidance and announcing that Ziemer had just countermanded Steiger—the number two official in the agency at the time—by invoking the name of the number one official. On a few previous occasions, I had seen career staff try to undermine political appointees by playing them off against one another, but had never seen it done so brazenly or in front of such a large group.

I didn't confront Jenkins directly. Instead, I told the group that Ziemer and Steiger had already asked us to look more deeply into the subject of messaging. Then I pointed out that the purpose of civilian-military cooperation, under the current administration, was to support both development and national security objectives. I noted, in addition, that USAID was already engaged in activities that didn't fit the traditional definition of development and were clearly intended to achieve national security objectives, such as media programs that refuted Russian disinformation and governance programs that exposed Chinese bribery of government officials.

After the meeting, several of my staff expressed to me their shock at the resistance to authority and change they had witnessed during the meeting. Two of them forwarded me articles on the general subject of bureaucratic inertia and hostility to change. A couple of the military officers assigned to my office told me that it was the worst bureaucratic backstabbing they had ever seen.

I told Ziemer what had happened, hoping that he would bring Jenkins into line. Ziemer was usually helpful when I asked him for assistance, but when it came to clashes between political appointees and career staff, he tended to back off. He did so again now.

"You are both big boys, so I am not going to tell you how to get along" was Ziemer's only remark. He did say I could press ahead with the messaging proposal, which I did. As my team and I moved forward on that front, Jenkins had his people snipe at us from a distance, while Jenkins himself sneaked over to the State Department to boast about USAID's strength in messaging and the value he personally brought to the table.

I also clashed with Jenkins over the agency reorganization, which took more and more of everyone's time as 2019 progressed. While reading one reorganizational document, I saw an assertion that an office in our bureau, the Office of Transition Initiatives (OTI), had "autonomy." Thus, it could make its own decisions about what to do and where to do it.

OTI was the agency's rapid action arm. It could hire companies within a few weeks to deal with political transitions, armed conflicts, and other situations that demanded action much more quickly than the standard acquisition cycle permitted. (The regular bureaucracy often spent a year or more on group discussion and document processing and wicket clearing before authorizing a contract.) Jenkins had formerly headed OTI, and the organization was staffed primarily by personal services contractors he had handpicked. That arrangement had made him the godfather of the personal services contractors, in addition to the civil servants, and it prevented interference in the organization's business by independent-minded foreign service officers.

Since his promotion to deputy assistant administrator, Jenkins had continued to preside over OTI, through godfatherly relations with his personally designated successor and the rest of the staff. At the end of 2018, though, a new political appointee, Owen Kirby, had arrived to serve as the office's deputy director. Kirby had begun questioning the office's unusual practices and the numerous ways that Jenkins was involving himself in those practices. A few months later, a deluge of complaints from OTI staff about the daytime inebriation of the office director provoked a crisis in which Kirby sided with the staff against the director. Jenkins tried to spare his protégé from removal, but the evidence against the director was so overwhelming that not even Jenkins could keep him in the job, though Jenkins did find him another job in the agency. Kirby became the office director, and soon he was insisting that Jenkins stop overriding the office director's authority and using OTI staff to do his personal bidding.

The intent behind the claim of OTI autonomy appeared to be the preservation of power in Jenkins's hands. Other political appointees and I had already raised concerns about the roles of Jenkins and OTI staff in deciding where the organization operated and what it did, as those were decisions political appointees should have been making. After conducting some additional research on the subject, I concluded that OTI had no legitimate claim to autonomy. The head of OTI was subordinate to the head of its bureau—Ziemer—just as every other office director was.

I raised the issue at a meeting of the bureau leadership group. Any references to OTI as autonomous should be deleted, I asserted. Jenkins blew his top. Congress had given OTI autonomy, he declared, and "consulting" with Ziemer was all that OTI needed to do with the political appointees.

Unconvinced, I took the matter to the USAID Office of General Counsel. The lawyers did their research and concluded, as I had, that OTI was not autonomous, but was under the authority of political appointees. The word "autonomy" was effaced from the planning documents.

Most of the other reorganizational controversies did not involve clear-cut legal issues, so I couldn't usually summon the lawyers to back me up. Decisions were made by votes of the bureau leadership group, which meant that when Jenkins and I disagreed, as we often did, the deciding vote was cast by Victoria. I believe she tried to be fair-minded, but also sensed that she knew she had more to lose by siding against Jenkins than against me. Jenkins had amassed great bureaucratic power over the years, and he would still be around after the Republican appointees were gone. On some of the points where Victoria sided with Jenkins, the stakes were too low for me to dig in my heels. On others, I worked hard to bring Victoria to my side. On a few particularly important matters, I sought the help of top political appointees, pointing out to them that career employees really shouldn't be allowed to overrule political appointees by outvoting them.

Among the most contentious issues was the staffing of the new bureau's offices. Having spent months coming up with new objectives and new tasks as mandated by the reorganization chieftains, each office—including mine—submitted requests for additional staff. Jenkins and Victoria had spent much of their time developing plans for the Office of Conflict Management and Mitigation, which everyone acknowledged had been a disaster, and they wanted to give that office most of the additional new personnel.

Jenkins claimed that CMC had no need for more staff, despite the fact that he was oblivious to most of the office's activities. I countered by pointing out the large number of new tasks expected of CMC following the reorganization. By this time, moreover, I'd become convinced that my office could make the best use of the additional people, because of shortages of competence and motivation in other offices. Considerable evidence supported that conclusion, though after making several pleas for more staff I began to worry that I might be catching swamp fever, with its insatiable appetite for bureaucratic resources.

Ultimately, this debate was cut off by a decision from above. We were notified in May 2019 that the unions and lawyers had determined that moving people around the agency would be exceedingly difficult and time-consuming, and therefore the staff numbers could be adjusted only for select offices. Some offices, including CMC, would be designated as "lift and shift," which meant that they would be put into the new organization without any changes at all to their personnel strength.

For more than a year, hundreds of staff had spent large chunks of time planning the reorganization on the premise that "form follows function." Now function had to follow form. The Reagan Building was rife with complaints that millions of dollars' worth of staff labor had been wasted because the reorganizational masterminds had failed to take the human resource constraints into account from the get-go.

During the deliberations about the new bureau, I learned of the existence of the Complex Crises Fund (CCF). This fund had started out at $10 million, and Jenkins was seeking to multiply it fivefold. Its vague title and description meant it could be used for just about anything in a conflict-ridden country. When I started asking probing questions about the Complex Crises Fund, I discovered that no political appointee knew anything about the money or how it was spent. This slush fund was, in essence, another form of patronage in the palm of Rob Jenkins.

The request to enlarge the Complex Crises Fund was included in the "Global Fragility Act," which took its name from an

Obama administration buzzword. USAID had spent all eight years of the Obama administration debating what "fragility" meant, and had never come to agreement. (It had something to do with weak governance in poor countries.) A number of Trump appointees, myself included, wondered why USAID was still using the term.

Jenkins personally lobbied congressmen and their staffs to authorize funding increases. Eventually Congress approved $30 million for the Complex Crises Fund and another $200 million for a Prevention and Stabilization Fund—both under the control of the new CPS Bureau—over a five-year period. These discoveries made clear to me that Jenkins's desire to lead the new bureau wasn't just about power and status, but also about money, and lots of it. With a fresh $230 million at his disposal, on top of the $250 million annual budget of the Office of Transition Initiatives, the head of the new bureau could steer vast sums to pet projects and preferred contractors.

The Complex Crises Fund was precisely the type of bureaucratic spending artifice that Steiger had told appointees to root out. I went into Ziemer's office and told him I'd learned that the Complex Crises Fund was doling out money without the knowledge or approval of political appointees. He said that he and I should meet with Jenkins, Morgan, and whoever else worked on the program to discuss it. Other experts were invited. In total, about ten people ended up taking part in the meeting.

Morgan began the meeting by describing the purpose of the Complex Crises Fund and the process for allocating money. She had a member of her staff describe some of the projects the fund had bankrolled. Ziemer expressed his appreciation for this fine work, then asked Morgan who made the decisions as to what was funded and what was not.

"I do," Morgan said.

"Why am I not the one who is making those decisions?" Ziemer demanded. He may have been too lenient toward career staff at other times, but this time he was calling them out in no uncertain terms.

Morgan beat around the bush with excuses and said that they would consult with Ziemer in the future. Jenkins looked on nervously, not saying a word.

"As the bureau leader, I need to have visibility and authority over the spending of money," Ziemer said, looking first at Morgan, then at the others. His deep, authoritative voice left listeners with no uncertainty about his meaning by the time he finished a sentence.

Morgan and Jenkins assured Ziemer they would make sure he had the opportunity to review and approve all disbursements from the Complex Crises Fund going forward. As they should have been doing all along.

Shortly after this meeting, a senior USAID official told me that Jenkins was being driven to desperation. First of all, I was digging into the bureau's finances and decision-making processes, which had been his levers of power. Second, Jenkins was losing influence at OTI because of the replacement of his handpicked OTI chief with a political appointee. Third and most menacing, Steiger had told Jenkins that he would not become the head of the new CPS Bureau. Evidently, Steiger had realized that placing a liberal Machiavellian career bureaucrat into the type of leadership position normally reserved for political appointees made no sense. It looked as though I would receive that position—the outcome that Jenkins had said would make him quit the agency where he'd worked for more than two decades.

Chapter 13

The Bureaucracy Strikes Back

On May 21, 2019, I was returning from a meeting when I saw a man I didn't know talking with my executive assistant outside my office door. Turning from the executive assistant toward me, he said that he needed to replace my computer with a new one, which he had brought with him on a cart. I replied that I had just received a new computer, and asked why he was replacing it already.

"I think they want to do some forensics on the hard drive," he said. "It's easier to take the whole computer than just the hard drive. They might have detected something on a scan. But they didn't tell me the specific reason."

Forensics? Taking the entire computer? Something didn't sound right. Was he one of those con artists who show up in office buildings to steal purses and computers?

"Do you know the name of the person who made the request to take the computer?" I asked.

He pulled out a piece of paper, which had the name of an individual and her email address. It looked legitimate. Besides, the building's security measures were probably good enough to prevent an outsider from entering the building. I wrote down the email address and told him he could go ahead and replace the machine.

Once he had installed the new computer and departed with the old one, I emailed the individual listed on the instruction sheet. I also emailed someone else I thought might know about it. Both came back with vague answers.

A short time later, I received an email from Jack Ohlweiler, the USAID lawyer who served as the agency's designated ethics official. He asked me to see him, so we set up a meeting in his office.

"I hear you have been asking about your computer," Ohlweiler told me. "I can tell you why it was taken. You are the subject of an investigation." He paused momentarily for effect. "Now, you shouldn't be alarmed. You shouldn't start drinking heavily. Around this place, people say that if a supervisor isn't under investigation, then he's not doing his job. I'm under an investigation right now."

Knowing nothing about agency investigations, I was reassured by the explanation that it was a routine occurrence.

"Can you tell me what the investigation is about?" I asked Ohlweiler.

"No," Ohlweiler replied. "I can't tell you. Depending on the outcome, you might not hear anything more about it. But in the meantime, you should be prepared to find qualified counsel."

Qualified counsel? That seemed concerning. Why should I be looking for a lawyer if it was probably no big deal? How could I even find a lawyer if I didn't know the subject matter of the investigation? But asking these questions would call Ohlweiler's judgment into question. Having seen the power of lawyers at the agency, I decided to avoid any question that might come across as a provocation.

I did raise a point of a less confrontational nature. "This investigation seems to be moving very fast," I said. "An OIG investigation into one of my subordinates began more than six months ago, and nothing seems to have happened with that one."

"Ah," said Ohlweiler, with the look of a professor answering an interesting question from a young law school student. "This investigation involves different authorities." He added that it was being conducted by a different entity within the agency, the Office of Employee and Labor Relations.

"I'm not sure whether you are aware of it," I said, "but I have reported several of my subordinates for wrongdoing. The most serious one led to the OIG investigation. As far as I know, the only reason why I would be the subject of an investigation would be a false accusation by one of those individuals."

"If that is the case," Ohlweiler said, "then it will certainly be taken into account."

I thanked him for the information and walked out.

Not until much later would I realize that investigations in the federal government are often far less benign than Ohlweiler had let on. And that they often serve as weapons of bureaucratic counterattack. And that they can be potent in their effects even if the charges have no merit.

Among the most stunning illustrations of these truths can be found in a 2018 National Public Radio story about whistleblower retaliation at the Department of Veterans Affairs (VA). The VA has long been the poster child for mistreatment of whistleblowers, thanks primarily to the frequent insertion of civic-minded veterans into a civilian workforce with leadership that often puts their own interests before their country and the veterans they are supposed to serve. As recounted by reporter Eric Westervelt of National Public Radio, Sheila Walsh joined the VA as a human resources official after twenty years in the Army and quickly discovered that she had stepped into a cesspool of corruption. She sought to rectify matters by reporting the corrupt acts in writing. "I went on the record saying I'm not going to participate in this level of corruption, illegal actions," she told Westervelt. "And so I became the enemy. Instead of them investigating the wrongdoing, they started investigating me."

Walsh was told to "stand down" on her reporting. Agency officials forced her to work in isolation, and confiscated her personal possessions. "They wanted me to feel humiliated, trying to break me down," Walsh said. "And they did break me down."

Dr. Julian Kassner, another VA employee who had previously served in the military, tried to combat graft in the department he'd been brought in to lead and was promptly subjected to an investigation on trumped-up charges. He was then fired with no explanation. "There are people at the senior level there," Kassner said, who "consider themselves the equivalent of a 'made man' in the mafia, that there are no rules that apply to them, up to and including fraud and record falsification."

On the same day my computer was taken, an email traveled from U.S. Special Operations Command through cyberspace to USAID. It contained a brief letter that purported to provide "derogatory personnel security information on Mr. Mark Moyer [sic]." The main paragraph stated: "Mr. Moyar authored a publication that contains numerous instances of classified information under the original classification authority of USSOCOM and sub-unified commands. This fact was established through post-publication review and results have been forwarded to the Department of Defense Insider Threat Management and Analysis Center-Unauthorized Disclosure Program Management Office." It also stated that my visitation privileges at SOCOM facilities had been suspended.

This message made its way to the USAID Office of Security, which had responsibility for the security clearances of all USAID employees. I caught wind of the allegation before the Office of Security took action on it, because a copy was sent to someone who had immediately sensed malevolent deceit and notified me. The word flabbergasted is a weak approximation of the astonishment that coursed through my veins when I learned of it.

In all my years at the Department of Defense, I had never heard of a "post-publication review." No one had been available to fulfill the government's obligation for prepublication review during the year before publication, but then two years after publication, someone suddenly had acquired the time and inclination to review something already available for everyone to see? It had to be a hit job, and the only people with motives for a hit job were the USAID employees I had reported for misconduct and their godfather, Rob Jenkins.

I didn't know whether top USAID leaders already knew about the SOCOM allegation, so I told them about it right away. My candor and my presentation of the facts, I hoped, would reassure them that I was in the right. Meeting personally with Bill Steiger, Tim Ziemer, Bob Leavitt, and Jack Ohlweiler, I explained to each of them why the SOCOM allegation lacked any merit. I kept all of the communications face-to-face, after one of them told me not to put anything about the matter in writing. At the time, this official led me to believe they were doing me a favor by avoiding the production of written records, but as events moved along I increasingly came to believe that the people who strenuously opposed the use of the written word did so not to protect me, but to protect themselves.

When I informed Ziemer, it was a busy Friday and he didn't have time to discuss it at length. On the following Monday morning, he pulled me aside after the weekly senior staff meeting.

"I was thinking about your situation over the weekend," he said in a caring tone. "At the end of one of my tours as a commanding officer in the Navy, I had accumulated a bunch of frivolous complaints from subordinates. It can happen when you try to do your job."

Ziemer's comment put me at ease. His next words, however, put me back on edge. "You may want to look at joining another team," he said with a look of solemnity. "Other agencies are in need of senior political appointees. Now, I am not telling you to join another team. But you ought to consider it." Only much later would I find out that by this time Ziemer already knew that additional complaints had been filed against me.

Ziemer explained that he didn't trust some of the people who were likely to be involved in reviewing my case, particularly John Voorhees. Other senior officials, he added, were only looking out for themselves. "You should make sure to look out for yourself," he said at the end.

I believed he was speaking sincerely, and wasn't part of the effort to unseat me, despite his past lenience with Jenkins and his prior service in the Obama administration. I was depressingly sure he was speaking the truth when he said that individuals involved in reviewing my case were not trustworthy, and that senior officials who should have been prepared to stand up for me would only watch out for their own hides. Events would prove him correct on both scores.

Ziemer's ominous message, with its premonition of an ambush in a bureaucratic dark alley, didn't convince me to flee. Running from bullies wasn't in my DNA. I believed I was in the right and would be vindicated. I'd worked hard for a year and a half to earn the leadership of the new bureau, and didn't want to relinquish it at the first sign of trouble. Finding another job would, in any case, take weeks, if not months, and I didn't think it would take that long to show that my book had not violated the federal non-disclosure agreement.

The investigation into my computer was proceeding. An agency official eventually informed me that nothing incriminating had been found on the computer. That wasn't surprising, since I hadn't stored anything on it. The USAID computer system didn't back up hard drives, so I had kept everything on the network drive, which USAID could access remotely at any time.

For the next three weeks, no one said anything to me about the SOCOM allegation. I began to believe that sanity had prevailed, that the absurdity of the allegation had been recognized by all. The four senior officials whom I'd notified about the matter had seemed sympathetic to my cause and receptive to my defense, and I hoped that they had already presented that defense on my behalf, squelching the feeble case once and for all. Here began a long series of misplaced hopes.

On June 13, 2019, I was sitting in my office when the phone rang. The small screen on the phone identified the caller as John Voorhees, the director of the USAID Office of Security. The guy Ziemer had said he didn't trust. Why was Voorhees, who never called me, calling me now?

I picked up the receiver. "Mark Moyar, CMC," I said.

"This is John Voorhees," came a gruff voice on the other end. "I need you to come down here to Security."

"I have a meeting that will start shortly," I replied. "I can come down at 2 p.m. May I ask what this is about?"

"Your security clearance," Voorhees replied, in the tone of a policeman who liked to throw his weight around. I would later learn that Voorhees had spent much of his career in the U.S. Army Military Police, an organization known for its gratuitous chest puffing.

"I'll be there at 2," I said, and hung up.

My security clearance. That didn't sound like a good topic of conversation. It had to be related to the SOCOM accusation.

I had a meeting at 1:30 p.m. with a USAID foreign service officer who was scheduled to join CMC soon and was in Washington from her current overseas deployment. I had been looking forward to the meeting, as we shared a wide array of interests, but the impending meeting with Voorhees tugged at my attention as we talked.

After that meeting ended, I took the elevator down to the USAID Office of Security. Walking up to the front desk, I gave my name. I was directed to a turnstile, and once through I was taken to a conference room, where I found two people waiting for me, neither of whom was John Voorhees. One was Tara Debnam, who ran the Security Office's Division of Personnel Security. The other was Nick Gottlieb, who a few months earlier had replaced Frank Walsh as the head of Employee and Labor Relations.

I had never met Debnam. I did know Gottlieb, having gone to him several times for help in addressing office personnel issues. We had gotten along well, based on what I had believed to be a mutual interest in holding toxic employees accountable.

"I'm sorry that we have to meet under these conditions," Gottlieb began. It turned out that he was there only to cover a few administrative details. Most of the talking was done by Debnam.

"I am suspending your security clearance," Debnam said. "We have received an allegation from U.S. Special Operations Command that you committed an unauthorized disclosure of classified information. You are being placed on paid administrative leave while this office conducts an investigation."

"Can you tell me whether this investigation is connected to

the seizure of my computer on May 21?" I asked.

"I don't know anything about your computer," Debnam replied. She looked at Gottlieb, who didn't say anything.

That was a surprise. If multiple parties within the agency were investigating me, wouldn't they know about each other's work?

"You are not aware of an investigation involving my computer?" I asked, to make sure there was no misunderstanding.

"No," Debnam replied.

"Who made the decision to suspend my clearance?" I asked.

"I did," she said. "Several authorities permit me to do so. I am suspending it on the basis of the allegation sent by SOCOM, which I received on June 3."

"If you received the information on June 3, and you consider the matter so serious that it requires suspending my clearance, why did you wait until today to suspend my clearance?"

Debnam did not answer this question and changed the subject.

"This suspension is not a presumption of guilt," Debnam continued in a timbre that conveyed fair-mindedness. "Right now, we have only an allegation. The purpose of the suspension is to allow for an investigation that will collect the facts and determine whether the allegation is accurate. You will have an opportunity to present any information you consider relevant."

It wasn't clear to me why they needed to suspend me from my job to investigate an allegation without any supporting evidence. But once again I decided that questioning someone's judgment was not the right call, so I didn't push the matter.

"We strive to resolve cases like this one quickly," Debnam added. "We try to complete the investigations in thirty to forty days." Debnam informed me that I had to relinquish my ID card and my cell phone immediately. I handed them over. An agency employee whom I considered a friend was waiting outside, and I was told that he would be escorting me out.

We went to my office to collect my briefcase and whatever else I needed to bring with me. I had no opportunity to speak with my staff before I was escorted out of the office. I tried to act as though nothing were unusual, believing that the appearance of a forced removal from my office would concede another victory to whoever was out to get me. During the walk into and out of the office, I chatted with my escort, who was no stranger to the office, so few people were likely to take notice.

As I was heading out, my eyes scanned the CMC office. Only one person was paying attention to me, Angela Greenewald. We locked eyes briefly. It was the first indication I received that she might be involved in the plot.

After leaving the CMC office, my escort and I proceeded to the rear entrance of USAID headquarters. I said goodbye, then stepped into the gleaming silver atrium of the Ronald Reagan Building. Heading to the nearest elevator bank, I took a ride down to the fourth floor of the basement, where my car was parked.

Only in the solitude of the drive home did the full weight of the clearance suspension hit me. The suspension and the imposition of administrative leave in response to an unsubstantiated allegation, I realized, supported the disheartening conclusion that Ziemer's suspicions about John Voorhees had been correct. If Voorhees had been interested in impartial justice and the effective functioning of the agency, he surely would have waited to receive corroborating evidence before authorizing the suspension.

During my time at USAID, I had learned that the agency rarely suspended security clearances, even when it received actual evidence of criminal activity. As a congressional inquiry would later find, USAID hadn't suspended a single clearance during the year 2016, and had suspended an average of fewer than nine per year in the ensuing years. USAID never suspended the clearance of Crnkovich even though he was investigated by the Office of Inspector General for criminal fraud and would eventually be forced out by incriminating evidence. Nor had the agency suspended the clearance of another subordinate of mine who, during a previous tour, had been reprimanded for having a problematic and undisclosed relationship with a Ukrainian national. Another USAID employee I encountered overseas had kept his security clearance after sexually harassing subordinates and locking his local girlfriend in a closet for prolonged periods.

After I had informed the Office of Security of my doubts about Bob Schmidt's eligibility for a security clearance, no action had been taken against his clearance, either.

The acquiescence of USAID leaders to the suspension confirmed Ziemer's prediction that self-interest would prevail over justice. It also increased the likelihood that the agency would decide to revoke my clearance, for the agency leadership had a role in the revocation process. A clearance revocation was a career-wrecking event, as it barred an individual from most, if not all, jobs in their field of expertise. If someone lost their clearance much beyond the age of thirty, moreover, they would find it difficult to move into a new field, because they would be ill-suited to the junior positions where most employees entered the profession. When Thomas Drake of the National Security Agency was stripped of his clearance and job in 2008 for reporting illicit surveillance of private citizens, he went from a senior executive in the government to a sales clerk at an Apple Store.

My mental armor, having been thickened over the years by religious faith, patriotic conviction, positive thinking, and hard experience, absorbed some of the blow and prevented it from knocking me to the ground. It did not, however, spare me from deep and painful mental bruising. The bruises hurt more than anything I could remember, except for the two miscarriages Kelli had endured and a life-threatening allergic reaction that had put our daughter in the hospital at age three.

When I got home, I was calm enough to explain the situation to the family in terms that made it seem less worrisome than it really was. I'd been suspended from my job because of a ridiculous allegation that had been made against me, I said matter-of-factly, and I'd be back at work soon, once a few people with common sense realized that I hadn't divulged the nation's secrets. The children took it reasonably well. My sons, in fact, found a degree of excitement in the prospect of a national news story that would expose outlandish scheming. Kelli, however, was understandably worried by the possibility that my job would be lost and my career left in tatters.

Chapter 14

Administrative Leave

I spent the next six weeks at home, largely in a state of isolation, preferring to avoid friends until the mess had been cleared up. The spurious accusation, I believed, would soon be debunked. Once that happened, my retelling of the story would culminate in my vindication, a far better ending than the current state of limbo.

During the investigation, I avoided contact with my CMC staff. Jenkins told the office that I was absent for unspecified reasons and that no one should contact me. I wasn't sure whether he was allowed to issue such instructions, but I didn't want to expose any of my staff to attack by the vicious jaws that were clamping down on me, so I didn't email or call them. For the same reason, I avoided contacting friends in other parts of the agency.

I later heard from people who had gone through similar ordeals that they had been isolated from other employees intentionally as a way of unnerving them. At least some of the bureaucrats responsible for suspending my clearance, I suspected, had hoped to break me psychologically, and their punitive and isolating measures certainly could have had such an impact. According to the British researcher Geoffrey Hunt, whistleblowers have an exceptionally high incidence of depression, anxiety, suicide, and other mental and physical illnesses. I attribute my ability to withstand the soul-crushing effects to the strength of my mental armor, as well as the support of family, the availability of productive activities, and the knowledge that the charges against me were untrue.

Although I wasn't breaking down, the ill effects of mental bruising continued to be felt. My blood pressure spiked, eventually compelling me to take blood pressure medication for the first time. Insomnia plagued the nights. The untold hours lying awake, a seemingly endless expanse of time, with my mind drawn toward the agonies of the predicament and the circumstances that had led to it, were among the worst times of the ordeal. Frequently I reminded myself of a lesson I had learned many years earlier, that pain can invite demons into the door, but can also arouse noble spirits that cast the demons out and bestow new wisdom. Resilience, equanimity, and love joined battle with the despair, rage, and hate that pain had conjured.

The battle subsided in daylight, when I had tasks to keep my mind occupied. With school out for the summer, I took turns with Kelli driving our children to sports practices and to the movies, and seized on opportunities to have lunch with them. Humans have an infinite capacity for taking things and people for granted, and pain is better than anything else at reminding us of the value of what we have. After a prolonged period when work had diverted my attention from family, this period of woe revived my appreciation for the gifts of family and good health.

I cannot say, however, that I spent most of my time carefully reaping the benefits of suffering. Although I knew that the path to wisdom and salvation runs through suffering, I was, like most humans, inclined to find ways to avoid it. The most effective way to ease mental anguish is distraction, and work the most effective means of distraction. I busied myself with my next book, the sequel to my earlier Vietnam War book *Triumph Forsaken*.

I also worked on a full-blown written defense, in preparation for the anticipated meeting with the investigators. The defense began with a description of the events surrounding submission of *Oppose Any Foe* for prepublication review. Then it turned to the anonymous accusation, noting that no one motivated by the desire to protect sensitive national security information would have made the accusation two years after the book's publication, because it would only draw attention to the book. *Operation Dark Heart* had gone from just another military memoir to a bestseller only when the government made known that it believed parts of the book ought not be published.

I produced a lengthy list of facts and analyses that pointed toward a conspiracy of whistleblower retaliation. One was the simultaneity of the two allegations against me. Another was the prior Defense Department employment of several of the suspects. Schmidt, Crnkovich, Greenewald, and Voorhees had served in the military and still had friends and acquaintances at the Defense Department who could have made the accusation against me. I wasn't told the name of the person at SOCOM who had complained about my book, but I did find out that the individual was a two-star general at Fort Bragg with ties to Greenewald. Prior to joining USAID, Greenewald had served at Fort Bragg as an Army Civil Affairs officer, and she owed her current job to Crnkovich, who had also worked in Army Civil Affairs after spending his earlier military career in the Military Police. Several of my staff had complained to me that Crnkovich had broken agency hiring rules to get Greenewald her USAID job.

Shortly before I was put on administrative leave, I learned Greenewald had stayed in regular communication with Crnkovich after his departure from CMC, even though Crnkovich had been told to avoid any interaction with the office staff. Upon learning of it, I asked Greenewald if she was communicating with Crnkovich, and she said it had been only a brief correspondence. A short time later, I received word that Greenewald and Crnkovich had recently visited Fort Bragg together.

When Greenewald had first joined the agency, midway into my tenure, I had enjoyed good relations with her. I sensed that she had become unhappy with me when I did not allow her to hold both the Special Operations Command and Central Command portfolios simultaneously. When she had interviewed for the job, Crnkovich had promised her both portfolios, but they

were two different positions, so I had to fill one of them with another employee. I had repeatedly gone out of my way to accom-
modate Greenewald, and had tried to help her after other staff
complained that she was belittling colleagues during meetings
and badmouthing people behind their backs.

I was sure Jenkins had a hand in this whole affair, because
Crnkovich and Schmidt were "his guys," and because he was obsessed with becoming the head of the new USAID bureau. After
the inspector general's investigation into Crnkovich began, Jenkins was overheard telling Crnkovich, "I have your back," and he
helped Crnkovich find temporary employment at the National
Counterterrorism Center. Months later, the agency's top lawyer
advised Jenkins to stop trying to help Crnkovich because of the
severity of the latter's offenses, but Jenkins kept helping him.

John Voorhees seemed willing to collude with Jenkins, Crnkovich, and Schmidt because of the agency's incestuous loy-
alties and debts. Voorhees had been a West Point classmate of
Schmidt's, and owed his job at USAID to Jenkins and Schmidt.
When Schmidt had chosen to flee CMC in August 2018, it was
Voorhees who had offered him sanctuary in his office. It was also
Voorhees who had brushed aside the doubts I had expressed to
investigator Lance Timberlake about Schmidt's suitability for a
security clearance. Later it would come to light that Voorhees
had aided Crnkovich in his efforts to obtain a job at the National
Counterterrorism Center.

My doubts about Voorhees's motives had germinated many
months earlier, well before Ziemer had shared his doubts with
me. One of the responsibilities of the Office of Security was
processing requests for Sensitive Compartmented Information
(SCI) security clearances for the agency's employees. USAID
could hand out lower-level clearances to its employees, but the
higher-level SCI clearance was granted by the CIA. For the small
number of employees who needed the higher clearance, Voorhees's office submitted information on the employee to the CIA,
which scrutinized it in ways known only to that secretive agency
before notifying Voorhees whether it was granted.

For reasons that included both incompetence and chicanery, my bureau took nearly six months to get my SCI paperwork to the USAID Office of Security. From there, the paperwork went to the CIA, as was confirmed in an email I received at the end of July 2018. Political appointees were supposed to be a high priority for SCI processing, and it was especially important for someone in my position, because an SCI clearance was required to attend numerous interagency meetings and visit certain Defense Department facilities. I expected to receive the clearance in a matter of weeks. After a month passed with no word, my office started contacting the Office of Security to find out what was going on. Voorhees's staff responded each time that he was addressing the matter with the CIA.

Summer turned into fall, then fall into winter, and still nothing happened.

Eventually, I started comparing notes with political appointees at USAID and other federal agencies, and learned that they too were encountering mysteriously long delays in obtaining their SCI clearances. One of them happened to know the individual at the CIA who processed the requests for USAID, and gave me that individual's phone number.

On February 15, 2019, I dialed the number. The individual promptly picked up. I told him I had been waiting for more than six months to receive my SCI and no one seemed to know what was taking so long. Could he help?

He asked for my name and social security number, which I provided.

"I can't find any record of you in our system," he told me.

"So that would mean that USAID hasn't submitted my information to you?" I asked, incredulous.

"Yes," he replied. "If they had submitted it, you would be in the system." He said he would get in touch with the USAID Office of Security to see what was going on. I thanked him and hung up.

My worst suspicions were confirmed. Bureaucratic incompetence wasn't the reason for this delay. It was bureaucratic sabotage. Voorhees had been intentionally sitting on my application while claiming that it had already been sent to the CIA.

From the experiences of some of my staff in obtaining SCI clearances, I'd already learned that Voorhees had the ability to move clearances through the CIA quickly when he wanted to, and, even more significantly, that Rob Jenkins influenced Voorhees's decisions on the timing of submissions. During my early days at USAID, when I had trusted Jenkins, I had told him I was looking forward to getting my SCI so I could start attending National Security Council meetings. I now suspected that Jenkins had asked Voorhees to hold up my clearance because he didn't want competition for the limited number of seats at these meetings, and because he knew that withholding my clearance would in general constrain my influence in the national security community.

Nearly two weeks then went by without an update on the clearance. On February 27, 2019, I decided to write to Voorhees directly. My SCI clearance request had been languishing without resolution since July 2018, I stated, and my staff had repeatedly inquired as to the status, only to be told that the CIA was sitting on it. Subsequently it had come to my attention that the request had never been received by the CIA. I asked Voorhees for his help in expediting the matter, and added that I wanted to meet with him to see where this request had run into trouble so that we could figure out how to avoid such problems in the future. Voorhees never responded to my request for a meeting. I did, however, receive the SCI in April.

My doubts about Voorhees and his office had risen still higher when I learned that his predecessor had been fired for misusing the Office of Security to settle personal scores. In 2016, the FBI had launched an investigation after receiving reports that office leaders were using fraudulent allegations to revoke the security clearances of their enemies. Top officials had allegedly planted phony evidence of collaboration with foreign powers on these individuals and then labeled them "insider threats." The FBI investigation ultimately resulted in the ousting of the director of the Office of Security, his deputy, two other managers in the

Office of Security, an employee in the USAID Office of Inspector General, and an FBI official assigned to USAID.

This scandal was known to almost no one outside of USAID. When I later mentioned it to civil liberties experts and congressional staffers who tracked such matters, they said they'd heard nothing of it, and expressed shock at both the nature of the misconduct and the fact that it remained hidden from view. Congress and the public, they commented, needed to know if senior federal officials with responsibility for security and access to personal information were committing crimes.

Later I learned that the head of security at another federal agency, William S. Fagan of the Securities and Exchange Commission, had similarly abused his power to retaliate against employees for reporting corruption. The sordid details were laid out in a 75-page lawsuit filed by a senior executive whom Fagan had ousted, David P. Weber. In 2012, Weber had joined the Securities and Exchange Commission as assistant inspector general, and had quickly received allegations that Inspector General David Kotz was spinning a web of conflicts of interest through intimate relationships with a subordinate and a lawyer representing victims of the Stanford Financial Group scandal. Weber reported his concerns about Kotz to the appropriate authorities. Weber also learned that his new office was already investigating security chief Fagan for criminal offenses that included steering contracts to personal friends, filling his office with friends and relatives, covering up sexual assault, and orchestrating reprisals against whistleblowers.

Fagan was apparently none too pleased that the new assistant inspector general was taking his job seriously. Based on vague complaints about Weber from a few employees, Fagan declared that Weber posed a "physical threat" to other staff. This declaration, carrying the weight of the agency's head of security, triggered the placement of Weber on administrative leave and the initiation of an investigation into the purported threat.

Investigators from another agency were eventually called in. They determined that Weber had posed no "physical threat" to anyone, and that Kotz had violated federal ethics standards by maintaining an unusually close relationship with an auditor. Because Fagan most probably knew Weber's office was investigating him, the investigators noted, "Fagan should have recused himself from any involvement in the investigation of, or subsequent action against, Weber."

The leaders of the Securities and Exchange Commission ignored the investigation's findings. They fired Weber, citing alleged offenses that the external investigation had disproven. In the end, Weber prevailed in his lawsuit, winning a $580,000 settlement. Kotz had left the agency by that time, but Fagan kept his job as head of the office of security despite all the evidence of improprieties.

During the preceding forty-eight years of my life, I had known next to nothing about the government's procedures for adjudicating security clearances. I had assumed that adjudication was governed by a set of government-wide rules and procedures. As it turned out, certain federal rules and procedures applied across all agencies, but each agency had enormous discretion in deciding how to apply them when granting and revoking clearances.

At USAID, a single individual decided whether an employee's security clearance should be revoked. According to agency regulations, that person was the deputy director of the Office of Security, but this job was vacant at the moment and therefore the duty belonged to the director, who was Voorhees. A clearance revocation could be appealed to a three-person panel. As shall be seen, however, bureaucrats could find ways to circumvent the appeal process.

Federal guidelines provided a list of transgressions that could warrant revoking a clearance, and a list of "mitigating conditions" that could offset them, and it was up to the adjudicator to decide how much to weigh each factor. A malicious adjudicator could revoke a clearance by giving great weight to a relatively minor infraction, or by ignoring major mitigating conditions. A case in point was Adam Lovinger, whose clearance had been revoked in 2017 for accidentally including an unclassified document that was later deemed "sensitive" in a stack of documents he had taken outside a secure area—after he had blown the whistle on his boss for contracting fraud in support of the scandalous Crossfire Hurricane investigation.

Conversely, a biased adjudicator could spare a favored individual who had committed serious offenses by giving greater weight to "mitigating conditions" of the most doubtful importance. Individuals accused of leaking classified information in the Crossfire Hurricane scandal had been permitted to keep their security clearances based on "mitigating conditions" such as "employee had 20 years of government service," and "employee was facing unprecedented challenges and pressures."

Once it was clear Voorhees would not recuse himself from my case for his relationship with Schmidt as he should have done, I contacted Bill Steiger to request that he prevent Voorhees from adjudicating. Knowing of Steiger's antipathy to email, I had someone hand deliver a letter to him on June 17, four days after the suspension of my clearance. In the letter, I stated that Voorhees was a close friend of individuals I had reported for waste, fraud, and abuse, whom I listed by name. I informed Steiger that Voorhees had already shown a willingness to misuse his authority against me by holding up my SCI clearance. In the name of impartiality, I wrote, someone else should be selected to serve as adjudicator.

Ten days later, Jack Ohlweiler informed me that Steiger had denied my request. Voorhees would adjudicate. Ohlweiler added that Steiger had forwarded my letter to Voorhees, on the dubious grounds that the letter was pertinent to the investigation. So the person adjudging me now possessed a letter containing my request that he be removed because of his bias. The forwarding of the letter to Voorhees appeared to be another fulfillment of Ziemer's prophecy that the leaders would look out only for themselves.

For the next several weeks, I heard nothing from the USAID Office of Security. I did, however, catch wind of another highly disturbing development. From friends inside the bureaucracy, I learned that Rob Jenkins had just talked Bonnie Glick into making him head of the new CPS Bureau.

Bonnie Glick had joined the agency in January 2019 as deputy administrator, the number two job in the agency. On personnel matters, she had taken over the pole position from Steiger, who, as may be recalled, had told Jenkins he wouldn't get the top job in the new bureau. Jenkins had used the full measure of his salesmanship to convince Glick to make him the head of the new bureau before she'd even interviewed the other leading candidate—me. I was appalled, but not surprised, for Jenkins had formidable sales skills, on top of his unquenchable thirst for power and his knack for intrigue and skullduggery. Some agency officials likened Jenkins to a used car salesman, and he certainly operated with the requisite slickness and duplicity, but the label didn't do him full justice. He possessed, in addition, the talents of a successful new car salesman. He could talk a soccer mom into purchasing a fully loaded Range Rover before she could visit the Ford dealership down the street where a similar vehicle was available for half the price.

To me, it looked like the Office of Security was stringing the investigation out while Jenkins stole the job I'd been expecting to receive. Could I afford to sit back and wait while Jenkins finished his coup? I couldn't stay at CMC if he took over the new bureau, as he would use his power to block my every move. There would be other jobs available at USAID if my clearance were reinstated, but they wouldn't possess the same level of influence over policy and resources as the head of a bureau.

I thought about contacting top agency leaders to forestall the plot. Deciding whether and how to seek help from above was one of the toughest choices for someone in a situation like this one. An appeal to Mount Olympus could bring a rapid and decisive resolution in your favor if the bureaucratic gods were on your side, but it could bring greater woe if they were not, and you usually lacked enough information to know for sure where they stood.

If the agency's senior leaders didn't have my best interests in mind, as events were beginning to bear out, then beseeching them for help might cause them to fear getting pulled into the quicksand with me. Yet if those leaders were inclined to sit back while the bureaucratic wolves tore me to shreds, a jolt might be required to convince them that there were good reasons to pull the wolves off. Some of those reasons would be purely ethical, but others involved self-interest. The White House would take a dim view of agency leaders if it learned that the Office of Security was prolonging a frivolous investigation into a senior political appointee while a rival from the career bureaucracy was pilfering his job.

I opened a blank email and put the addresses of Green, Glick, and Steiger in the "To" box. The investigation, I began, seemed to be going nowhere. No one from the Office of Security had contacted me, and according to Ohlweiler, no one had provided any evidence to support the allegation against me. For the benefit of Glick and Green, whose familiarity with the situation was uncertain, I reiterated my belief that the allegation against me was a false one that had been planted as a means of retaliation. After reading it over and making refinements, I clicked send.

Jack Ohlweiler contacted me two days later to say the agency leadership would not be responding to my email. He also warned sternly against contacting other leaders in the government, because it made me look guilty. Keep to yourself and let the process play out was his recommendation, as the process would be fair in the end. I decided to take his advice and refrain from further communication with higher authorities, so as to await the allegedly fair process. It was a decision I would come to regret.

During my years in the military world, I had grown to admire leaders who stood by their subordinates in times of need. General George S. Patton once remarked, "There's a great deal of talk about loyalty from the bottom to the top. Loyalty from the top down is even more necessary and is much less prevalent. One of the most frequently noted characteristics of great men who have remained great is loyalty to their subordinates." As the leader of an office, I had put in extra effort to help subordinates who had met resistance from others in the agency, needed support in finding their next assignment, or were enmeshed in a dispute with a co-worker. As a subordinate of the agency's front office, I expected the same type of downward loyalty from the agency's leaders. I had loyally and vigorously heeded their exhortations to bring the bureaucracy and the money under control, yet when the bureaucrats fought back, the senior leaders weren't rushing forward to help defend me, but instead were staying in the rear and shoring up their personal defenses.

History, I knew, was replete with egomaniacs who had stomped on people below them on the ascent to the top of the executive branch. Whether it was Aaron Burr, J. Edgar Hoover, or Richard Holbrooke, they drove subordinates like rental cars, unconcerned about the damage caused by their awful driving habits. It made me wonder if looking out for the welfare of subordinates was a trait peculiar to a select number of military leaders and was out of place in the world of federal civilian bureaucracy.

I had to remind myself that history had also recorded executive branch leaders who were not power-hungry narcissists and had cared for the people below them as well as those above. Individuals like George Marshall, Stephen Hadley, and Joseph Dunford had made it to the top by leading others as they would wish to be led. According to most of the leadership studies I'd read over the years, leaders who looked after their employees had happy employees, and happy employees were more productive than unhappy employees. So bureaucratic backstabbing and abuse of subordinates wasn't a universal prerequisite for success. But perhaps it was a prerequisite in the numerous places in the federal government where self-absorbed backstabbers proliferated.

My encounter with Jack Thompson in the bowels of the Reagan Building took place two weeks later. Buoyed by Thompson's statement that the void of evidence against me remained unfilled, I allowed hope to flicker. When, in the subsequent days, my home phone received calls from unknown numbers, I entertained hopes that the caller was Mark Green, or even Donald Trump, phoning to tell me he'd learned I had been fraudulently targeted for reporting corruption, to thank me for standing up to the corrupt officials, and to reward me with a promotion. Each time, however, the caller turned out to be only a political pollster or a seller of extended car warranties.

For the final two weeks of the six-week investigation, I heard nothing from anyone at USAID. I interpreted it as another good sign, on the presumption that I would have to be informed if actual evidence emerged.

Chapter 15

Justice in the Administrative State

On July 23, I received an email from Diana Leo, the USAID liaison to the Presidential Personnel Office. It read: "This is formal notice that you are to report to duty at the Ronald Reagan Building on July 24, 2019, at 1:00 p.m. Upon your arrival, proceed to the 13.5 Street Entrance and inform security at the gate that you have an appointment in the Badge Office, Room B2.6."

That was it. No mention of the outcome of the security clearance investigation.

Why the badge office? I wondered. If I were to be reinstated in my job, I would need to get my badge back. So the badge office seemed a good sign. The email didn't instruct me to bring a lawyer with me, which might have been the case had they been planning to revoke my clearance. Another good sign. That night, I went to bed feeling more hopeful than at any time since I had been escorted out of the building.

The next day, I put on a suit and drove to the Reagan Building. I arrived at the badge office at 1 p.m.

The first person I saw was Jack Ohlweiler. His presence wasn't a good sign. A lawyer didn't need to be there if they were just reissuing a badge.

"Let's go in here," Ohlweiler said, opening the door into a meeting room next to the badge office. It was the same room where Jack Thompson had questioned me two weeks earlier. Diana Leo showed up, and she and I followed Ohlweiler into the room. I sat down across from them.

I was expecting they would tell me that my clearance had been either revoked or reinstated. If the former, then they would explain to me the procedures for appeal. If the latter, we could exchange pleasantries and laugh about how silly the whole thing had been.

I hadn't counted on a third possibility. Even had I counted on one, I never would have imagined the bureaucracy could have settled on an option as unlawful and unethical as the one it chose.

Ohlweiler pulled out a single sheet of paper and handed it to me. He gave me a moment to read it. The document began: "This letter is formal notification that the Agency will terminate your Administratively Determined (AD), Excepted Service (Political) appointment at USAID, effective July 24, 2019." It went on to say that in the original appointment letter of February 2018, "the Agency placed you on notice that you would be serving in a temporary appointment without time limitation, and you serve at the pleasure of the Administrator of USAID. At this time, we thank you for your service and wish you the best in your future endeavors." The letter provided no reason for the termination of my employment. It was signed by Diana Leo, White House Liaison.

A wave of dark foreboding swept through my brain as I read the letter. I could feel my body temperature rising, though fortunately the room was cool and I didn't break into a sweat. Later, I would realize that this piece of paper would be an important asset to me in the complaint I filed with the USAID inspector general against the agency. But at the moment, I could think only in the most negative terms.

After reading the document, I looked up at Ohlweiler and Leo.

"As you are aware," Ohlweiler began in his haughty manner, "a political appointee can be terminated at any time with or without cause. After reviewing the matter, John Voorhees concluded that your clearance would have to be revoked because of the information provided by the Department of Defense. If we were to go through the revocation process, it could take another thirty days, and at the end you would have your clearance revoked and would no longer be able to work at the agency. The agency leadership decided that it would be better for everyone if you were terminated immediately. This way, your clearance isn't revoked, the investigation comes to an end, and there are no other adverse personnel actions for you. So thank you for your service." He paused, giving me a moment to digest this information, then added that there would be no severance pay or extension of benefits.

"I know this must be difficult," he continued in a gentler voice, "so I am here to answer any questions you might have." By now, I had spoken with Ohlweiler enough and heard enough about him from others to know of his deftness at playing the nice guy while simultaneously twisting the knife in the victim's back.

I took a deep breath. "When this process started six weeks ago," I said, "Tara Debnam told me that the SOCOM allegation was not a proof of guilt. The purpose of the investigation, she said, was to determine the accuracy of the allegation. When Jack Thompson interviewed me several weeks later, he said that SOCOM never provided evidence to support the allegation that was made against me. So how could Voorhees have concluded that my clearance had to be revoked?"

"The allegation came from another federal agency, so John had to treat it as gospel," Ohlweiler said. "There is no need for them to give us supporting evidence. We had another case where DoD sent us adverse information about a USAID employee, and we had to accept it as true."

My head was now spinning. What law professor had taught him that no evidence is needed for an action that requires due process, as a clearance revocation does?

"Now, John and I did do some due diligence," Ohlweiler went on. "I spoke on the phone with the two-star general and colonel who reported this, and they read me a few passages from the book, which sounded like they were classified."

Sounded like they were classified? This assertion was no less mindboggling. I don't think that any judge in the United States, not even the flakes in California or Vermont, would have found someone guilty on the basis of a lawyer's hunch.

"What did the passages say?"

"I can't tell you," Ohlweiler said, then added, "I don't know where you got that information."

"So you don't know whether it was classified, and you don't know whether it was already in the public domain?" I responded. "As I wrote in my sworn statement, I published only information in the public domain, and the courts have ruled that former government employees are permitted to publish information that is already in the public domain and was not obtained during the course of employment."

Ohlweiler responded, "John Voorhees and I were both in the military, so we know what we are talking about."

"When we had spoken earlier," I said, "you told me I'd have an opportunity to respond to any specific allegations from SOCOM by showing John Voorhees where the information came from. I never received the opportunity to do that. For USAID to renege on that promise and claim that I was guilty based on a one-sentence accusation from SOCOM is a denial of due process rights."

"I don't see any due process violations," Ohlweiler said.

"Under due process, I would have the opportunity to see the evidence against me," I replied. "I haven't seen any evidence."

Ohlweiler usually fired back without pause, but he now appeared flummoxed. After a moment, he made the strange argument that I had possessed access to the incriminating evidence when I had written the book. He also cited SOCOM's suspension of visitation privileges at its facilities, which he said indicated that SOCOM had made a determination on the information.

"SOCOM never gave me the opportunity to respond to the evidence it supposedly used in drawing that conclusion," I countered. "So there was no due process."

Ohlweiler then fell back on the contention that another federal agency's claim had to be considered as "gospel." He added that the involvement of a two-star general and a colonel showed that the claim was legitimate, and not the product of a disgruntled employee at USAID seeking to retaliate against me. I had the sense that he had previously overawed civilians who were unfamiliar with the military by invoking the authority of a general.

"Can you tell me the name of the general who claimed to know that I had published classified information?" I asked.

"No."

"How do you know that this general wasn't the friend of a USAID employee I'd reported for waste, fraud, and abuse?"

"I don't think a general would stick out his neck for a disgruntled USAID employee. And I don't think SOCOM would stick out its neck unless you had divulged something very damaging, because otherwise it would be putting itself on the line."

I asked whether the Department of Justice had reviewed the case. Ohlweiler said that the Justice Department typically would conduct a review of an alleged classified leak, but would only act under certain circumstances. He said I probably wouldn't hear from them if they chose not to act.

"Who made the decision to fire me?" I asked.

"Deputy Administrator Glick, in her capacity as the alter-ego of the administrator."

"Does Administrator Green know about it?"

"Yes, he is aware of it."

"What about the White House?"

"Yes, it was cleared through the White House."

"Has Bonnie Glick read the five-page sworn statement I provided?"

Ohlweiler hesitated a moment, then said, "I don't know."

So the person who had fired me based on an unsubstantiated charge may not have even heard my side of the story. Maybe that was why she hadn't shown up herself, but had instead sent Ohlweiler. The reason for her absence, though, could have been that she didn't like confrontation or the delivery of bad news, whereas Ohlweiler, by all appearances, positively enjoyed both.

"What exactly is the status of my clearance now?" I asked.

"Your clearance has been put on inactive status."

"What if I want to get another job requiring a security clearance?"

"Then your case will be reviewed by the agency seeking to hire you," Ohlweiler said. "You might want to start by talking with DOPSR, to straighten out the question of whether you leaked classified information." His utterance of the word "leak" was particularly annoying. That term was used when someone slipped secret information to a journalist or a foreign intelligence operative, not when someone with a thirty-day non-disclosure agreement published information after giving the government a year to review it.

When I subsequently mentioned Ohlweiler's recommendation about contacting DOPSR to one of the nation's most distinguished security clearance lawyers, he said that it was misleading and ill-informed. If I went to the Defense Department to try to clear my name, he said, they would probably either ignore me or cause me additional trouble for bothering them. I would need to find an agency or company that was willing to hire me for a cleared job with the knowledge that they would have to go through the hassle of resolving the suspended clearance.

Ohlweiler then mentioned offhandedly that I could seek legal assistance from Mark Zaid, whom he described as a leading expert on prepublication review. I informed him that I had already spoken with Zaid. Weeks earlier, in fact, I had asked Ohlweiler if USAID would consult with prepublication experts, since it had none on its staff, and he had replied that USAID would bring in whatever experts were needed. Now it was clear that the agency had brought in no experts, and relied instead on the opinions of Ohlweiler and Voorhees, which were at odds with the law.

"Earlier in this process," I said to Ohlweiler, "you told me to let the process play out and warned me not to contact people of influence I knew elsewhere in the administration, as that could give the impression that I was guilty. So I refrained from contacting important people I knew, believing I'd have the opportunity to contact them during the thirty-day appeal period if my clearance were revoked. I have now been deprived of the opportunity to seek support from higher political levels, since the appeals process has been taken away."

Ohlweiler made no attempt to defend himself against the charge, but moved on to another topic. He said that my termination was being handled quietly, and therefore word of my difficulties wouldn't spread outside the agency. Apparently he thought I would find comfort in that fact and would keep quiet to avoid embarrassment.

I found no such comfort. As I saw it, keeping everything hush-hush would play into the hands of the saboteurs, who naturally wanted their dirty deeds to remain hidden. Silence might not do me any good, either—with my job gone and my security clearance in a precarious limbo, I probably couldn't melt back quietly into the workforce right away. Nor was I the type of person who would rather accept a thrashing submissively than take on the risks of hitting back. I knew better, though, than to tip my hand to Ohlweiler by informing him I would do something other than crawl away into obscurity.

At the end of the meeting, I looked at both Ohlweiler and Leo. Maintaining eye contact while talking is not one of my strengths—in fact, I am quite poor at it—but in this moment of outrage my eyes bore down upon them. "You are sending a terrible message to others in the government," I warned. "This action tells everyone that the agency will allow career staff to sabotage one of the few political appointees who tried to hold staff accountable for bad behavior. Managers will conclude that they are better off tolerating misconduct and poor performance, because if they try to impose discipline, they could get fired based on unsubstantiated allegations instigated by their subordinates."

Ohlweiler and Leo looked back at me blankly.

On the way out, Ohlweiler reverted to the faux compassion he had displayed at the start of the meeting. He said he knew that this was an unfortunate situation, and he felt badly about how it had worked out for me. I shook hands with him and Leo and walked away.

Chapter 16

Aftershocks

For the last time, I passed through the atrium of the Reagan Build-ing en route to the parking garage. The shock of the moment was intense, but not as intense as it had been when I'd been escorted out six weeks earlier, because by this time I had prepared myself mentally for the possibility that the Office of Security would re-sort to bureaucratic witchcraft. I had been caught off guard, how-ever, by the decision to fire me rather than revoke my clearance. It had taken me by such surprise that I hadn't had time to think through all of its consequences before the meeting was over.

As I drove home, those consequences took shape in my head. The immediate termination was even more pernicious than it had first appeared. By convincing Bonnie Glick to fire me in-stead of reaching a decision on my clearance, Voorhees and Ohl-weiler had pulled off an incredibly audacious and devious stunt. In order to revoke my clearance, Voorhees had needed to cite evidence, and he had needed to disclose the evidence to me so that I would have an opportunity to contest it. Apparently he had been unable to obtain evidence showing that I had harmed national security, as otherwise he would have used it to revoke my clearance. But he had figured out that the agency leadership had the authority to punish me without evidence. So it looked like he had conned a top agency leader into believing that he had the evidence to punish me in his way, and she then had used her authority to fire me.

I wasn't sure whether Voorhees and Ohlweiler really believed that the words of other agencies had to be treated as "gospel." Tara Debnam had certainly understood that there is no gospel in the world of due process when, on the day she had suspended my clearance, she had acknowledged that the SOCOM allegation was not proof of an infraction on my part, but rather an accusation that had to be proven by evidence. To suggest that evidence was optional would give dictatorial powers to the purveyors of the gospel, permitting them to retaliate with impunity against whistleblowers or other enemies by soliciting unsubstantiated allegations from friends at other agencies.

Voorhees and Ohlweiler had been exceptionally brazen in thinking they could get away with this grandest of sucker punches. In the past, they had gotten away with persecuting career employees who lacked political connections, possessed few means of communicating with the public, and were afraid of making waves. They must have realized that a senior political appointee who had published six books and was willing to report multiple staff members for corruption might fight back with greater force and perseverance. Evidently they were confident that their support within the federal bureaucracy was so deep that they could thwart me, too.

I mulled over the role of Bonnie Glick. She didn't appear to be the primary culprit, but she didn't appear to be blameless, either. Firing a senior executive deserved greater care than she had shown. She should have spoken to me to hear my side of the story before arriving at any decision, or at least read my sworn statement. She had demonstrated gutlessness by sending Diana Leo, a very junior political appointee, and Ohlweiler, a dodgy career lawyer, to deliver the news instead of coming herself. The agency's head, Mark Green, subsequently decided that Glick had botched the notification, as he would personally deliver the news of firing the next time a political appointee was ousted.

I'd met with Glick only once, shortly before the suspension of my security clearance. Although Glick had still been relatively new to the agency at that time, she'd already alienated many of the people around her. Agency staff, career as well as political, faulted Glick for an imperious management style, and believed that she was being manipulated by senior career employees who had maneuvered into her good graces through flattery and favors, among them Rob Jenkins. Front office employees groused that Glick was neglecting the official responsibilities of her position to pursue pet interests and accumulate personal connections outside the agency.

The loudest complaints from the staff concerned a conflict of interest that was flagrant even by USAID standards. Glick's husband, Paul Foldi, was a lobbyist for international development contractors. And he wasn't just any lobbyist, but the top lobbyist for the mega-contractors that received most of the $20 billion USAID spent each year on contracting. With Glick's appointment to the number two position at USAID, a single household owned commanding positions at two of the cornerstones of the aid-industrial complex.

Foldi headed the Council of International Development Companies, a component of the Professional Services Council. Funded by government contractors to the tune of $6 million per year, the Professional Services Council billed itself as "the voice of the government technology and professional services industry" and "the most respected industry leader on legislative and regulatory issues related to government acquisition, business and technology." The organization "helps shape public policy, leads strategic coalitions, and works to build consensus between government and industry." In other words, the Professional Services Council lobbied the government to advance the special interests of government contractors, which mainly concerned maximizing the profits of those contractors, as opposed to the interests of the taxpayers, which concerned maximizing the effectiveness of taxpayer dollars.

During the Obama era, the Professional Services Council had strenuously opposed the efforts of USAID Administrator Raj Shah to reduce the power of the mega-contractors. When Mark Green had advocated procurement reforms with that same objective during the first years of the Trump presidency, Foldi and the council had objected to them, too. Green, to his credit, had ignored the lobbyists and directed his staff to undertake new procurement and budgetary reform initiatives. Numerous eyebrows were raised, therefore, when the wife of Paul Foldi began shutting those initiatives down.

Foldi, a former congressional staffer, and Glick, a former foreign service officer, epitomized the new breed of plutocrat that had emerged in Washington with the federal spending sprees of the early twenty-first century, parlaying regular government jobs into higher-paying gigs where they serviced fellow plutocrats with no-bid contracts, exorbitant consulting projects, and other by-products of massive government spending. I'd encountered some of the plutocrats among the Trump appointees at the Defense Department, but most of the appointees I knew at USAID had never belonged to the upper crust of this new Gilded Age. They had come from either the lower echelons of the Washington institutions, which didn't pay nearly as well, or from a city or town far removed from the swamp. Many of them, indeed, had been motivated to join the administration by Trump's pledge to drain the swamp of the self-serving parasites, and had stayed true to that principle throughout their time in office, as would be verified by their inability to obtain jobs in the aid-industrial complex after leaving the government.

Federal conflict-of-interest laws expressly prohibited government employees from working on matters affecting their spouse's financial interests—the very type of work that Glick was now doing at USAID. Jack Ohlweiler, as the agency's designated ethics official, was supposed to review the relationships between employees and their spouses and flag conflicts of interest, but he didn't advise Glick or other agency leaders that Foldi couldn't remain the nation's top aid lobbyist while his wife became the second-in-command at the top aid agency. When other agency officials began complaining about the conflict of interest, Ohlweiler allowed Glick to keep things going by having her sign a recusal from specific contracts, which did nothing to prevent her from thwarting broad reforms or promoting the general interests of the aid industry, which were indistinguishable from the interests of her husband. In the process, Ohlweiler showed a willful blindness to a conflict of interest of his own—he was at this very time seeking Glick's support for his promotion to the newly vacant job of deputy general counsel.

Because I'd received only small fragments of information about Glick's involvement in my termination, I couldn't rule out the possibility that she'd fired me merely because the career staff had duped her into believing I'd committed a felony offense. The circumstantial evidence, however, gave reason to suspect that her decision had been influenced by a desire to remove a potential threat to two of her main objectives—stifling procurement reform and keeping her conflict of interest under wraps. By reporting senior officials for unethical acts that included procurement abuse and conflict of interest, I'd put myself high on the list of agency employees who might at some point call attention to her machinations.

I returned home to deliver the devastating news to my family. Then I called one of the lawyers who had been providing me legal advice *pro bono*. When I told him what had happened, he was nearly as astounded as I was. USAID, he said, had pulled a fast one in order to deny me the ability to see the evidence and file an appeal.

The lawyer advised me to file a whistleblower retaliation complaint with the USAID Office of Inspector General. First, though, he said I should request permission to resign. A resignation would give me a "clean SF-50," a reference to the standard form for federal employee personnel actions. If I sought to work for the federal government again, the potential employing agency would scrutinize the SF-50 that had been completed at the time of my departure from USAID, and a resignation would look much better than a compulsory termination.

On July 25, I called Nick Gottlieb and asked if I could submit a resignation. I also told him that I had accumulated leave that had not yet been used, and requested that I be considered a paid employee until my leave ran out. After checking with higher authorities, Gottlieb consented to this arrangement. Two days later, I submitted a letter stating that I was resigning effective August 3.

Gottlieb also informed me that USAID would not allow me to retrieve my belongings from my former office. Everything would be packed up by contractors and handed over to me off premises. Weeks went by without further communication, so I started sending emails to Gottlieb and others inquiring about the status, but without result. Later, when reading about other federal whistleblower cases, I learned that withholding personal belongings is a common means of harassing and intimidating whistleblowers on their way out the door.

In the aftermath of my firing, I figured that someone from the senior leadership at USAID would contact me, at least to offer condolences, if not assistance in getting on with my life. I had worked with a sizable group of USAID leaders who knew I'd been fired unceremoniously and who didn't know whether it had been justified. Some of them had encouraged me to report waste, fraud, and abuse, and had thanked me when I had done so. But none of them attempted to reach me. I tried contacting a few of them by email, and received no response.

It's easy to second-guess leaders when you haven't been in their shoes, so I tried thinking through the matter from their perspective. If one of my subordinates had reported five people for waste, fraud, and abuse and then had been fired based on an unsubstantiated allegation about a book published two years earlier, would I ignore him? Or would I contact him to see how he was doing and offer help in finding another job?

I believed that I would have gone the second route. But perhaps I underestimated the fear that the career bureaucrats had put into even top political appointees. The success of Voorhees, Ohlweiler, and Jenkins in destroying me may well have convinced agency leaders they would suffer a similar fate if they gave any sign of extending a hand in my direction.

I did receive communications from some former subordinates and peers. Although there had been no announcement of my departure, and almost no one had any idea why I'd disappeared six weeks earlier, word of my firing and its dubious circumstances was spreading. Speaking with these individuals dulled the pain, though it also generated new worries since some of them believed that the people who had torn me down me would come after anyone deemed to have collaborated with me.

Several friends suggested that I contact the White House Presidential Personnel Office to complain about my treatment, and to see if I could obtain an appointment at another agency. I requested a meeting with Katja Bullock, the person in that office responsible for USAID appointments. She agreed to meet on August 2 at her office, in the Eisenhower Executive Office Building, next to the White House.

I'd never met Bullock before. Most of what I'd heard about her came from press stories belittling the Presidential Personnel Office, the most sensational being a *Washington Post* story of March 30, 2018, entitled "Behind the Chaos: Office That Vets Trump Appointees Plagued by Inexperience." Bullock herself was far from inexperienced, but the *Post* had taken her to task for helping four family members get jobs in the Trump administration. The media, though, had a tendency to exaggerate the faults of anyone and anything connected to the Trump administration, so I really had no idea what to expect.

I wanted to inform Bullock of all the dishonest and malicious tricks that had been played against me. For that reason, I brought with me several key documents, including a summary I had written about the travesty. Arriving early for our 1 p.m. meeting, I passed through the multiple layers of security at the Eisenhower Executive building, then took a seat in the waiting room outside Bullock's office.

When I was shown in, Bullock greeted me warmly in the accent of her native Germany.

"What have you been told about my departure from USAID?" I asked after we sat down.

"Diana Leo informed me that you were not able to keep your security clearance," she said, "and you had to leave USAID because a security clearance is required for USAID employees."

"She gave you that information before I was fired?" I asked.

"No," Bullock replied. "I only heard about it after you had been fired."

"I was told that the termination had been cleared with the White House in advance."

"No."

Her brow furrowed into a look of concern. Her mind, like mine, was processing the apparent fact that several people at USAID had choreographed my firing without obtaining White House clearance, and then had lied to me about obtaining White House clearance. My ire was heating up, and I hoped that Bullock's was, too.

"Did you know that they handed me a written termination?" I asked. "I had to come back to them later to request an opportunity to resign, at the recommendation of my lawyer."

"They should have given you the option of resigning before firing you," she said. "They also should have offered you the opportunity to find a job at another agency. It could have been an agency where a security clearance is not required." More evidence that USAID had intentionally railroaded me.

Bullock said she had sent my CV to some agencies that didn't require a clearance, and was waiting to hear back. She hadn't sent it to the agencies that most closely matched my expertise, such as the Department of Defense and the Department of State, because those jobs required a clearance and she had been told that I couldn't hold one.

"USAID put me on administrative leave for six weeks and conducted an investigation, which, as far as I know, produced no evidence," I said. "To fire me without any evidence was to violate my due process rights."

"Unfortunately, political appointees are not entitled to due process," Bullock said.

"It's true that political appointees can be fired without due process," I responded, "but security clearances cannot be taken away without due process." From my briefcase, I pulled out a page and handed it to her. It contained the official USAID policy stating that "whenever an adverse security clearance action is initiated, the individual subject to the action must be afforded due process." Had I been afforded due process, I explained, I would have been able to appeal an adverse decision to an independent authority; obtain the evidence against me through discovery; present my own evidence; call witnesses; and cross-examine opposing witnesses. After she had read the page, I told her that I had brought other documents demonstrating that I had been mistreated, and that I wanted them shared with top officials at the Presidential Personnel Office and the Office of White House counsel.

"PPO and the Office of White House Counsel can't really do anything about the treatment of appointees at the agencies," Bullock said. "It's up to the heads of those agencies."

Now I had a better understanding of why bureaucrats were pushing around their political appointees at so many agencies. Having been sold down the river by a political appointee who had been manipulated by career bureaucrats, I needed the White House personnel office to stick up for me, but that office was taking the position that the White House wouldn't do anything to protect its own appointees.

Bullock then said she would call Diana Leo to see if she could learn anything further. Picking up her phone, she dialed Leo while I sat in attentive silence. Leo answered, and the two of them conversed for several minutes. I could only hear Bullock's side of the dialogue. She was asking very basic questions about my firing, another indicator that she had been given very little information about the events.

After Bullock hung up the phone, she relayed what Leo had just told her. Bonnie Glick had made the decision to fire me based on the claim from the USAID Office of Security that I was certain to lose my clearance. That confirmed what Jack Ohlweiler had told me. This confirmation would prove valuable when, in the months to come, USAID attempted to deny that anyone had threatened to revoke my security clearance—after realizing that such a threat would confer whistleblower protections on me.

"It's too bad that USAID couldn't reassign you to another job," Bullock added.

Much later, I would learn that USAID had been lying about that, too.

I told Bullock that several career staff had deliberately broken rules and laws to expel me from the agency because I'd tried to implement White House policies and resist corruption. She asked for their names, which I gave her. When I spoke the name Jack Ohlweiler, she perked up. "Jack Ohlweiler," she said, rolling her eyes. "He has already caused me problems with two other people."

At the end, Bullock reiterated that she would try to help me find a job at an agency that didn't require a security clearance, and said she would call Bonnie Glick to see if anything else could be done, but added that she doubted anything could be done to get my job or my clearance back. Distraught at the tepidness of her interest, I decided not to give Bullock the stack of documents I had brought with me. Best not to give my most valuable weapon to a person who seemed to lack enthusiasm for the fight.

Only long afterwards would I find out that Bullock was an old friend of Bonnie Glick from the world of Maryland Republican politics, and had been instrumental in the hiring of Glick. When other political appointees at USAID had criticized Glick, I also learned, Bullock ran interference for her at the White House. In my quest to undo the deeds of Glick, I had unknowingly sought the help of her tribal chief.

Had this catastrophe occurred earlier in the Trump presidency, I could have gone to senior leaders I knew at the White House. H. R. McMaster and John Kelly would have intervened on my behalf, I believed. Those two, however, had departed, leaving me without friends at the top who could send a rescue plane to retrieve me from the desolate island where I was now stranded.

At USAID, the rest of the pieces fell into place for Rob Jenkins once I was gone. On August 30, the agency sent out a notice that Jenkins would head the new CPS Bureau as soon as it came into being. A short time later, Congress passed the Global Fragility Act, which gave the new bureau $230 million over five years for the Complex Crises Fund and the Prevention and Stabilization Fund.

The job of CMC Director was filled temporarily with a career employee who knew better than to cross Jenkins. Together he and Jenkins undid the changes I had made and the initiatives I had started. They rewarded Angela Greenewald for betraying me by promoting her to GS-15, making unusual arrangements for her to work at Fort Bragg where her boyfriend lived, and giving her both the Special Operations Command and Central Command portfolios.

The only favorable development during this otherwise dismal period was the expulsion of Crnkovich from USAID. He left the agency on August 1, 2019. I had never been privy to the details of the inspector general's investigation into Crnkovich, but did learn that investigators had amassed enough incriminating information to force Crnkovich out—no small feat in the case of a well-connected career federal bureaucrat. His ouster reassured me that my original decision to report him to higher authorities had been correct—at least from the perspective of governmental integrity, if not the perspective of my own career.

Yet even this development had a dark side. I soon received word that Crnkovich was working at the Department of Defense, which meant that USAID had not touched his security clearance or notified the Defense Department of Crnkovich's clearance-related problems. Had Defense officials been notified that Crnkovich had been kicked out of another federal agency for fraud, they would not have hired him into a job requiring a security clearance. By contrast, the USAID Office of Security had inserted a note in my record stating that anyone considering me for a clearance should call USAID, at which point they would be informed of the SOCOM complaint. John Voorhees and Jack Ohlweiler had given better treatment to Crnkovich after the emergence of highly incriminating evidence of criminal fraud than they'd given to me after an agency investigation had produced no evidence that anyone was willing to stand by.

Chapter 17

Out on the Streets

As the delay in the return of my personal belongings increased, so did my worries that the USAID Office of Security was ginning up new troubles. I learned that it had asserted control of my former office, locked the door, and sent its personnel inside on several occasions. Having heard that staff from the Office of Security had planted false evidence during the insider threat scandal of 2016, I feared that the office would play the same trick again.

Apparently, my adversaries were by now content with the damage they had already inflicted, for I received no news of additional allegations against me. After continued badgering on my part, some contractors finally packed up my belongings and I was permitted to retrieve them on September 9. Once the agency no longer could claim it had found evidence of espionage interspersed with my office files, I filed a whistleblower retaliation claim with the USAID Office of Inspector General.

Because I had been a political appointee, I wasn't covered by the Whistleblower Protection Act as most federal employees were. The exclusion of political appointees from the act was mystifying. As temporary employees, political appointees could assume greater risks than other employees in reporting waste, fraud, and abuse, and hence were especially deserving of whistleblower protections. Political appointees were, nevertheless, covered by Presidential Personnel Directive 19 and law 50 U.S.C. § 3341, which prohibited actions against whistleblowers that adversely affected their eligibility for access to classified information. In my complaint, I noted that USAID had taken multiple actions that had adversely affected my eligibility, including the suspension of my security clearance, the threat of a clearance revocation, the involuntary termination of my employment, and the notification of the Presidential Personnel Office that I could not hold a security clearance.

In order to receive the protections of PPD-19 and 50 U.S.C. § 3341, a federal employee must demonstrate submission of a "protected disclosure" prior to the alleged retaliation. A "protected disclosure" is a disclosure of waste, fraud, abuse, or other violation of a law, rule, or regulation, and it must be made to a qualified individual, such as a supervisor, an agency leader, or an inspector general. In my complaint, I presented evidence of protected disclosures involving five different USAID employees.

The USAID Whistleblower Protection Coordinator, Tanner Horton-Jones, contacted me to set up a meeting. On September 24, I met with him and the lead investigator, Special Agent Sean Bottary, at the Marriott Hotel in Fairfax, Virginia. Seated at a table in the large, open lobby, we spent most of the meeting going over the details of the whistleblower retaliation claim. Horton-Jones assured me that his office was going to look into the case with the utmost seriousness. He added, however, that because the Whistleblower Protection Act did not apply to political appointees, they were treating my case solely as a waste, fraud, and abuse hotline complaint, not as a whistleblower complaint. As a result, Horton-Jones said, the Office of Inspector General was under no obligation to complete the investigation within a specific time frame.

Horton-Jones made no mention of PPD-19 or 50 U.S.C. § 3341. The omission was highly suspicious. As the agency's whistleblower coordinator, he must have been aware of their provisions and their applicability to political appointees. Rather than raise the matter during this meeting, I would follow up afterwards via email, which would give me a written record of the agency's position.

In my email to Horton-Jones, composed later that day, I stated that I was eligible for the protections of PPD-19 and 50 U.S.C. § 3341 because I had been subjected to actions affecting security clearance eligibility after making protected disclosures. Horton-Jones emailed back that while those protections applied to political appointees, I was not eligible for its protections because the agency had not revoked my security clearance and had not initiated its clearance adjudication and appeal process. Horton-Jones didn't say whether this interpretation had sprung from his own mind, or had come from that of his boss, Nicole Angarella, the general counsel of the Office of Inspector General. As I was later to learn, Angarella was a highly controversial figure, having been promoted to the job of top lawyer over more experienced and competent lawyers by Inspector General Ann Calvaresi Barr, who counted Angarella as one of her protégés.

When I described this interpretation of PPD-19 and 50 U.S.C. § 3341 to several of the nation's premier security clearance lawyers, they called it an absurdity. They pointed out that the CIA had previously tried to use this same interpretation to deny whistleblower protections to one of its employees, Andrew Bakaj, until an investigation by an external inspector general had determined that Bakaj was indeed entitled to the protections and had been the victim of whistleblower retaliation. These lawyers also noted that nothing in PPD-19 or 50 U.S.C. § 3341 indicated or implied that employees could be denied protection if the agency did not fully adjudicate the clearance. Furthermore, they said, both the directive and the law left no doubt that federal employees were protected against the threat of clearance revocation. I put this ammunition in my pocket and awaited an opportune moment to load it.

In the meantime, I was scrambling to find employment, which is far from easy for a middle-aged white male conservative scholar, no matter how broad his experiences, accomplishments, or professional contacts. When I had signed on with the Trump administration, I'd expected to stay to the end of the Trump presidency and have time in the last months of my tenure to amass a bouquet of attractive job offers, at think tanks, non-profit organizations, and government contractors, where I could keep contributing to the causes of the U.S. government and the American people. I then would carefully select the bouquet's most beautiful flower. Now I was down in the dirt, scrounging for whatever might be poking out of the ground at the moment.

The executive experience on my resumé was shorter and less impressive than anticipated, thanks to my firing. To prospective employers, moreover, I would have to explain why I left USAID without another job lined up. If I told an employer that corrupt bureaucrats and lawyers had used a bogus allegation to get me fired, they might suspect that so extraordinary a tale had to be the fanciful invention of someone who had been fired for a legitimate reason.

Katja Bullock's efforts to find me a job at another agency came up empty. None of the Washington think tanks were hiring for senior national security experts at the moment. Nor were there promising opportunities at colleges and universities. The politicization of academic hiring had become even worse since my last foray into the academic job market, owing to the retirement of the last open-minded professors of the Silent Generation and their replacement with leftists who believed the faculty had to be kept free of ideological deviants.

Had there somewhere been a glimmer of hope for a conservative academic like me in 2019 at a "mainstream" university, it would have been snuffed out as soon as the faculty learned I possessed the one attribute that registered even higher on academia's deplorability scale than conservative thinking—service in the Trump administration. Whereas universities routinely fell over themselves to hire veterans of Democratic administrations, not a single Trump appointee was offered a tenure-track or tenured academic appointment after working in the administration. The only people who left the upper ranks of the federal government during the Trump era to find loving arms in academia were the anti-Trump lawyers who had abused their power in Crossfire Hurricane and the Mueller probe—Peter

Strzok (Georgetown University), James Comey (Howard University), Andrew McCabe (George Mason University), Sally Yates (Georgetown University), and Andrew Weissmann (New York University).

At Harvard, to cite one of numerous examples, more than 200 people signed a petition demanding that the university "refuse to serve as a tool to launder the reputations of those who crafted and enabled the Trump administration's anti-democratic, anti-immigrant, racist, and morally reprehensible abuses." The petitioners called on Harvard to "commit that it will not hire or affiliate with any senior official in the Trump administration or Congressional leader who was complicit in the administration's immoral actions." Harvard President Lawrence S. Bacow further discouraged faculty from dispensing fellowships and teaching positions to Trump veterans by warning that anyone seeking to appoint such people should "be prepared to defend why an individual is worthy of recognition."

Only one former Trump appointee received a Harvard fellowship at the end of the Trump administration. And it wasn't just any Trump appointee, but Bonnie Glick. Her fellowship, a semester-long appointment at Harvard's Institute of Politics, would be announced one week after Trump left office. Plenty of Trump appointees had records of achievement and scholarship that would have merited a Harvard fellowship, but Glick wasn't one of them.

I would join other Trump administration veterans in wondering whether Glick had obtained the fellowship by bestowing favors on Harvard while she had been USAID deputy administrator. That type of graft occurred all too often in the top echelons of big government and big academia. USAID and Harvard, in fact, had their own history of exchanging contracts and jobs.

During the 1990s, under J. Brian Atwood's leadership, USAID had doled out $57 million in contracts to the Harvard Institute for International Development to promote economic reform in the former Soviet Union. Most of the contracts were awarded without competitive bidding. Atwood subsequently received a teaching job at Harvard's Kennedy School of Government. Although two Harvard professors who received these contracts eventually had to pay the U.S. government a whopping $31 million settlement for violating conflict-of-interest rules, Atwood never received any punishment.

Employment in the aid industry was similarly governed by ideology. During my time at USAID, I'd regularly encountered former political appointees who worked for the development contractors and NGOs that implemented USAID programs, the vast majority of them veterans of Democratic administrations. Despite the evident distaste for Republicans, I figured it wouldn't hurt to apply. Tracking the job opportunities as they popped up on Indeed, LinkedIn, Devex, and other job sites, I promptly applied to positions that matched my expertise and experience.

After receiving automated email receipts, I heard nothing from any of them until months later, when I received automated email rejections. At first I wasn't sure whether this treatment was simply the result of general hostility to conservatives and Trump appointees, or whether I had been personally targeted. Rob Jenkins possessed influence with many of the organizations that had received my applications, thanks to the decades he'd spent advocating for their industry, steering contract dollars into their bank accounts, and placing protégés in their workforces. I wouldn't have been surprised had Jenkins put in a bad word for me, either preemptively or in response to an inquiry from someone reviewing my application. In 2021, however, I would begin to lean toward the explanation of general hostility, because the Trump appointees who left USAID at the end of the Trump administration were to fare no better than me in obtaining jobs with the aid companies and non-profits, except for a few who had shirked their duties as political appointees and curried favor with aid plutocrats and swamp monsters.

The defense industry was the other place where I cast my line. The biggest problem here was my security clearance status, as any company interested in hiring me might have to spend months trying to restore my clearance. Eventually, I found one company that was willing to help. In the fall, it sent the Department of Defense a request to reactivate my clearance so that I could work on a classified project. Such requests are often granted within a month. The Department of Defense security clearance office, however, did not provide an answer after a month, nor after two months, nor three, despite repeated prodding from the company. The silence would persist for nine months.

In November, I began some part-time consulting at a company that specialized in unclassified work on terrorist financing and other financial crimes. I began driving into Washington several days a week to work at the company's office. An urban office is not often associated with spiritual rejuvenation, but for me the experience of returning to a productive team environment was a relief after months of sitting at home in uncertainty. The company's employees were amiable and passionate about their work, and the tasks at hand restored a sense of normalcy and order. The immediacy of the work also encouraged me to think more about my future, and less about the past.

The past, however, kept creeping back. A few days after I started the new work, one of my former USAID employees, whom I'll call Joyce, received a strange email from USAID Employee and Labor Relations demanding answers to questions about her job and her interactions with me. I'd kept hearing that the people who had taken me down were causing problems for anyone they considered to have been a supporter of mine, but this action took matters to a new level. A subsequent investigation would reveal that this incident had been sparked by a complaint from John Voorhees against Joyce.

Joyce sought assistance from the civil service union and a private lawyer. They helped convince the agency that the complaint was groundless, allowing her to keep her job and her clearance. A persistent pattern of harassment, however, convinced Joyce to quit the agency several months later.

The campaign against people who had supported me would help convince my former deputy, Stephanie, to leave USAID for the private sector. This news was especially saddening, for the government desperately needed people of her quality. I believed that she could have risen to one of the highest positions in the agency had she stayed. Among the most important reasons for the ineffectiveness of the federal government is its aptitude for alienating and driving out its best people.

Chapter 18

Dereliction of Duty in the Office of Inspector General

In the middle of December 2019, the Office of Inspector General informed me that it had completed its investigation. The rapid completion meant the investigation had played out in one of two ways, I surmised. One good, the other bad.

Under the good scenario, Calvaresi Barr had directed her staff to review the case rapidly and thoroughly, out of a desire to get to the truth posthaste. An email she had sent me on December 6 had given me hope on this score. "I have had regular updates from my staff and understand that they have been diligently working on appropriately addressing the concerns you have raised," she had written.

Under the bad scenario, the inspector general had allowed her staff to perform a very shallow review that acquitted the agency. I knew little about Calvaresi Barr, but I figured that the facts of the case were so strongly in my favor that any sensible inspector general would avoid this option.

Because I had initiated the complaint, I was permitted to request a copy of the investigation report. I did so immediately, and received it by email on December 19, 2019. All told, the report was three pages in length. When I mentioned that fact to individuals familiar with inspector general reports, they said the document had to be something other than the investigation report. The report couldn't possibly be that short. But upon further exploration, we found out that the three-page document was the report.

The first page of the three merely summarized the charges I had made in my complaint of September 11. The report's substance, if it could be called that, took up scarcely more than one page. The first "substantive" sentence provided this revelation: "The investigation revealed that Mr. Moyar authored a publication entitled: '*Oppose Any Foe: The Rise of America's Special Operations Forces*.'"

The ensuing findings were no more enlightening. The report offered a short chronology of events, almost all of which were contained in the complaint I'd submitted. I looked quickly through the brief paragraphs until I reached the conclusion on the third page. It read, "The information USAID has indicates that applicable policies and regulations were followed in this matter and that Moyar's allegations against Voorhees are not substantiated."

Upon reading that sentence, the hopes I had placed in the Office of Inspector General collapsed. The investigation's complete lack of seriousness and the document's Orwellian language gave me the feeling that I was reading a North Korean report to the International Atomic Energy Agency. It made me question whether the game of politics was so corrupt that those who were unwilling to lie, cheat, and steal should not bother playing.

After my initial shock at reading the investigation report had passed, I analyzed the document in detail. Certain basic features were unusual. The name of the report's author had been redacted, but the author's organizational affiliation was still shown— the "USAID OIG Middle East & Asia Division." Normally, a document of this type would have been sent by Calvaresi Barr, or else another senior official not assigned to a geographic region, since the complaint had nothing to do with that region. Had the inspector general deemed the complaint too unimportant to assign it to a more senior official?

The designated recipient of the report, whose name had also been redacted, worked at the Office of General Counsel, when normal practice would have been to send the report to the head of the agency. Months later I would receive a copy of this document with fewer redactions, which revealed the name of the recipient to be Jack Ohlweiler. A report of this nature should never have been sent to Ohlweiler, since I had accused him of serious wrongdoing in the complaint. If the report had really needed to go to the Office of General Counsel first, it should have been sent to one of Ohlweiler's superiors. The fact that it had been issued to Ohlweiler also heightened my suspicion that Ohlweiler had been colluding with the inspector general. The flimsy exoneration of USAID, and the arguments made for it, were strikingly similar to what Ohlweiler had said to me himself about the case.

The redacted document gave no indication of the investigation's duration. I assumed that the investigation had been completed in mid-December, given Calvaresi Barr's assertion on December 6 that her staff were "diligently working on appropriately addressing the concerns you have raised." I would later learn that the report had been completed on October 3, 2019—just ten days after it had begun with my interview at the Fairfax Marriott. Clearly, no serious investigation could have been conducted in such a short period of time. The only diligence taking place in December had been diligence in stalling.

The report's chronology omitted most of the facts I had presented in my complaint, including all the ones that demonstrated my eligibility for whistleblower protection. I had given Bottary a lengthy list of people to interview, but the report mentioned none of them, and it gave no other indication that anyone on the list had been interviewed. I contacted several people on the list to see if they had been interviewed, and none had heard from Bottary or anyone else in his office.

After tallying up the deficiencies, I sent a response to Calvaresi Barr. It listed a total of fourteen key points from my complaint that the report had failed to address. In addition, I faulted the USAID Whistleblower Protection Coordinator, Horton-Jones, for failing to advise me of my whistleblower rights and remedies and for wrongfully denying that I was protected in any way by PPD-19 and 50 U.S.C. § 3341.

Over the Christmas break, while awaiting Calvaresi Barr's response, I plumbed the history of inspectors general to see what insights it might offer. It turned out that the USAID Office of Inspector General, like the USAID Office of Security, had a recent history of abusing its power. In 2014, eight USAID auditors and employees had complained to Congress and the *Washington Post* that Acting Inspector General Michael G. Carroll had systematically removed negative information from the office's audits. The *Post* reviewed twelve audits produced between 2011 and 2013 and found that negative information about USAID and its overseas offices had been excised in more than four hundred places. Carroll, it was believed, wanted to shield USAID leaders from criticism so that they would appoint him to his position permanently. The publication of these allegations resulted in the withdrawal of Carroll's nomination for the job and his forced retirement from the government.

The person who had been most active in reporting Carroll's transgressions was Robin Marcato. I didn't learn the details of Marcato's story at this time; that wouldn't happen until the end of 2021, when I met her and read the transcript of her 2018 hearing before the Merit Systems Protection Board. (Although she was a liberal Democrat and I was a conservative Republican, our shared abhorrence of the corruption at USAID would ensure that we hit it off smashingly.)

As an employee in the Office of Inspector General during Carroll's tenure, Marcato had first taken information about the adulteration of audits to the USAID whistleblower ombudsman, who at the time was Jerry Lawson. Lawson admired Marcato's integrity and intentions, but warned her against telling anyone what she had learned. "Do not report this, because they will try to destroy you," Lawson advised. At the Merit Systems Protection Board hearing, Lawson explained that he had discouraged Marcato and others from blowing the whistle because he'd read about a whistleblower lawyer conference where "not a single lawyer would say that he would recommend to their clients that they report misconduct because retaliation is so prevalent."

Marcato chose not to retreat in the face of danger. After she received direct orders to falsify a report, she notified a congressional staffer of this and numerous additional acts of fraud. Congressional staff brought Marcato's concerns to the attention of several legislators. Senator Tom Coburn, Republican of Oklahoma, was so appalled by Marcato's disclosures that he complained directly to Carroll. To placate Congress, Carroll offered a ritual sacrifice. He arranged for the resignation of the Assistant Inspector General for Audit, Tim Cox, who had done much of Carroll's dirty work. Once congressional interest subsided, Carroll paid Cox lavish sums to work for the agency as a contractor. Marcato reported this trickery to Congress as well.

Because Marcato had first raised most of these same issues internally, Carroll and other top leaders in his office figured that Marcato must have been Senator Coburn's main source. They began looking for excuses to punish her. At Marcato's hearing before the Merit Systems Protection Board, Lawson testified that Carroll "was encouraging whistleblower retaliation," and that the problem continued after Carroll's retirement, when a protégé of his named Cathy Trujillo took charge. Robert Ross, the top official for management in the USAID Office of Inspector General, testified that Trujillo had put intense and incessant pressure on him to discipline Marcato because Trujillo and her associates "wanted at all cost to get [Marcato]."

In November 2015, Ann Calvaresi Barr took over from Trujillo as inspector general. At the outset, Calvaresi Barr told the staff that she intended to support whistleblowers, fanning the hopes of employees like Marcato, Lawson, and Ross. Lawson was so encouraged that he sent Calvaresi Barr a memo urging her to investigate acts of retaliation against Marcato.

Calvaresi Barr did not respond as anticipated. Instead of requesting a whistleblower retaliation investigation, she called for an investigation into Marcato. She steered that task to the

Department of Defense inspector general, where both she and Trujillo had a friend named Glenn Fine, whose record with whistleblower complaints was as checkered as theirs. Trujillo, one of the foremost perpetrators of the retaliation, personally contacted Fine about initiating the investigation into Marcato.

While that investigation was taking place, Marcato saw other indications of a lack of integrity on the part of Calvaresi Barr. In December 2016, Marcato notified a congressional investigator that Calvaresi Barr had given misleading testimony to Congress. In February 2017, she reported that an audit on Haiti had mysteriously disappeared from the USAID OIG website.

The Department of Defense inspector general completed its investigation into Marcato in the summer of 2017. The Report of Investigation faulted Marcato for a few minor infractions that had not previously been considered grounds for terminating USAID employees. Yet presiding USAID official Jason Carroll, whom Calvaresi Barr had brought with her from the Department of Transportation, used the report as justification for firing Marcato. USAID never fired any of the employees implicated in the far more serious offenses Marcato had reported, such as providing false information to Congress, deleting negative information from audits, destroying records, and retaliating against whistleblowers.

Marcato concluded that the decision to fire her must have come from Calvaresi Barr herself. "I don't think the whistleblowers had a chance with Ann," Marcato said at the hearing. "I don't think she cared about whistleblowers or anything. I think she cared that I was an impediment to her having people who said yes all the time and did what they were told, just like Mike Carroll."

My research also revealed that in the four decades since its inception, the community of inspectors general and their staffs had evolved into a guild, resembling the guilds of shoemakers and blacksmiths during the Middle Ages. The guild had its own association, the Council of the Inspectors General on Integrity and Efficiency, which met regularly for workshops, conferences, and an annual awards ceremony. (One suspected that the ceremony had the nauseating self-congratulation of the Oscars, without the celebrity glitz or high fashion.) When a job opened up at one agency's inspector general office, chances were good that it would be given to someone from another inspector general office.

The members of the inspector general guild, like those of other guilds, jealously guarded admission and information. They were averse to calling out fellow members for bad behavior, because the merest hint of impropriety could create enemies inside the guild, damage the guild's reputation, and invite external scrutiny and interference. The guild was intent on policing itself, by means of the Integrity Committee of the Council of the Inspectors General on Integrity and Efficiency. Allowing a committee dominated by inspectors general to police the inspectors general had confirmed the fact that the inspectors general were as susceptible to favoritism and corruption as other humans. The committee refused to investigate most of the accusations it received, dragged its feet on many of the others, and in at least one case—Marcato's—allowed the retaliators to turn the investigatory weaponry against the whistleblower. Several prominent whistleblowers, in addition to Marcato, had accused the committee of ignoring well-substantiated allegations in order to protect fellow inspectors general. Among the allegations it passed over were the overpayment of salaries to the inspectors general of the National Reconnaissance Office and National Security Agency, by totals of $150,000 and $18,000 respectively. For years, members of Congress had demanded an overhaul of the Integrity Committee along with greater congressional authority and oversight, but the inspectors general had fended them off with token gestures.

The Integrity Committee was manifesting its deficit of integrity at this very moment with its refusal to investigate allegations brewing at the Department of Homeland Security. This agency's leaders had sent the Integrity Committee evidence of misconduct involving three senior officials in its Office of Inspector General, Jennifer Costello, Diana Shaw, and Karen Ouzts. Sorry, not interested, said the Integrity Committee.

Trump-appointed officials as well as the liberal Project on Government Oversight lambasted the Integrity Committee for failing to look into the allegations.

In this case, unlike most others, the agency's leadership found a way around the Integrity Committee's intransigence—hiring a private law firm to conduct an independent investigation. After interviewing fifty-three people and reviewing forty-two thousand emails, text messages, and documents, the investigators concluded that the three officials had fostered "an atmosphere of mistrust and unprofessionalism to the detriment of the agency and its mission." The three of them, who were known within the office as the "Mean Girls," were found to have employed the usual hairpulling techniques of toxic leaders, such as retaliating against "any employees they thought were in the way of their personal goals and agenda." According to the report, "the work environment became so bitterly hostile that employees who left the agency during this period cited dissension and tension as contributing factors for their departures."

The investigation drove the Mean Girls out of the Department of Homeland Security. Diana Shaw, however, managed to obtain an even more senior job within the inspector general guild, becoming the deputy inspector general of the State Department. Twice thereafter, she became that agency's acting inspector general when a politically appointed inspector general resigned. She hung on to this new job even after the law firm's damning investigation was made public.

On the few occasions when the Integrity Committee was willing to investigate an inspector general, it moved at an excruciatingly slow pace. In April 2017, the committee received complaints from Senator Charles Grassley and several other powerful senators about the inspector general of the Federal Housing Finance Agency (FHFA), Laura Wertheimer, and members of her senior staff. The senators had been inundated with whistleblower reports about the inefficiency of Wertheimer's office, her termination of audits in response to pressure from the agency head, and her hiring of individuals who lacked the specified qualifications. Nearly a year elapsed before the Integrity Committee launched an investigation, which it placed in the hands of another agency's Office of Inspector General. Three more years would pass before the Senate received the investigation's results.

Wertheimer and her chief counsel, Leonard DePasquale, invoked spurious legal arguments to deny the investigators access to documents, and threatened subordinates with harmful consequences if they shared information with the investigating team. Despite this obstructionism, the office's staff gave the investigators enough information to compile a devastating indictment of Wertheimer's leadership. The Report of Investigation stated that Wertheimer had "abused her authority by creating and fostering a culture of abuse and intimidation for her staff, which particularly focused on those who were, or whom she perceived to be, providing information to Congress and/or the [Integrity Committee]." Wertheimer, the investigators determined, had retaliated against a senior executive who had met with congressional staff by nicknaming him "weasel" and distributing copies of a children's book entitled *Weasels* to members of her staff. One employee in the Office of Inspector General told investigators that Wertheimer had mocked his weight in front of a roomful of people, which in his words was "the most degrading and embarrassing thing." He commented that "as a mature adult, I should've been able to stop right there and say, 'Boss or not, time out. That's unprofessional and you don't get to talk to me that way.' But I was afraid of her. I mean I still am afraid. She's the big boss."

The Integrity Committee concluded that Wertheimer had "engaged in conduct that undermines the integrity reasonably expected of an IG," and that "misconduct of this nature warrants consideration of substantial disciplinary action, up to and including removal." Wertheimer hung on to her job for two more months before pressure from Senator Grassley, watchdog organizations, and enraged federal employees finally convinced the Biden administration the time had come for her to go. She suffered the usual fate of the senior career bureaucrat exposed for gross misconduct, compulsory retirement.

Three weeks after Christmas, I received a response to the critique I'd sent Calvaresi Barr. It came not from her, but from Suzann Gallagher, the acting assistant inspector general for investigations. Gallagher opened by stating that "the OIG Office of Investigations found that the actions taken by USAID leading up to your voluntary resignation were not retaliatory, but were predicated on United States Special Operations Command's (SOCOM) referral that you had included classified information in your published work. The OIG found that, solely in response to the information from SOCOM, USAID's Office of Security (SEC) suspended your clearance pending further review. This review ceased upon your voluntary resignation, and SEC did not render an adjudication on your eligibility for a clearance."

Now they were defending the agency by claiming I couldn't be a whistleblower because I had voluntarily resigned and nothing had been done to my security clearance. Did the Office of Inspector General really think that I had voluntarily left the agency, after I had informed them I had received a written termination notice on July 24, 2019? Did they think I hadn't bothered to keep a copy of that document? Or a copy of the resignation letter I'd signed three days later? It was smart of Calvaresi Barr to let so fraudulent a claim come from the pen of an underling.

Gallagher went on to claim, "None of the actions taken by USAID with regard to your clearance violate the whistleblower protection or other due process provisions of PPD-19 or 50 U.S.C. § 3341, the controlling statute." Gallagher was not a lawyer. What lawyer had produced this fatuous text I did not know. Presumably the wording had been sanctioned by the general counsel of the inspector general, Nicole Angarella. But anyone should have been able to tell that the law did not support the agency's claim to innocence, as it prohibited not only clearance revocation but the threat of clearance revocation.

After reading Gallagher's email, I wrote to Mark Green directly to give him and the agency one more chance to deal with the matter before I sought help elsewhere. "I have refrained from writing to you for many months because I had thought that OIG was going to take seriously my allegation of whistleblower retaliation," I emailed Green on January 10, 2020. "During my employment at USAID, I tried to contact you directly on two occasions, and on both occasions I was rebuked by gatekeepers. I do not know what gatekeepers and filters are restricting your access to information, but I do know that others at the Agency have in the past tried to conceal information from USAID leadership to advance their own agendas rather than those of the Agency, so I am now sending information to you directly." I laid out the basic facts of the case, and explained why I believed the inspector general's investigation was inaccurate, shallow, and biased.

Green did not write back. Instead, USAID General Counsel Craig Wolf emailed me a response. Wolf had joined the agency as a political appointee just as I was leaving, so I had never met him. I hoped that as a political appointee, Wolf would be sympathetic to my cause.

He wasn't. In the style of a company man, Wolf wrote, "The Administrator spoke to me about your most recent email and asked that I reply to you on his behalf. As you know, the OIG reviewed your whistleblower complaint from September 11, 2019, and found no evidence that the actions taken by USAID prior to your voluntary resignation were in retaliation or reprisal for your allegations concerning certain USAID staff." There they were again, the words "voluntary resignation." Wolf then asserted that the USAID leadership "agrees with and accepts the findings and conclusions of the OIG investigation and considers this matter closed."

I never found out exactly what had led Wolf to leave me twisting in the wind, but I did receive some possible clues several months later. When the agency solicited applications for my permanent replacement as CMC Director in the spring of 2020, I learned, Wolf applied for the job. My increasingly pessimistic mind guessed that Jack Ohlweiler, in his capacity as the agency's designated ethics official, had assured Wolf there was nothing unethical about applying for a job after blocking the return of the prior job holder by falsely claiming he had voluntarily resigned. I also heard from several individuals at the agency that numerous political appointees distrusted Wolf because of his close personal ties to Bonnie Glick and certain career bureaucrats.

Wolf's email brought to a close my four-month effort to obtain help from USAID officials. With agency leaders unwavering in asserting that a written notice of involuntary termination could be described as a voluntary resignation, I wasn't going to get any further by banging on their door. It was time to find new places to knock.

Chapter 19

Going Outside

Before my brush with the USAID Office of Security, civil liberties hadn't been a subject that aroused much interest in me. The Obama administration had become entangled in several scandals involving flagrant violations of civil liberties, such as the IRS's targeting of conservative groups and the NSA's collection of phone metadata, and those misdeeds had served as useful reminders that Democrats could violate civil liberties as readily as Republicans. As I and many other conservatives saw it, however, they reflected the sins of a few top officials, rather than a broader, systemic problem.

I had thought that private citizens didn't really need to worry about governmental surveillance if they weren't doing anything wrong. Although as a conservative I had a natural suspicion of the government, conservatives like me had a soft spot in our hearts for those working in the military and other security-related fields, as we viewed those fields as particularly valuable, and we knew that they often attracted individuals of high patriotic spirit. Surely, I thought, U.S. officials in charge of programs that watched Americans and collected their personal information had been carefully vetted and would exercise their powers fairly and honestly.

It turned out I was wrong. The targeting of personal enemies by the Office of Security in 2016 had shown that security bureaucrats could flagrantly abuse their authority and their access to information. The same office had committed abuses against me, and the USAID Office of Inspector General and multiple Department of Defense entities had joined in the criminality.

Nor until now had I paid much attention to whistleblowers, apart from seeing them in popular movies, like the one where Julia Roberts took on a sleazy electric company, and the one where an uncharacteristically portly Russell Crowe blew the whistle on the tobacco industry. I had admired those who put themselves at risk to tell the truth and stop criminal activity, yet at the same time I had held the common perception that people often claimed whistleblower status merely to divert blame from themselves, advance an ideological agenda, or reap millions of dollars in damages. In addition, I had bought into the stereotypical depiction of the whistleblower as a misfit—a timid gnome with dandruff and rumpled polyester pants whose cubicle contained only his action figure collection and photos of his cat. I was unaware that the perils of whistleblowing tended to scare off the most self-serving of individuals; that many whistleblowers never received a penny; that punitive damages for whistleblower retaliation against federal employees were far lower than the multimillion-dollar settlements paid out occasionally to private-sector whistleblowers; and that whistleblowers were more often an organization's high flyers than its cellar dwellers.

Although the federal whistleblower protections of PPD-19 applied to me, I wasn't a typical whistleblower, at least not as the term is generally defined by laymen. According to popular perception, a whistleblower is a worker bee who reports illegal activity by management. The modest status of such whistleblowers makes them easy targets for retaliation by managers, since the managers can smack them with instruments of discipline on questionable or baseless pretexts.

Most of the misconduct I reported, by contrast, involved my subordinates. As a manager, it was my duty to report such misconduct. It is often believed that managers do not get punished for reporting bad behavior as do the rank-and-file because they have the support of upper management, if they are not themselves part of upper management. Research on whistleblowing, however, has shown that managers, and especially middle managers, frequently suffer retaliation for reporting waste, fraud, and abuse. Retaliation against middle managers is believed to be so widespread because they often assume they have enough status and security to right the wrongs and withstand any blowback, only to find that upper management is often willing to throw conscientious managers under the bus in order to protect themselves or their organization.

Humans are creatures of experience, attaching greater weight to what we have lived than to what we have heard—which isn't always a bad thing, since much of what we hear is wrong or incomplete. We care more about problems that have affected us personally than those we have only read about in the newspaper or seen on television. Having been personally wronged through due process violations and bureaucratic fraud, I now cared very much about civil liberties and whistleblower retaliation. I was ready to go to war.

The inspector general's whitewash left me with one last administrative remedy—PPD-19, Section C. It was one of the protections that Horton-Jones, the ostensible Whistleblower Protection Coordinator, had neglected to mention to me. Under this section, employees who exhausted the whistleblower process with their agency's inspector general could request an external review by a three-member panel, chaired by the Inspector General of the Intelligence Community.

Prior to January 2020, I had not retained a lawyer, but had instead been the fortunate recipient of free legal advice from several of the nation's top security clearance lawyers. Now that I was down to the last chance and short on time, I decided that I ought to hire a lawyer who could help me write the appeal, and who knew arcane rules that could work to a client's advantage. Lawyers jousted with each other in legalese, and I didn't speak that language.

I was referred to Kel McClanahan of National Security Counselors, an organization that provides low-cost legal advice to whistleblowers and other individuals beset by security clearance problems. Speaking with him by phone, I related the particulars of my case. He outlined his extensive experience with the use of security clearance actions as instruments of whistleblower retaliation, and expressed a strong interest in defending me, demonstrating the sort of passion I expected would be necessary for a long legal slog. When McClanahan offered to take my case on a contingency basis in deference to my lack of a job, it sealed the deal.

While McClanahan worked on the appeal to the intelligence community inspector general, I sought help from Congress. By law, current and former federal employees are permitted to share information with Congress that could be deemed inappropriate for sharing with other audiences. In the middle of January, I sent information on my case to a variety of congressional staffers. What happened to this information once it reached Capitol Hill was never clear to me. I heard secondhand that it provided ammunition to Republican staffers who were arguing that the administration needed to be more vigorous in protecting political appointees from scurrilous attacks by career bureaucrats.

Some of the information I sent to Congress found its way to conservative journalists. The first news article about my case was written by Susan Crabtree, a seasoned reporter at *RealClearPolitics* who had written numerous articles on corruption and whistleblowing at federal agencies. Published on January 17, 2020, the article laid out the facts of my case and contrasted my treatment by USAID with the kid-glove handling of Eric Ciaramella, the whistleblower whose allegation had triggered the impeachment of President Trump one month earlier.

For the article, Crabtree interviewed Sean Bigley, a security clearance lawyer who at this moment was representing two dozen pro-Trump clients who faced similar security clearance problems. Only one of Bigley's clients, Adam Lovinger, had been mentioned in the press; the others had chosen to remain in the shadows, fearing that speaking out would hurt their chances for regaining their clearances.

"There is no question that federal law, policy, and precedent all support Dr. Moyar's position," Bigley told Crabtree. "This case cries out for congressional and potentially law enforcement intervention," he said. "More broadly, Dr. Moyar, and the many other administration officials subjected to similar abuses, need to know that the White House has their back. A message needs to be sent from the top that this type of behavior will not be tolerated."

Crabtree also interviewed Brett Max Kaufman, a lawyer at the American Civil Liberties Union, whose organization had joined Columbia University's Knight First Amendment Institute in suing the federal government for inefficiencies and abuses in the government's prepublication review system. "The indefinite withholding of prepublication clearance, based on the experience of our plaintiffs, is a huge problem," Kaufman said. Agencies were ignoring the time limits that were supposed to serve as "a bedrock First Amendment protection against government licensing schemes such as this."

The story came to the attention of Senator Grassley, Republican of Iowa. No one in Congress had done more to protect whistleblowers than Grassley. His commitment to whistleblower protection, pursued relentlessly since he had joined Congress in 1975, had earned him hero status among whistleblower advocates of all political persuasions. Senator Grassley and his staff began asking pointed questions that the USAID inspector general could not ignore.

The combination of public exposure in the media and behind-the-scenes pressure from Congress compelled USAID to reopen my case. On February 5, a USAID official informed McClanahan that the Office of Inspector General was conducting a new investigation. He promised that the office would be investigating the matter much more thoroughly this time around.

It was the first positive news I had received in quite a while. It looked like there might finally be real scrutiny of the events of the past year. The reopening of the investigation allowed McClanahan to suspend plans for filing an appeal with the intelligence community inspector general. If the reopened investigation were as thorough as advertised, it would vindicate me and we would have no need for that option of last resort.

On March 13, Mark Green announced that he would be stepping down as head of USAID. For the next few days, the media frothed with conjecture over the succession, after rumors circulated that Deputy Administrator Bonnie Glick—who by convention was the natural successor—might not come out on top. The aid-industrial complex favored Glick and touted her to the administration and the press. Correspondent Michael Igoe of *Devex*, the preferred publication of the aid-industrial complex, reported that "prominent outside development leaders" were "lobbying for Glick to take over." This backing reinforced the perception among USAID staff that Glick was beholden to the interests of her husband and the development contractors for whom he lobbied.

The efforts of the aid-industrial complex came to naught. On March 17, Trump gave the job to John Barsa, who had been the USAID assistant administrator for Latin America and the Caribbean. According to an acquaintance of mine with knowledge of the deliberations, Glick's summary termination of my employment had been one of several factors in the decision to snub her. Another factor had been the recent departure of Katja Bullock, her White House patron. The newly appointed head of the White House Presidential Personnel Office, John McEntee, had ousted Bullock as part of a campaign to remove political appointees who hadn't sufficiently supported Trump's policies.

In April, Trump began addressing a problem that should have been addressed earlier in his administration: the inspectors general. On April 3, he fired Michael Atkinson, the intelligence community inspector general, and three days later sacked Glenn Fine, the acting inspector general at the Defense Department. He also announced the nomination of five new inspectors general at agencies that had been lacking presidential appointees in those positions. The next day, Jonathan Swan of *Axios* reported, "Sources close to President Trump expect him to fire more inspectors general across his government. . . . Conservative allies of the president have told him that these I.G.s are members of the 'deep state' trying to undermine him. Trump appears to have embraced that view."

Trump's firings sparked a flurry of partisan denunciations from journalists, pundits, lawyers, and congressmen. On Twitter, Senate Minority Leader Chuck Schumer charged that Trump was purging "honest and independent public servants because they are willing to speak truth to power and because he is so clearly afraid of strong oversight." Walter Shaub, who had run the Office of Government Ethics under Obama, tweeted that the country was "entering the end game with the potential fall of the Inspector General community. The government is failing us, safeguards that took two centuries to build have crumbled, and fascism is eyeing this republic like lunch."

The defenders of the incumbent inspectors general ignored the actual faults and misdeeds of Michael Atkinson and Glenn Fine, which were considerable. It was Fine who had obliged Ann Calvaresi Barr by responding to a whistleblower retaliation complaint with an investigation that faulted only the whistleblower, Robin Marcato, and resulted in her termination. Under Fine's leadership, the Defense Department's inspector general office had repeatedly been accused of giving short shrift to whistleblower complaints and shielding senior officials from accusations of whistleblower retaliation.

Two days after Fine's removal, Susan Crabtree reported in *RealClearPolitics* that "many of Trump's closest advisers and allies believe several inspectors general—some serving in acting roles and first appointed during previous administrations—have become a thorn in the side of his presidency, working to undermine his agenda and sabotage some political appointees' efforts to carry it out." Crabtree's sources also said that "a driving force behind the Trump camp's frustration with Fine is a longstanding impasse into a whistleblower reprisal case against defense analyst Adam Lovinger." I had recently become acquainted with Lovinger because of the similarity of our calamities. Having seen his clearance revoked, he had been forced to spend the last three years scrounging for work outside his area of expertise.

Crabtree's article mentioned Calvaresi Barr, too. "The USAID inspector general," she reported, "is not among those Trump has so far publicly moved to replace, although her name has circulated on a recent list of top IGs who should be replaced." This news must have set off panic in a number of USAID offices. From what I knew, the USAID inspector general deserved to be the next one shown the door.

The USAID Office of Inspector General had originally promised McClanahan that the report of the new investigation would be completed in March. But when March came, it said the investigators were still investigating. We could not tell whether they were really still investigating, or just stalling, as they had done the last time.

On the afternoon of Friday, April 24, the inspector general's office informed McClanahan that the report had been completed and forwarded to the head of the agency. I was permitted to request a copy of the report, which I did that afternoon. I was hoping that we might receive it that same day, as we had been told that it had been prepared for release earlier that week, but it didn't arrive that day.

On the following Monday, I kept checking my email for the report. Nothing. Another week went by without a word. Then, finally, it came by email on the evening of May 4.

Chapter 20

The Inspector General Reports Again

When I opened the file on my laptop, I first looked at the page count. It was 224 pages. A 224-page report certainly sounded more thorough than a three-page report. Maybe the inspector general really had looked into every nook and cranny.

The first brief taste of hope was followed, however, by morsel after morsel of bitter disappointment. If the first report had been a canapé of biased investigation, sloppy analysis, and muddled dissembling, the second was a veritable smorgasbord. Ann Calvaresi Barr and at least two other senior U.S. government executives had been involved in producing this shoddy report, indicating, first, that the government had selected its executives poorly and, second, that large amounts of taxpayer-funded money had been wasted in producing the report. The investigator listed on the report was the same one who had been listed on the ridiculous first report, Sean Bottary.

At the front of the file was a brief cover note from Calvaresi Barr to John Barsa, which contained a boilerplate pledge on protecting whistleblowers. "My office's mission is to safeguard and strengthen U.S. foreign assistance through timely, relevant, and impactful oversight," Calvaresi Barr stated. "Ensuring the right of individuals to report wrongdoing without fear of reprisal is essential for accomplishing that mission. Therefore, assessing and responding to allegations of whistleblower retaliation committed by Agency management is a top priority for my office as is ensuring that these complaints are investigated in a timely and thorough manner."

The cover letter was dated April 24, but the investigation report was dated February 18. So the updates we'd received in March and April attributing delays in the release to deeper digging had indeed just been another delaying action.

Most of the 224 pages consisted of either U.S. government documents that were not specific to my case or documents that I had provided with my complaint. The actual investigation report was just eight pages. Of the fourteen points I had identified as major omissions in the first report, eleven were nowhere to be found in the eight-page report, and the other three received only superficial coverage. Some of the key individuals had been interviewed this time around, but the interviewers had often failed to ask hard questions, and had not followed up when someone provided an evasive, dubious, or inconsistent answer. Many other key individuals had not been interviewed at all; only two of the thirty-five people I'd recommended had been interviewed. The three people I'd identified as central orchestrators of the retaliatory scheme hadn't been interviewed and weren't even mentioned in the report. And yet the report claimed that there remained no "undeveloped leads."

The report didn't repeat the earlier claim that I was ineligible for whistleblower protections because I had "voluntarily resigned." Instead, it acknowledged that Diana Leo had "notified Dr. Moyar that he would be terminated" on July 24, 2019. Such a stunning reversal should have caused investigators to question why the acting assistant inspector general for investigations and the agency's top lawyer had asserted in writing that I had resigned of my own volition, and why they had used that assertion to deny me whistleblower protections. But the report made no mention of these fictitious claims or their implications.

A thorough whistleblower investigation would have begun by examining the origins of the accusation against the alleged whistleblower. The investigators had received information from me, and perhaps from others, about the two-star general and his links to USAID. Yet neither the report nor any of the attached documentation said a word about him, or any other Defense Department employee.

The report stated that the USAID Office of Security had obtained information from the Department of Defense Insider Threat Management and Analysis Center (DITMAC) indicating that my book contained classified information, and asserted that this information vindicated the initial SOCOM accusation and the decision to suspend my clearance. The specifics of the DITMAC information, however, had been redacted from the version of the report that we received, which was puzzling since the report was not classified. The report continued, "Based on the SOCOM information, USAID political appointees, after consultation with the White House, made the ultimate decision to issue a letter of termination to Moyar."

This sequencing, along with other statements in the report, led the reader to believe that USAID had possessed the supposedly incriminating insider threat information before the decision to fire me. The only reference to receipt of the information from Insider Threat Center, however, indicated that USAID personnel reviewed it on January 27, 2020—more than six months after I had been fired. The agency was defending the Office of Security's actions by citing evidence it apparently obtained only long after the taking of those actions.

The report made no mention of the First Amendment rights and court rulings I had cited in my lengthy sworn statement. It was mute on the thirty-working-day time limit for prepublication review specified in the non-disclosure agreement. Instead, it invoked the logic of the administrative state, citing as sole authority the policies and officials of the Department of Defense. The department was allowed to take as long as it wanted to review my manuscript, the report's authors maintained, because that was what the department's bureaucrats said.

The accompanying interview transcripts contained substantial redactions, but even so they shed more light on matters than the eight-page report. John Voorhees told investigators that before suspending my clearance on June 13, 2019, he had "contacted SOCOM for amplifying information on the letter. SOCOM did provide supporting, classified documentation." Voorhees said that "once he had the additional information, he advised Deputy Administrator Glick, Chief of Staff Steiger, and Attorney Ohlweiler he was 'on firm ground for suspension.'"

Voorhees's use of the term "supporting" in reference to this documentation suggested that it contained corroborating evidence. But other interviews indicated that it did not "support" the accusation, but merely "validated" it. Tara Debnam, who must have seen this documentation since she was the one who had actually suspended the clearance, had told me on the day of suspension that USAID had received only an allegation, not supporting evidence.

Although the report did not directly address the pivotal question of whether Voorhees had threatened to revoke my clearance, several interviewees spoke on the subject, including Voorhees himself. In his statements to the investigators, Voorhees sought to avoid any appearance of having threatened to revoke my clearance, and in such strenuous terms as to suggest he had learned after my departure that threatening to revoke a clearance could land him in hot water. He told the investigators that "the subject of firing or termination never came up in his conversations with [Deputy Administrator] Glick, [Chief of Staff] Steiger, or Attorney Ohlweiler." He "would never discuss revocation with them, only suspended status." Voorhees didn't explain why he would never tell top agency officials about revoking my clearance when those officials would need to know if one of their employees lost the clearance required to perform his job. Nor did anyone ask Voorhees to explain this discrepancy.

Several other interviewees contradicted Voorhees on this point. Jack Ohlweiler admitted telling me at the July 24 meeting that "the next step was revocation and without a clearance or access, Moyar could not do his job anymore." The investigators didn't ask Ohlweiler to explain how he had reached the conclusion that revocation lay in my immediate future. His admission, however, made clear that someone had convinced Ohlweiler that I was headed for revocation—and the someone in question could only have been the person with exclusive responsibility for rendering decisions on USAID security clearance revocations: John Voorhees. Ohlweiler, in fact, had said on the day I was fired that Voorhees had determined my clearance would have to be revoked.

When the OIG investigators interviewed Diana Leo, she too confirmed that Glick had fired me because she had been persuaded that I would otherwise lose my clearance. According to the transcript, Leo attested that "the conversation revolved around Moyar not being able to do his job without a security clearance." There was only one way I could find myself without a security clearance—if it were revoked by John Voorhees.

The most significant interview was the one with Bonnie Glick herself. Until reading this transcript, I had known only what other people had said about Glick's role in the matter. Because Glick had made the decision to fire me, her words assumed paramount importance.

In response to the interviewer's question, Glick asserted that "Voorhees never told her that Moyar needed to be fired or used the term 'revoke' at any time." Glick may have been playing a semantic game, of the sort often employed by bureaucrats in sticky situations, or she may have been on the receiving end of a semantic game played by Voorhees. In conversations with Glick, Voorhees might have used a word other than "revoke," such as "withdraw" or "take away." Bureaucrats often resort to such verbal sleight of hand when they are up to no good, in case they ever face questioning from an inspector general or a member of Congress. It was also possible that Ohlweiler had conveyed the word "revoke" to Glick and thus technically Voorhees had never uttered the word to her.

Whatever the case, Glick's next words provided powerful new evidence that Voorhees had indeed informed Glick—either directly or through someone else—that he was ready to revoke my clearance. Glick stated that she "knew that Moyar performing his job was contingent on a security clearance. If Moyar could not obtain the clearance, then removal needed to be considered." She added that "retaliation was not a part of the decision. Only that Moyar needed a clearance to perform his job."

Glick's reference to my inability to "obtain the clearance" represented either a misstatement or a misunderstanding on her part, for I already possessed the clearance, even if it was suspended. But Glick showed that she understood the basic issue at hand—whether I would lose my clearance—when she said that the decision to fire me was based on the consideration "that Moyar needed a clearance to perform his job." Again, the only way I would no longer possess a clearance to perform my job would be if John Voorhees revoked it.

If one accepted *Merriam-Webster*'s definition of *threaten* as "to announce as intended or possible," then Glick's statements to investigators led inescapably to the conclusion that Voorhees had threatened to revoke my clearance—one of the actions expressly prohibited by the whistleblower protection statute. In addition, Glick's account confirmed that this threat had induced her to take two actions that crossed another legal line by adversely affecting my eligibility for access to classified information—the involuntary termination of my employment and the notification of the Presidential Personnel Office that I couldn't hold a security clearance.

The failure of the investigators and Calvaresi Barr to delve into the conflicting testimony on this crucial point ranked among their most egregious faults. They could have followed up with Voorhees, Ohlweiler, Leo, Glick, and others for additional details that would have clarified who had said what, and who had contradicted whom. They could have confronted Voorhees with evidence from other witnesses indicating that he had in fact spoken of revoking my clearance. Such additional probing might well have led to the conclusion that Voorhees or others had lied in their initial statements. That conclusion could have had potential criminal consequences for those individuals, and would have lent additional credence to my whistleblower retaliation claim.

The interview transcripts shed light on several additional complaints that had been leveled against me during my time as CMC Director. I already knew about one of them, the one that had resulted in the seizure of my computer, which I'll call accusation number two. Jack Ohlweiler provided new details in his interview, recounting that someone had alleged that "Moyar was using Temporary Duty (TDY) to write a book, and using his government computer to write a book, while on government duty." Ohlweiler said that examination of my computer had determined that it "did not contain any evidence to support the allegation."

Ohlweiler had told me early on that the investigation into accusation number two seemed to have been an act of retaliation by someone within USAID. Yet the new investigation report said nothing about the accuser's motive in making an accusation that had been disproved. Nor did it give any clue as to that person's identity.

The existence of accusation number three, which had previously been unknown to me, was revealed in the interview with Ohlweiler. "Moyar had an ethics opinion on file with respect to a website for the sale of all his published books," he stated. I had never requested any ethics opinion, as it had never occurred to me that a personal website with information about my books and links to those books on Amazon.com would present a problem. Just about every author had such a website in 2019. That website, in fact, dated back to my prior federal service at the Marine Corps University more than a decade earlier. So someone else had lodged a complaint about the website and the Office of General Counsel had considered it so unimportant that they had never contacted me about it.

When the investigators interviewed Rob Jenkins, he told them about additional accusations that had been made to the

Office of Inspector General. He recounted hearing that "people were going to the Inspector General for various issues about Moyar relating to management and travel." Evidently these allegations against me had not been compelling enough to trigger an investigation, either, for I would have been interviewed had there been one. In yet another curious omission, the report of the Office of Inspector General failed to mention that its own personnel had received these unsubstantiated allegations.

Any competent investigator in a whistleblower retaliation case should have seen in these accusations a pattern of retaliation and duplicity. The next step should have been an examination of the origins of the complaints. But that step had not been taken.

The investigators performed no better in addressing my allegation that Voorhees had deliberately slow-rolled my SCI clearance. The report exonerated Voorhees simply by taking his word for it. "When interviewed," the exonerating section stated, "Voorhees explained that the CIA is responsible for processing all USAID SCI clearances and that the SCI process is outside of USAID's control." In actuality, USAID had partial control of the process, because it submitted the employee's information to the CIA, and in my case it had used that power to delay the completion of the process for many months.

During the interviews, the investigators rarely asked questions about motives for retaliation against me. That topic did, however, come up during the lone interview they conducted with a CMC employee. That person told them that "people in the office wanted Moyar gone because he held them accountable."

The investigators now had plenty of dots to connect. I had blown the whistle on Crnkovich. I had been fired on account of an unsubstantiated claim because that claim was treated as gospel by John Voorhees, a member of Jenkins's network. Jenkins and Voorhees had tried to arrange a period of refuge for Crnkovich at the National Counterterrorism Center, and later helped him get a permanent job at the Department of Defense. Voorhees had given sanctuary to another member of the Jenkins network, Schmidt, after I had authorized a review of his prior management of CMC. It shouldn't have been hard to connect the dots and dig deeper. But the investigators and Calvaresi Barr didn't connect any of it.

The inspector general seemed to be trying very hard to protect someone, at the risk of her own reputation. Was she trying to protect top agency leaders, as Michael Carroll had before her? Was she intent on squelching a whistleblower for exposing the misdeeds of other agency officials, as she had done to Robin Marcato? Did she owe favors to my accusers or other individuals whose actions were obviously problematic, like Voorhees and Ohlweiler? Or had Jenkins found a way to manipulate her, too? All seemed plausible.

Chapter 21

The Department of Defense Inspector General

Back in September 2019, I had submitted a complaint to the Department of Defense's inspector general, similar to the one I had sent to its USAID counterpart a short time earlier. I had been advised that the Defense Department inspector general could cover aspects of the case that USAID might be unwilling or unable to explore. Those would include the actions of the two-star general and other Defense Department personnel.

The next month, I had received a preliminary reply. "We forwarded your complaint to the Directorate for Whistleblower Reprisal Investigations (WRI) for analysis," it read. "WRI has declined to exercise its discretionary authority to investigate your complaint." No explanation for this decision was given. The message continued, "An inquiry of the non-reprisal aspect of your complaint will be conducted and you will be notified when your complaint is closed and how to obtain a copy of releasable records."

Senator Grassley had previously denounced the Directorate for Whistleblower Reprisal Investigations and its head, Marguerite C. Garrison, for monstrous ethical violations. According to his sources, he said in April 2017, senior managers in her directorate were guilty of "tampering with investigative reports and then retaliating against supervisory investigators who call them to account." These revelations were "sparking allegations that a 'culture of corruption' is thriving in the Inspector General's office."

Garrison survived that attack, as well as a media story in March 2020 that exposed her behavior to a much larger audience. That story concerned an investigator on her own staff, Steven A. Luke. In 2018, Luke had contacted Senator Grassley's office about a case involving Robert Cardillo, head of the National Geospatial-Intelligence Agency, who had been accused of violating agency travel rules. Luke had investigated the claim, and concluded that it lacked merit, but Garrison pressured him into reaching a different conclusion.

Luke was a man with a strong sense of moral duty. His email signature contained this quote from Johann Wolfgang von Goethe: "You can easily judge the character of a man by how he treats those who can do nothing for him." In the face of Garrison's pressure, Luke refused to back down. Ultimately, Garrison relented, and Cardillo was exonerated.

Favorable outcome notwithstanding, the experience took a heavy toll on Luke. According to Amy Mackinnon, who wrote a lengthy story on Luke for *Foreign Policy*, Luke's wife said that "it was the worst work-related stress she had ever seen him under. He was frustrated, preoccupied, and beginning to look for other jobs."

Luke subsequently contacted Grassley's office to relate his frustrations. "I felt bullied, berated, and belittled unless I acquiesced to go along with everyone else and write the ROI [Report of Investigation] as a substantiation," he informed Grassley's staff in an email. Luke scheduled a meeting with a member of Grassley's staff for February 4, 2019. A few weeks before the meeting took place, however, Luke was found dead in his car trunk outside the inspector general's headquarters building. The police ruled it a suicide. Luke had a history of depression, but his wife believed that the job stress had contributed to the outcome.

When Mackinnon contacted Grassley for her story, the senator told her, "The tragic suicide of Steven Luke may be part of a long-standing pattern of alleged investigative misconduct, retaliation and bullying in the directorate where Luke worked. This abusive culture has apparently been allowed to exist unchecked for far too long."

On April 29, 2020, after more than six months of waiting, I received a short email from the Defense Department's inspector general. It stated that my complaint had been "closed," and that "the DoD Hotline is not authorized to release case information or documents." I was informed that I could file a Freedom of Information Act request to obtain case records. McClanahan submitted a request.

The Defense Department responded to the request on June 5, stating that the Joint Staff, SOCOM, and USAID were reviewing relevant documents. The only document of significance received on this day was an email dated October 10, 2019, which gave a short explanation for the decision of the Directorate for Whistleblower Reprisal Investigations to turn down the case. The directorate, it stated, declined the case because it "lacks jurisdiction over the complaint, or the complaint was clearly filed in the wrong forum." Strangely, the email didn't say which of the two was the actual reason, or provide evidence to support either one.

Meanwhile, McClanahan was continuing to seek answers about the disposition of my security clearance. Someone at the Defense Department informed him that my clearance was going through an adjudication process, based not on the complaint that I had published classified information, but on a complaint that I had published the book without governmental approval. If that were the case, then I was being held up by an accusation that I hadn't waited indefinitely for the government's permission to publish something that the government didn't deem objectionable, after giving the government far longer to review the manuscript than required by the non-disclosure agreement.

We also learned, in late June, that the Defense Department adjudicators were still waiting for USAID to send them information on my case. The Defense Department acknowledged that it had been working on my case for at least five months, so USAID should have sent the information long ago. No one could or would tell us why it hadn't arrived at Defense.

At this stage, we were receiving assistance from Quinton Brady, a sharp young lawyer who worked for Senator Grassley. Brady was pressing USAID and the Defense Department for answers, and as a member of Grassley's staff he could get information from bureaucrats who wouldn't give McClanahan or me the time of day. Brady learned that USAID was defending itself by citing a letter signed by the two-star general who had made the original accusation. The letter alleged that I had disclosed classified information, but didn't provide the specifics. USAID was simply arguing that I was guilty "because a two-star general said so." When USAID disclosed this defense to Brady, he replied that Senator Grassley and his staff couldn't buy the claim that a general's words had to be treated as holy writ. They had seen individuals of higher rank than a two-star general lie, cheat, and steal.

Brady received other, even more preposterous excuses from the Defense Department for what they had done to me. Someone told him I had misused a SOCOM helicopter. In years past, official business had made me the passenger on SOCOM helicopters from time to time, but I had never been in a position to determine whether or how to use one. Another person claimed that the response of SOCOM to my manuscript had been delayed for many months by a change in the book's title, one that I hadn't shared with the government. Brady was therefore most interested when I forwarded him an email showing that I had notified the Defense Department of the change of title in August 2016.

Brady told me he'd been appalled by the shoddiness of the USAID inspector general's investigations. In addition to omitting interviews with the people I'd identified as perpetrators of whistleblower retaliation, he observed, the inspector general had failed to review any relevant emails. Any competent investigator, he said, should have looked at the email records in this type of case.

Even with Brady's help, things were still moving slowly. Bureaucrats at USAID and Defense would promise him something, but then fail to deliver, and he'd have to call them weeks later to ask again. It seemed like a major break would never come.

It finally came on July 7. That morning, I opened my email inbox to find a message with the subject of "Clearance Update." The sender was an employee of the company that had been trying to hire me for the past nine months. The Defense Department, it read, had granted me a clearance.

The long night of clearance limbo, more than a year in duration, was over at last. Someone in a position of authority—I didn't yet know who—had finally determined conclusively that I hadn't spilled secrets in the book. They had rejected the claim, advanced by the USAID Office of Security and Office of Inspector General, that I was incriminated by the cachet of the two-star general and the mysterious documentation provided by the Defense Insider Threat Management and Analysis Center six months after my firing. They also rejected the argument that I had erred in not waiting indefinitely to publish. Now I could get a cleared job. And I had ironclad proof that I had been fired on false grounds.

Beaming in exaltation, I informed family first. Then I notified McClanahan, Brady, the Presidential Personnel Office, friends at USAID, and others who had helped. After many months of battling back and forth, we now had our opponents on their heels. As they retreated, we would pursue with our cavalry.

Chapter 22

Twilight of the Trump Administration

More good news arrived the next morning. *Politico* reported that Rob Jenkins had just lost his grip on the leadership of the nascent CPS Bureau. Although Jenkins had been designated the head of the new bureau shortly after my termination, bureaucratic lethargy and the COVID-19 pandemic had delayed the official formation of the bureau until now, nearly a year later. The White House, *Politico* stated, was transferring a senior political appointee, Pete Marocco, from the Pentagon to USAID to serve as bureau head. Marocco assumed the position on July 8, 2020.

On a less positive note, the press coverage made plain that several media outlets were embarking on a crusade to discredit Marocco and other Trump appointees at USAID. The reliance of the media crusaders on self-serving USAID bureaucrats for information was as obvious as a third grader's reliance on his father for the construction of his Pinewood Derby car. Nahal Toosi and Daniel Lippman were listed as the authors of the *Politico* article, but, as USAID staff pointed out in a flurry of communications with one another and with me, the article sounded like it had come straight from the mouth of Rob Jenkins.

Marocco's arrival, Toosi and Lippman reported, "is being greeted with all the excitement of a root canal." According to the article, anonymous career officials alleged that Marocco "frequently undermined career staffers" who didn't go along with his plans. After fitting Marocco into the role of Voldemort, the reporters presented Jenkins as Harry Potter. "The possibility that Marocco could lead the conflict prevention bureau upset some USAID staffers in particular because a widely respected career official was supposed to get that role," the authors stated. "That employee, Rob Jenkins, is 'beloved' in the agency, one of several USAID officials said in praising him."

In the months to come, Marocco was the subject of several more hit pieces, based on the words of anonymous agency officials. Colum Lynch, Robbie Gramer, and Jack Detsch of *Foreign Policy* assailed Marocco on September 2 for cutting funding to programs that didn't support the Trump administration's national security priorities. The trio sounded as indignant as subversive career bureaucrats that a White House appointee would try to align federal programs with White House policies.

In another *Politico* article, published later in September, Toosi and Lippman reported that "experienced staffers" had sent the USAID Office of Inspector General a thirteen-page complaint about Marocco. The complaint "alleges that Marocco is requiring that he personally approve all office expenditures over $10,000 and be notified of all spending below $10,000 in an office with an average annual budget of $225 million." Apparently the bureaucrats who authored the complaint thought the political leadership shouldn't see how they were spending taxpayer dollars in that office, the Office of Transition Initiatives. (OTI)

Even more ominously, the journalists reported, "Marocco has also undermined a number of senior and working-level staffers at OTI, including Rob Jenkins, a longtime USAID official and former head of OTI, whose role has been reduced by Marocco. Jenkins has been excluded from 'many' meetings and even told by Marocco to hang up on a recent call he didn't want Jenkins on." Yes, the dreaded compulsory phone call hang up. This was the same Rob Jenkins who had excluded me from "many" meetings.

From my sources in the agency, I learned that Marocco was crossing swords with Glick, Ohlweiler, and Jenkins over the hiring of my successor as CMC Director. After my departure, Jenkins had talked Glick into converting the job from a political appointee position into a career senior executive service position, which ensured that the holder would stand below Jenkins in the civil service hierarchy, possessing none of the independence of a political appointee. Jenkins and Ohlweiler had then found their way onto the hiring committee, and had filtered out highly distinguished candidates while pushing their underqualified cronies through to the final round. The hiring panel awarded the job to a Jenkins protégé and sent the selection to the agency front office without going through Marocco, who as the head of the bureau should have been in the approval chain.

When the agency circulated the customary action memo for the hire, Marocco marked his disapproval on the document and added a comment stating that the hiring committee had violated federal hiring rules. Another political appointee listed on the signature page, the agency's deputy chief of staff, likewise disapproved of the action memo, and on the same grounds. Chief of Staff Steiger, however, wasn't prepared to stick his neck out to block a candidate who was backed by the uberbureaucrats, Ohlweiler and Jenkins. Steiger gave his approval to the hire and berated Marocco in front of other staff for objecting in writing. Marocco told Steiger what the USAID human resources bureaucrats had repeatedly told me—that wrongdoing needed to be documented in written form because otherwise it would be impossible to hold the perpetrators accountable.

Ohlweiler and Jenkins urged John Barsa, the acting agency head, to approve the hire despite the two written disapprovals. If Barsa didn't sign off, they warned, the candidate who had been chosen by the hiring committee could sue the agency for not heeding the hiring committee. This argument rested on not only the bogus premise that the agency head was merely a rubber stamp for the hiring preferences of subordinates, but also the even crazier premise that this candidate knew she was the hiring committee's top choice—she wouldn't have known that fact unless the members of the committee violated confidentiality protocols and divulged the information to her. Nevertheless, the menacing warnings of Ohlweiler and Jenkins convinced Barsa to acquiesce in the hiring of their preferred candidate.

At the beginning of August 2020, in response to a Freedom of Information Act request, the government sent McClanahan the SOCOM inspector general's inquiry into my Defense Department hotline complaint. Issued on February 11, 2020, the document was as short as the initial report from the USAID Office of Inspector General—just three pages. Of even greater concern, most of the text had been redacted on the grounds that disclosure would violate personal privacy. It was a glaring misuse of the privacy exemptions of the Freedom of Information Act— those exemptions are intended to keep people from seeing information in someone else's personnel file, not to keep people from seeing information in their own file.

In one of the few unredacted sections, the SOCOM inspector general tersely categorized my hotline complaint as "unsubstantiated." Only one sentence in the entire visible text amounted to something other than regurgitation of information I had provided in the complaint. The sentence stated that the suspension of my access to SOCOM facilities in May 2019 "pre-dated the Hotline Complaint and therefore did not occur as a result of Dr. Moyar filing a complaint."

Somehow the SOCOM inspector general had construed the crux of the matter to be whether my complaint of September 2019 had provoked the SOCOM access suspension of May 2019. This interpretation was "insane," in McClanahan's words. Neither of us had ever alleged that someone had traveled back in time to perpetrate retaliation.

After a quiet August and September, the month of October began with a bang. On October 1, *Politico* and *Foreign Policy* reported that Pete Marocco had decided to take an extended "personal leave" from his job as leader of the new bureau, for a period that ran at least into early November. The reporters linked the development to a recent "town hall" meeting where career employees had complained about Marocco in front of his boss, Jenny McGee. One unnamed USAID employee told a reporter that Marocco "was raked over the coals" during the town hall event. "It was professional, but ruthless."

According to the media reports, the Trump administration had not indicated whether Marocco would be returning, but Nahal Toosi noted in *Politico* that "multiple USAID officials said they were elated that Marocco was taking leave and expected it would be permanent." In the absence of Marocco, the bureau would be run by Rob Jenkins.

Jenkins had chalked up another victory. He had forced out a second senior political appointee who had stood in the way of his ambition to lead the bureau he believed he'd been born to lead. No one was saying publicly that Jenkins had orchestrated Marocco's downfall, but it was obvious to those inside the agency that Jenkins had plucked the media's strings until the front office couldn't take it any longer.

On October 7, after weeks of uneventful waiting, McClanahan received a new version of the USAID inspector general's 224-page report. It came in response to a request he'd filed nearly six months earlier under the Freedom of Information Act and Privacy Act. By law, federal agencies were supposed to respond to such requests within twenty business days, about one-sixth of the time it had taken USAID in this instance. The cover letter explained: "The United States Agency for International Development (USAID) regrets the delay in responding to your Freedom of Information Act (FOIA) and Privacy Act (PA) request. Unfortunately, USAID is experiencing a backlog of FOIA requests. Please know that USAID management is very committed to providing responses to FOIA requests and remedying the FOIA backlog."

The new version contained many more redactions than the version we had received earlier, some of them bordering on farce. Just three pages out of 224 displayed unredacted information that we hadn't been able to see in the earlier version. Those three pages, though, contained several bombshells.

All three of these pages belonged to the transcript of the Jack Ohlweiler interview. The most valuable of the newly revealed material was an affirmation by Ohlweiler that "[redaction] informed [redaction] that he would have to revoke Moyar's clearance if he was not fired." McClanahan and I already had enough information to tell with near-complete certainty which names had been redacted from this sentence. Everything pointed toward Voorhees as the first name, and either Ohlweiler or Glick as the second.

If, in fact, Voorhees had made this statement to either Ohlweiler or Glick, then he had lied to the investigators when he had told them that "the subject of firing or termination never came up in his conversations with Deputy Administrator Glick, Chief of Staff Steiger, or Attorney Ohlweiler," and that he "would never discuss revocation with them." In addition to violating criminal statutes prohibiting individuals from knowingly and willfully making false statements to federal investigators, those words proved that Voorhees had crossed the line of threatening to revoke a security clearance.

The new version of the Ohlweiler transcript also exposed other defects and deceits in the arguments that Ohlweiler and Voorhees had advanced in engineering my termination. In another passage that appeared to involve Voorhees and Ohlweiler, a redacted individual said that even if Voorhees revoked my security clearance, I might be able to retain my clearance by appealing the decision to a three-person panel. It was the first time I'd seen someone at USAID acknowledge on the record that the permanent revocation of my clearance was not a foregone conclusion. Now it looked as though Ohlweiler and Voorhees had duped Glick into firing me by claiming that the loss of my clearance was certain when they themselves knew it to be less than certain.

McClanahan forwarded the new material to Quinton Brady. Senator Grassley's staff could, we hoped, confirm the names in the document. They might be driven to further action by the new evidence of felonious lies to investigators, and by the indifference of investigators to receipt of those lies.

The presidential election, meanwhile, came to a head. As in 2016, Trump was trailing in most of the polls prior to election day, and most of the mainstream media was predicting his imminent doom. On election night, Trump again confounded the pollsters with unexpected state victories, but this time he came up short in a few key states. Several days later, once the final vote tallies dribbled in from the battleground states, Biden came out on top.

USAID reemerged in the news that same day, November 6. Early in the afternoon, Josh Rogin of the *Washington Post* tweeted the text of an email from Jack Ohlweiler to John Barsa, which stated that Trump's appointment of Barsa as acting head of USAID in April was limited by statute to 210 days, and hence Barsa would have to return to his prior job by midnight. With the end of Barsa's temporary appointment as agency head, Ohlweiler informed Barsa, "Bonnie Glick will then be the only person who has all the authorities to act as the Administrator and therefore will be the titular 'Head of the Agency.'"

It sure looked like Glick had joined forces with Ohlweiler to cook up the confrontation, in order to dislodge Barsa and vault herself into the top position. Since Glick's arrival at the agency twenty-two months earlier, she and Ohlweiler had cut several shady deals. Ohlweiler, in his capacity as the agency's ethics attorney, had done Glick a massive favor by overlooking the conflict of interest posed by her husband's lobbying job. Glick, for her part, had given Ohlweiler the freedom to do whatever he wanted, without concern for his ostensible boss in the Office of General Counsel. When Ohlweiler had laid his specious legal arguments about my case on the table, she had obligingly picked them up and used them to fire me.

Prior to the coup attempt against Barsa, the most prominent collaboration between Ohlweiler and Glick had involved the agency's hiring of the chief acquisition officer. In an agency whose main function was procuring the services of development organizations, this job was critical to ensuring that billions of taxpayer dollars were spent properly. The position of chief acquisition officer had always been held by a foreign service officer, and in 2019 the agency assignment system had awarded it to a foreign service officer named George (not his real name). This selection was widely praised in the agency, for George was considered an outstanding and incorruptible contracting officer. Bonnie Glick, however, wanted to fill the position with a civil servant of less exalted reputation who was a personal friend of her lobbyist husband.

Ohlweiler stepped in to clear the path for Glick's preferred candidate. He warned George that he could lose his security clearance and his employment if he didn't step away from the chief acquisition officer position. Old allegations could be dredged up, Ohlweiler intimated. Best if George slinked away quietly into another job and kept his mouth shut. The threats convinced George to withdraw from the job and take an overseas assignment.

Ohlweiler and Glick knew that removing a respected foreign service officer from a critical foreign service position in favor of a less respected civil servant would not pass muster with certain officials in the approval chain. Their solution was as simple as it was audacious—cut those officials out of the chain. By the time these officials learned that a tiny crew had been laying the bureaucratic brickwork in secret, the mortar was already dry, and at that point no one in authority had the courage to summon a wrecking ball. The foreign service union and other foreign service officers went to Congress to accuse Glick of breaking agency rules by filling a foreign service position with a member of the civil service. A Senate committee found their argument persuasive and asked the USAID Office of Inspector General to investigate. Unsurprisingly, that office looked the other way.

Details of the unholy alliance between Ohlweiler and Glick had reached the White House and Capitol Hill through multiple channels. Those details, plus other complaints about Glick, plus the leaking of the email about Barsa, convinced the White House to send Glick packing. At 2:45 that afternoon, the White House informed Glick that she needed to resign by the end of the day or else she would be fired. She refused to submit a resignation letter, so at 5:00 p.m. the White House issued her a termination letter. The White House assigned Barsa to the deputy position that Glick had held, enabling him to continue running the agency in an acting capacity.

On November 20, the Presidential Personnel Office contacted me to ask if I would be interested in working at the Department of Defense. I had spoken with the personnel office after the restoration of my clearance four and a half months earlier, but it had done little hiring in the period leading up to the election, reportedly because a looming shakeup would take place after the election. The firing of Secretary of Defense Mark Esper on November 9 had unblocked a number of appointments that had been in the pipeline, mine included. But unless the election result were overturned by the Trump campaign's lawsuits—which appeared highly unlikely—this appointment would give me very little time at the Pentagon. Taking a job there would, nevertheless, provide further evidence that USAID had used a fraudulent allegation to oust me, since the allegation had originated in the Defense Department. It would also provide a bit of money as well as health insurance. I replied to the Presidential Personnel Office that I remained interested in working at Defense.

The White House Liaison Office subsequently informed me that I would be appointed to the position of deputy assistant secretary of defense for security cooperation. In that job, I would supervise a multi-billion dollar enterprise that supported foreign security institutions and promoted their cooperation with the United States. I knew the subject matter intimately. I accepted the job at once.

Chapter 23

The Worst Day

In the middle of December, I was informed that Senator Grassley's office expected to send USAID public letters about my case on December 23. Although I didn't know what the senator would write, I knew it would benefit my cause. These sorts of letters typically drew public attention to wrongdoing and compelled agencies to hand over information that could help verify whistleblower retaliation claims.

On the morning of December 23, the alarm clock went off at 4:30 a.m., so that Kelli could drive our son Trent to an imaging center for a 6:00 a.m. MRI on his hip. For several months, Trent had been undergoing physical therapy for what the orthopedic doctors had thought was a sports-related muscle strain, but the therapy hadn't alleviated the problem, so now they were checking to see if the hip cartilage had been damaged. After Kelli shut off the alarm, I drifted back into sleep, thinking pleasant thoughts about the imminent appearance of Senator Grassley's letters on his website.

When they returned home, Kelli confided to me that the MRI technician had told her she needed to talk to the orthopedist within hours, not a week later as originally planned. We soon were on the phone with the orthopedist, who stated that the MRI had detected a bone abnormality. The radiologist wasn't certain about the diagnosis, he said, but it could be Ewing sarcoma, a highly aggressive cancer. The orthopedist's office had already set up an 11:00 a.m. appointment for Trent with an oncologist who specialized in bone surgery.

Kelli and I were both stricken with the unique, indescribable terror produced by endangerment of one's own child. By light-years it outdistanced any horror of the past eighteen months. Neither mental armor, nor manly composure, nor rational contemplation of statistical probabilities, nor Christian faith in the afterlife could prevent the horrible saw from cutting into the soul.

During the darker moments of the past eighteen months, I had been bolstered by the knowledge that my children would be free to carry on with life regardless of what happened to me. Now even that stanchion had been torn away. Raging at the heavens, I demanded, like Job, to know why God was inflicting such pain.

When we met with the oncologist, he said that the bone looked abnormal on the MRI, but didn't show the characteristics of Ewing sarcoma. He couldn't tell if it was another type of cancer or something less serious, so Trent would have to undergo a biopsy. Because the holidays were approaching, the biopsy wouldn't take place until early January.

We left the medical building and returned to our car at 12:30 p.m. When we were on the road, at 12:35 p.m., my cell phone rang. The phone number didn't look like that of a robocaller, and the area code suggested it might be related to my pending Pentagon job, so I answered.

The person on the other end identified himself as Michael DeMark of the Washington Headquarters Service. He said he was working on my background investigation for the deputy assistant secretary of defense position. He wanted to email me a document, which he described as a Statement of Reasons from the Pentagon's clearance adjudications facility. The words "Statement of Reasons" sent ice up my spine. I'd only heard that term used for the denial or revocation of a security clearance.

After a moment's hesitation, I asked why I was being sent a Statement of Reasons. DeMark said that it was "coming down" from the incident at USAID that had led to my departure in 2019. When I asked him what the purpose of the Statement of Reasons was, he gave the impression of being unfamiliar with security clearance procedures, saying that it probably was related to a security clearance denial or suspension. (Later I found out that he was intimately familiar with all matters pertaining to security clearances.) He didn't mention the word revocation, which was slightly reassuring, since a revocation was slightly worse than a denial.

I should have asked more questions, but the shock of a Statement of Reasons combined with the visit to the oncologist had me out of sorts. DeMark said he would email me the Statement of Reasons in the next five to ten minutes, and that I should sign it on two pages, then return it to him. I gave him my email address and said I would have a look at the document. The conversation ended there.

Kelli and I had promised Trent we would take him to the restaurant of his choice after the appointment with the oncologist. While we were waiting for the food to arrive, I downloaded the email from DeMark on my phone. The Statement of Reasons began with the assertion that "a preliminary decision has been made" to "revoke your eligibility for access to Sensitive Compartmented Information."

Until a few hours earlier, I would have considered a security clearance revocation the worst event of my life, a trauma warranting descent into the deepest realms of despair. But now I knew it wasn't the worst—learning your child might have cancer beat it, hands down. This new perspective robbed the revocation of some of its sting.

The initial pain of the sting was further reduced after lunch when I read the Statement of Reasons in its entirety. Considering that the Department of Defense had granted me a clearance five months earlier, I feared that whoever was now trying to revoke that clearance had devised a cunning plot to justify and implement the revocation, backed by new fictions or distortions designed to make the harmless appear sinister. Maybe they had tracked down childhood friends to reconstruct my middle-school transgressions. Or perhaps they would go after me for my tardiness a couple of years earlier in submitting one of our family's automobiles to the state of Virginia for its annual safety inspection.

The text of the Statement of Reasons, however, promptly dispelled any notion that I was under attack by an evil genius from the subterranean chambers of the Pentagon. I wasn't up against Hannibal Lecter, but Rosco P. Coltrane.

A well-crafted Statement of Reasons contains pages of incriminating evidence and analysis. This one contained just a few hundred words, and it didn't introduce new information, but only attempted, in the most outlandish fashion, to find wrongdoing by contorting a few existing facts. One or more people, it seemed, had decided to revisit my clearance and substitute their own judgment for that of the person who had adjudicated it earlier in the year. Who these people were and why they had done it joined the long list of questions that McClanahan and Brady were trying to answer.

The Statement of Reasons didn't claim that the book contained classified information or otherwise release-prohibited information. Instead, it asserted, "You knowingly and willfully disclosed the information without official and formal approval by DOPSR. You violated DOPSR policy and your Nondisclosure Agreement made with the Federal Government. Your failure to comply with Federal Government Security Standards, which resulted in your suspension of access to facilities and equipment for Unauthorized Disclosure of protected United States Government Information, reflects questionable judgment and unwillingness to comply with rules and regulations, which raises questions about your reliability, trustworthiness, and ability to protect classified or sensitive information."

This accusation was the same one the Department of Defense had considered in the early summer, the one it had found sufficiently unpersuasive that it had granted me a clearance on July 7. Whoever had written it into the Statement of Reasons had done nothing to make it more convincing. That person clearly hadn't the slightest understanding of prepublication review, a fact underscored by a reference in the text to "republication review."

In writing my book, the document continued, I had kept "classified, sensitive, proprietary, or other protected information" on an "unauthorized information technology system, i.e., your personal computer." Consequently, "your misuse of information technology is a security concern." The Statement of Reasons didn't explain what "classified, sensitive, proprietary, or other protected information" had been stored on my personal computer, a computer that had never been in the possession of the government.

I forwarded the Statement of Reasons to McClanahan. He directed me to hold off on signing the Statement of Reasons until he could obtain additional information from the Defense Department.

After getting past the shock of the Statement of Reasons, I turned my attention to an email McClanahan had forwarded to me at 12:39 p.m., when I had been on the phone with DeMark. Attached to the email were the two letters Senator Grassley's office would be posting online that afternoon. The first of the senator's letters, addressed to John Barsa, began: "I write to you today with concerns regarding potential whistleblower reprisal against Dr. Mark Moyar by the United States Agency for International Development (USAID), its failure to properly investigate that reprisal despite clear evidence of wrongdoing against him, a potential pattern of abuse within USAID relating to security clearance suspensions, and additional allegations of retaliatory practices involving security clearances." Finally, some encouraging words on this miserable day.

Grassley blasted the USAID Office of Inspector General for the handling of my whistleblower retaliation claim. The office had failed to investigate the possibility that "USAID took action against Dr. Moyar as a result of his subordinates, and possibly members of SOCOM, engaging in a coordinated effort to remove him from his position for making those disclosures." The SOCOM Office of Inspector General, Grassley continued, had "bizarrely" indicated that my complaint invoked the concept of time travel. The senator faulted the inspectors general of both USAID and SOCOM for failing to obtain emails and other communication between the individuals involved in the case.

Grassley asked Barsa to respond no later than January 20, 2021, to a series of questions. "Are you aware of the individual that allegedly contacted SOCOM to allege that Dr. Moyar had written and published a book without obtaining clearance from DoD?" Grassley asked. "If so, when did you become aware of this? Who was this individual?

"Was then-Deputy Administrator Glick advised that USAID would have to revoke Dr. Moyar's security clearance if he was not fired? Who advised DA Glick of this? Why did that person advise DA Glick that Dr. Moyar would have to be fired?"

Pegged to these questions was a footnote that cut straight to the pivotal issue of why I had been terminated. Voorhees had "stated that the subject of firing or terminating Dr. Moyar 'never' came up in conversations with DA Glick or a USAID attorney," and "the subject of revocation would never be discussed with Glick or the USAID attorney." But, Grassley continued, Ohlweiler had answered in the affirmative when asked if he had said that "the Director of Security informed DA Glick that Dr. Moyar's security clearance would have to be revoked if he was not fired." His text filled in the names in the key sentence from the previously redacted Ohlweiler interview—Voorhees had indeed told Glick that he would have to revoke my clearance. The contradictory statements of Voorhees under oath were now laid plain, and in the public record.

One of the attachments to Grassley's letter was an unredacted version of the SOCOM inspector general report of February 11, 2020, which contained several eye-popping revelations. On July 19, 2019, it stated, the SOCOM deputy chief of staff had spoken with Voorhees about "USAID's request for copies of the actual pages of the book" that contained the ostensibly prohibited information. The SOCOM deputy chief of staff told Voorhees that he "saw no reason SOCOM could not share the relevant information with USAID given the gravity of the situation with a senior official being the subject."

Previously, I'd been told that SOCOM had not been willing to share the specifics of the allegation with USAID, and that USAID had relied on the word of a two-star general as the evidence against me. Why hadn't I heard that SOCOM had eventually offered to turn over the pages? Why hadn't Voorhees mentioned the pages to the investigators from the Office of Inspector General when asked about the information he'd received from the Defense Department? The most plausible explanation was that he realized upon inspection that the pages didn't support the accusation of unauthorized disclosure. At that point, a fair-minded person would have reinstated my clearance, rather than claiming, as Voorhees apparently did, that he needed to revoke my clearance on the "gospel" theory of unsubstantiated accusations.

The unredacted SOCOM inspector general's report also revealed that both the Pentagon's Unauthorized Disclosure Program Office and the SOCOM Security Office had conducted reviews of the book after its publication. The government, apparently, was willing to devote more resources to penalizing former employees than to protecting their First Amendment rights through prepublication review. More to the point, this revelation showed that multiple reviews of the manuscript had taken place and yet none had resulted in adverse notices in my security clearance record or prevented the reinstatement of my clearance in July 2020, let alone triggered a criminal prosecution. The consensus evidently held that I hadn't published any material that government rules and the non-disclosure agreement prohibited me from publishing.

Grassley's second letter, addressed to Ann Calvaresi Barr, reiterated many of the points made in the first. "It is unclear as to how USAID OIG can come to the conclusion that none of Dr. Moyar's allegations could be substantiated if USAID did not conduct a complete and thorough review of easily obtainable information," Grassley stated. He asked Calvaresi Barr to answer questions similar to those that he had posed to Barsa, plus the following:

"Why did USAID OIG choose not to include any mention or reference to several complaints about Dr. Moyar to USAID OIG by members of USAID which were found to be unsubstantiated in the Report of Investigation?

"How many complaints against Dr. Moyar originated from subordinates Dr. Moyar had previously reported for wasteful, fraudulent, or abusive conduct? Of these complaints, were any substantiated?

"Did USAID OIG attempt to interview or speak with members of SOCOM? If not, why not?

"Did USAIG OIG attempt to interview or speak with members of DOPSR? If not, why not?

Calvaresi Barr had a lot to answer for. No doubt she would be thinking about the letter over the Christmas holiday and deciding how to respond. There was no way for her to get out of it now, I thought.

Chapter 24

False Dawn

It so happened that Ann Calvaresi Barr did find a way out. On January 1, 2021, while everyone in the media and the government was watching football or sleeping off the effects of New Year's Eve revelry, USAID posted a notice online with the header, "U.S. Agency for International Development Inspector General Ann Calvaresi Barr Retires from Federal Service."

The notice didn't explain why she was retiring. People who had seen Grassley's letter to her one week earlier were liable to suspect that the letter's scalding contents had influenced her decision. Senior officials who engaged in the sort of dereliction alleged in the letter seldom got punished with a fine or jail time, but instead were forced to leave. As mentioned earlier, Calvaresi Barr's immediate predecessor, Michael G. Carroll, had been forced into retirement for wrongfully purging negative information from the office's reports.

A desire to spend more time with grandchildren or relax on the beach definitely didn't cause her to step down. Upon leaving the inspector general position, she went through the revolving door to take a high-paying job at Deloitte, a megacontractor that had received over $2 billion in USAID contracts over the past several decades. During Calvaresi Barr's time as inspector general, her office had conducted dozens of audits of Deloitte programs, so one couldn't help wondering whether Deloitte had hired her as payback for overseeing the same type of see-no-evil investigations she'd overseen in my case.

Calvaresi Barr had a moral, if not legal, obligation to respond to the senator before leaving the job she'd held for the past five years. She'd still been a federal employee when Grassley had written the letter to her, and she had presided over the two investigations into my case. Had she been convinced that her office had acquitted itself well, she would have been eager to defend her staff and her reputation. But she didn't send the senator a response. Instead, she punted the task to her successor.

I hoped to hear news about my clearance and the prospective job right after the holiday break, but for the first few days of the new year my inbox received only messages about miracle cures for baldness and two-for-one sales at Joseph A. Bank. Then, on January 6, I received a phone call from Michael DeMark of the Washington Headquarters Service.

DeMark repeated his earlier request for me to sign the Statement of Reasons. I replied that my lawyer was handling the response to the Statement of Reasons. I also asked him if I would be able to start the new job while the process of contesting the Statement of Reasons played out. He said I couldn't start until the background investigation was completed, and the background investigation couldn't be completed until the Statement of Reasons was adjudicated. This adjudication would take many weeks, if not months. By then, Trump and his appointees would be long gone, along with this job. Thus, no matter how outlandish the Statement of Reasons might be, it had killed my chances of serving as deputy assistant secretary of defense.

At noon that day, Trump spoke at the National Mall. I didn't watch his speech on TV, nor did I watch the ensuing riot, as so many other Americans did. I was preoccupied with the Pentagon imbroglio and, more importantly, my son's health. Trent's biopsy was scheduled to take place the next day. The fear surrounding that test had detached me emotionally from the partisan bickering, making the news reports from the Capitol feel as distant as historical accounts of congressional feuding over the War of 1812.

One of the few benefits of my inability to start the new job was my availability to accompany Trent to the biopsy. On the morning of January 7, Kelli and I took Trent to Inova Fairfax Hospital. The two nurses who greeted Trent at the diagnostic center were magnificent. Through their attentiveness, compassion, and good cheer, they swept away most of the gloom that hung over the event. They joked with Trent about his lack of the ailments and frailties they normally saw in patients, his absence of jeweled body piercings that could interfere with the diagnostic equipment, and his disinterest in forms of recreation that were getting other people through the COVID-19 era like drinking and smoking and drugs. The medical poking and prodding were made to seem no more unusual than brushing teeth or cutting fingernails. They practically had us thinking we were there to test Trent for strep throat, not cancer.

Neither the Capitol riot of the previous day nor any other political subjects ever came up in our conversations with the nurses. We never had any idea whether they were Republicans or Democrats. They had no idea of our political affiliation. The absence of politics was a refreshing change in an era when people too often obsessed over the subject.

The nurses treated Trent as they must have treated all their patients—with as much kindness as they would have shown a member of their own families. At a time when pundits and politicians were calling the United States a nation of execrable racists, the love for others shown by these nurses epitomized what I had seen many times before—Americans attaining the highest levels of human goodness. It served as a reminder that the human capacity for love is one of the most compelling signs of God's existence. Surely the mere evolution of organisms out of primordial microbes could not have created something as powerful and glorious.

The biopsy procedure took place without incident. We'd have to wait another week to receive the results. Because of the COVID-19 pandemic, we wouldn't meet with the doctor in his office, but instead would speak with him virtually, via Zoom video.

The meeting took place on January 14. When the doctor appeared on the screen, he didn't spend even a second on small talk. Instead he immediately said that the biopsy had revealed the presence of Ewing sarcoma. A fiendish cancer, intent on spreading aggressively throughout the body, capable of changing itself to evade the most advanced medical treatments.

Trent would have to spend the next six months undergoing chemotherapy and radiation treatment. The second half of his senior year in high school would be dominated by hospital visits, and he would have to forego dreams of building on the sports successes of his junior year, which had included a fourth-place finish in the 1,000-meter run at the state track and field championship.

Kelli and I were as crushed as we had been three weeks earlier when the term Ewing sarcoma had first been uttered. Trent, sitting between us, was astonishingly composed.

In the midst of this horror, things seemed to turn strangely in my favor at the Pentagon. Late on a Friday afternoon, I received an email from Heather (not her real name), my main contact at the White House Liaison Office. It was the first time she had contacted me in nearly a month. Under the subject line of "On Boarding Monday," she wrote, "We are looking forward to having you join the team Monday. Please plan to arrive at 0900 at the Pentagon Visitors Center."

I immediately emailed McClanahan to see if he knew how this turnaround had come about. He was as dumbfounded as I was.

It looked like someone had intervened to override the revocation process and bring the background investigation to a successful conclusion. Ideally, that person had realized that the revocation had all been a sham and had torn up the Statement of Reasons, but it was also conceivable that someone had decided to continue reviewing the allegations in the Statement of Reasons while I proceeded with the job. I informed the White House Liaison Office that I would be at the Pentagon Monday morning at 9:00 a.m. I'd already completed the onboarding paperwork, which had been sent to me through an online portal, so I'd be ready to hit the ground running.

Rising early on Monday morning, I donned my sharpest attire and drove to the Pentagon. The streets and highways were devoid of traffic, for the COVID-19 pandemic was still keeping most government employees and contractors at home. It was an exhilarating drive, full of thoughts about how rejoining the government—even if only for a short time—would further revive my reputation and my career. I reached the Pentagon much earlier than anticipated, just after 8:00 a.m. Parking at one of the garages nearby, I read a book in the car while awaiting the appointed hour.

At 8:30 a.m., just as I was preparing to trek across the vast Pentagon parking lot, my cell phone rang. It was Heather. She had just learned that my security clearance information hadn't yet come through, so I wouldn't be able to start the onboarding process today. Apologizing profusely for the late notice, she remarked, "This isn't how we usually operate." She hoped to receive the necessary information by 10:00 a.m., which would allow us to reschedule my onboarding for the following day.

Two hours later, Heather sent me an email. "Unfortunately," she wrote, "I just spoke with the Security Manager who informed me that he is awaiting documentation from you and that he does not believe this will be corrected this week. I am very sorry for the inconvenience this caused you and the late notice." That documentation, I concluded, must have been the response to the Statement of Reasons—the first step in the revocation appeal process that would keep me sidelined well past the end of the Trump presidency. I wouldn't be rejoining the Trump administration after all.

Joe Biden's inauguration took place on January 20. A peevish Trump refused to attend, but he did not attempt a Hitlerian overthrow of the democratic system or chain himself to the Resolute Desk as his detractors had prophesied. Instead, he departed the White House early that morning on the presidential helicopter, Marine One, which took him to Andrews Air Force Base for a connecting flight to his Florida residence.

On the day after the inauguration, I received a phone call from DeMark.

"I have some information concerning your security clearance," he said.

"You need to provide it to my lawyer, Kel McClanahan," I replied. "He sent you an email saying that any communications concerning me should be routed to him."

"I can't give the information to him, only to you," DeMark said.

That seemed odd. Since when were government officials forbidden from communicating with the lawyers of people who faced career destruction at the hands of the government?

"Are you prohibited from talking to my lawyer by an official rule of the Washington Headquarters Service?" I asked, referring to DeMark's employer. The Washington Headquarters Service had its own checkered history of misusing its power.

"That is correct," DeMark replied.

I was even more surprised by this assertion. Who knew what additional claims of dubious validity were on deck? I let him continue.

"There is no longer a need for you to respond to the Statement of Reasons," DeMark said, "because you are no longer under consideration for a job."

"Is that because the deputy assistant secretary position went only through January 20?"

"Yes."

"What is the status of my clearance now?" I asked. "If someone looks in the security clearance database, will it say the clearance has been revoked or not?"

"It will say that there are actions pending," DeMark answered. "Nothing will be adjudicated until you are a candidate for another job requiring a clearance."

"What happens to the Statement of Reasons?"

"It will remain in your file."

"If I get offered a job at an agency other than the Department of Defense, what will happen?"

"That agency will then adjudicate the Statement of Reasons."

So they were doing to me what USAID had done to me a year and a half earlier—depriving me of any opportunity to contest the charges until I was offered another job requiring a clearance. To get such a job, I'd again have to find an employer who wasn't put off by the allegations and was willing to wait many months for a faceless authority to pass judgment on it.

A few days later came the climax of another subplot, this one involving the media. The publication of Grassley's letters the previous month had captured the attention of Amy Mackinnon of *Foreign Policy*, the reporter who'd chronicled Steven Luke's travails at the Department of Defense inspector general. I had never met her before, but McClanahan knew her and believed she would be an ideal person to write about the new developments. An excellent writer, she had a strong interest in whistleblowers and unscrupulous inspectors general, and she could reach a large audience—*Foreign Policy* had named her story on Steven A. Luke its most influential article of 2020.

I spoke with Mackinnon twice on the phone, each time for close to two hours, with McClanahan listening in. I put her in touch with large numbers of other people who could provide relevant information. Several of them subsequently told me she had contacted them and spent more than an hour asking them questions and listening to their answers. She clearly had an affinity for the story.

During my second call with Mackinnon, on January 12, she mentioned that a dozen other USAID employees had corroborated my story, and noted that they had revealed actions at USAID that were "insane." She was putting the final touches on the story and hoped that it would run by that Friday, January 15. Things were looking up on the media front.

For the rest of the week, I visited the *Foreign Policy* website repeatedly, but each time there was no sign of the article. On Friday afternoon, I checked in with McClanahan, and he expressed hope that it would run early the next week. But that week came and went without an article.

On January 25, McClanahan informed me that *Foreign Policy*

had decided not to run Mackinnon's article. Her editors had told her, much to her dissatisfaction, that they were uncomfortable with the fact that most of the interviewees had insisted on anonymity. They claimed to be averse to criticizing a federal agency and its employees on the basis of anonymous sources.

A more dishonest excuse would have been difficult to conceive. For more than a year, I had been collecting *Foreign Policy* articles on the internal workings of USAID and the Defense Department, a dozen all told. Every single one had relied heavily or exclusively on anonymous sources. That is, after all, how journalists typically obtain information about problems at federal agencies. Government employees don't give the press unflattering information about the government unless they are granted anonymity, as otherwise they would face termination or other severe punishments. The *Foreign Policy* article deriding Pete Marocco on September 2, 2020, for example, had stated, "This article is based on interviews with more than 20 former and current U.S. officials, congressional staffers, and outside experts, most of whom only agreed to speak on condition of anonymity due to the sensitive nature of internal administration deliberations."

Most of the *Foreign Policy* articles trashing the Trump administration, it should be added, didn't address matters as serious as my case. The publication's criticisms of Marocco had centered on his determination to implement the administration's policies and his exclusion of Rob Jenkins from meetings and a phone call—not exactly startling occurrences in the federal government. So why had they killed what should have been one of their stories of the year? Had the Jenkins network managed to sway the publication's leaders? Had the leaders decided that the magazine shouldn't be casting a former Trump appointee in a favorable light?

Foreign Policy purported to be a politically neutral publication, but its liberal bias was as obvious as that of the *New York Times* and NPR. It published few articles by conservative authors, and seldom portrayed conservatives as positively as liberals, unless they were bashing other conservatives. Among the articles that *Foreign Policy* saw fit to print while I was awaiting the publication of Mackinnon's article were "No Amount of Swagger Can Dress Up Pompeo's Legacy. The outgoing secretary of state prioritized his political ambitions over America's interests." And "This was a great week for America. But the country's system is broken in ways even Biden is unlikely to fix." And "Why Race Matters in International Relations: Western dominance and white privilege permeate the field."

As I sat in my family room that evening, burning oak logs in the fireplace, I was surprised by my serenity in the face of what appeared to be another huge setback to my hopes for obtaining justice. I'd expected Mackinnon's article to put great pressure on the Defense Department and USAID, and to vindicate me in the eyes of the broader world. I'd put her in touch with numerous people and encouraged them to speak with her by assuring them she'd report the story fairly. It would be hard to convince those people to talk to a reporter again after this story went nowhere. Although my rational mind still knew that cancellation of the article was a serious gut punch, I was not troubled by it as I would have been troubled before. In comparison with the ogre of pediatric cancer, everything else looked like a gnat.

Chapter 25

Lying to Congress

On March 19, 2021, Senator Grassley's office published a document he had received from USAID in response to his letter to John Barsa. The document had been sent on January 26, and had been signed by a career official rather than by Barsa, who evidently had lacked the time or interest to meet the senator's request before the Trump administration ended. Unsurprisingly, the career staff members who had produced the response had done their best to clear the agency's employees of wrongdoing. Grassley's long list of questions, though, had forced them into difficult choices between handing over facts—which would expose the misdeeds of agency employees—and engaging in evasions or falsehoods—which would further undermine the agency's credibility and expose the respondents to charges of lying to Congress. They chose the former in some instances, the latter in others.

The agency's responses to two key questions fit plainly into the falsehood category. In answering the senator's queries about whistleblower reprisal claims and investigations, the agency stated that it "is not aware of any claims of reprisal," and "has not had any reprisal investigations." Of course, the agency was well aware that I had filed a reprisal claim and that it had resulted in two investigations by the agency's Office of Inspector General. This dishonesty begged the question of how many other reprisal claims and investigations the agency was concealing.

The second lie was the agency's reply to the question "Are you aware of the individual that allegedly contacted SOCOM to allege that Dr. Moyar had written and published a book without obtaining clearance from DoD?" The agency's answer was a flat "No." Senator Grassley and his staff already possessed evidence to the contrary. USAID officials had previously told them that the accusation had originated with a two-star general, and had cited that individual's elevated rank as evidence of the accusation's veracity. In addition, Grassley's staff knew from my retelling that Ohlweiler had mentioned to me a two-star general of purportedly biblical authority. The only logical reason for the agency to lie about its knowledge of the accuser's identity would be to prevent Senator Grassley and McClanahan from linking the accuser to Crnkovich.

The agency's response to Grassley contradicted the inspector general's report on the agency's ability to reassign me while the clearance dispute was adjudicated. Bonnie Glick, it may be remembered, had told the inspector general's investigators that she'd fired me because the supposedly imminent clearance revocation would have rendered me incapable of holding not only my existing job at USAID but any other job at the agency. When asked by Grassley now, eighteen months later, whether I could have been reassigned rather than fired, the agency told a different tale: "Former Deputy Administrator Glick understood that a reassignment was a possible alternative, but chose not to pursue one."

The agency was now acknowledging that a key premise of the termination decision had been false. From my admittedly jaded perspective, it looked like a few agency officials had intentionally concealed or mischaracterized the reassignment option during the summer of 2019 in order to ensure that I was fired. Whether Bonnie Glick was a party to, or a victim of, this duplicity was not clear and, at this point, not very important. The career bureaucrats must have been changing their version of events now because they realized that admitting to use of this false premise would make them criminally liable. Unsurprisingly, the agency didn't say who had made the false claim in 2019, preventing us from pursuing the perpetrator.

The response sidestepped the critical questions of what John Voorhees had said to Bonnie Glick and Jack Ohlweiler about revoking my clearance and whether Voorhees had lied about it to investigators. Pressed by Senator Grassley to divulge who had advised Glick that my clearance would be revoked if I were not fired, the agency didn't mention Voorhees at all in its response, despite the fact that the senator had pointedly referenced Voorhees in posing the question. Instead, it stated that Ohlweiler had told Glick that because the Defense Department had accused me of a serious offense, "there was a very low probability Dr. Moyar would have his clearance reinstated."

In most of his prior statements to me, to other agency officials, and to investigators, Ohlweiler had spoken of certainties, not probabilities. He had conveyed the certitude of my guilt in advancing his "gospel" theory of bureaucratic accusation, and in persuading Glick to fire me. In the recently redacted interview transcript, however, he had acknowledged the possibility that revocation wasn't certain. Now we had an even clearer assertion that the outcome was a matter of probability rather than certainty.

Ohlweiler appeared to have changed his tune because of the answer the agency was compelled to give to another of Grassley's questions. This question read as follows: "Would USAID have revoked Dr. Moyar's security clearance if he had not resigned?" The question forced the agency to choose between asserting that it possessed such overwhelming evidence that no amount of due process could have saved me, which was a very high bar, or admitting that revocation was not foreordained, which would discredit the rationale for firing me. The agency must have recognized that it could not clear the high bar, and thus was obliged to choose the second option. The agency gave this reply: "This is an unknown, as Dr. Moyar did not complete the full due process after the suspension of his clearance. He left the Agency with his clearance in suspended status."

The agency explained that Ohlweiler had based his "very low probability" assessment on the fact that the Defense Department had "referred [Moyar's] case to the DoD Insider-Threat Team and to the U.S. Department of Justice for prosecution." McClanahan and I had long suspected that someone at the Defense Department had referred me to the Justice Department for prosecution, but we had never before seen proof. This revelation confirmed that the Justice Department had determined the allegation lacked merit, since Justice would have confronted me long ago had it intended to prosecute me. It also proved that Ohlweiler and others at USAID had known of the referral to the Justice Department from the beginning. And from there we could deduce that they had learned as well of the refusal to prosecute. Agency officials and the Office of Inspector General should have included the Justice Department's findings in their analyses of my case, but had never done so. It was as if an employer had justified firing an employee by citing an allegation of grand larceny against the person without mentioning that the district attorney had declined to prosecute the person for lack of evidence.

In reply to a question from Grassley about the Defense Department's reinstatement of my security clearance in July 2020, the agency stated, "USAID communicated directly with the U.S. Department of Defense regarding this issue. Based on that conversation, we understand that DoD reinstated Dr. Moyar's clearance in error. To our further understanding, DoD has realized this error, has since taken action to correct it, and has suspended Dr. Moyar's clearance in the same way USAID suspended it."

Someone from USAID, it was now clear, had spoken with Defense officials before the Defense Department had sent me the revocation notice in December 2020, and had convinced the Department to reverse its own position. That sort of intervention could easily qualify as whistleblower retaliation, particularly if it involved Voorhees or Ohlweiler, the two people most likely to have been on the USAID side of that conversation. Because that intervention had resulted in a revocation notice rather than just a suspension, moreover, it guaranteed me the whistleblower protections of PPD-19 and 50 U.S.C. § 3341.

Senator Grassley proceeded to send a letter to Acting Administrator Gloria Steele to get to the bottom of this interagency communication. "After Dr. Moyar had his security clearance reinstated, did USAID, in any capacity, have contact with the Department of Defense (DoD) to allege or imply that DoD had made a 'mistake' of reinstating Dr. Moyar's clearance?" he demanded. Then came two questions that really made me chuckle. "Has USAID ever mistakenly reinstated a security clearance of an individual accused of leaking classified information? If so, how many security clearances has USAID mistakenly reinstated and when?"

The senator also informed Steele that, in answers to his prior queries on security clearance suspensions, USAID had disclosed that the agency hadn't suspended a single security clearance during the last year of the Obama administration, the most distant year for which the agency provided information. From 2017 to 2020, by contrast, the agency had suspended the security clearances of thirty-four employees. Grassley remarked, "The response I received seems to indicate a potentially troubling pattern of suspensions" at USAID. This pattern, he added, appeared consistent with "a purported rise in security clearance suspensions across the federal government" during the Trump administration.

What was more, Grassley observed, USAID reported that only ten of the thirty-four employees in question had "completed the full adjudication process." The agency claimed it had been unable to adjudicate the others because "if an individual leaves the Agency prior to the completion of the adjudication process, USAID loses jurisdiction to finish the process." Here was another mind-blowing revelation. More than 70 percent of employees whose clearances had been suspended had received neither a verdict on their case nor an opportunity to appeal an adverse verdict to a review panel with the protections of due process. The agency didn't divulge how many employees it had deprived of adjudication by firing them or forcing them to resign, as it had done to me; some might have left voluntarily, out of fear that an unfavorable outcome was certain. But I knew that I wasn't the only one who had been wrongfully denied an opportunity to contest the charges with the benefits of due process.

The rise in clearance suspensions and the high percentage of suspensions that were never adjudicated caught the interest of the *New York Times*. In an article published on March 19, reporter Julian Barnes wrote, "The agency that distributes foreign aid suspended more security clearances during the Trump administration than it had previously, according to a Republican senator who said the increase could demonstrate retaliation against whistle-blowers." Barnes briefly described my case, and noted, "While some have tried to prevent the use of security clearance suspensions as a way to punish workers, lawyers and experts said the practice has continued."

The article was short and appeared only in the online edition, but it did get some attention in USAID circles. A few days after its publication, I was contacted by Father John Anderson. An ordained Orthodox Christian priest, Anderson had joined USAID as a political appointee in the latter part of the Trump administration. He had previously worked as a career employee at the Department of Justice, where he had run afoul of entrenched bureaucrats for reporting corruption in the U.S. Marshals Service. I'd heard that Anderson had become the acting head of the CPS Bureau during the final weeks of the Trump administration, after Pete Marocco had departed, but I hadn't learned what had happened to him during those weeks.

Anderson told me that during his stint as acting bureau head, Rob Jenkins had stabbed him in the back as regularly as he had stabbed Pete Marocco and me. When Anderson had tried to obtain information on the bureau's activities, Jenkins and his cronies had resorted to all the ruses of stalling and deception in the bureaucratic repertoire. Although Jenkins had lost his ally Bonnie Glick during the Trump administration's waning days, he had managed to co-opt several other senior political appointees in his efforts to amass power and thwart the Trump agenda. Later I was to hear from other sources that Jenkins and Ohlweiler had strongarmed some of these appointees with threats, and had won over others by promising to help them secure post-Trump employment at USAID-funded organizations.

Shortly after I met Anderson, I learned from other former appointees of another disturbing incident near the end of Trump's presidency. In October 2020, I was told, career USAID staff had butted heads with political appointees over an online video in which a career agency employee had admitted to obstructing Trump's policies and leaking to the press. The video was the recording of a two-hour Zoom event entitled "Democracy Defense! A Guide for Federal Workers," which had been hosted on the evening of October 28, 2020, by Feds for Democracy and Democracy Kitchen, two groups with histories of teaching federal workers how to derail the Trump administration.

Over 150 people had logged on that evening for what was supposed to be a secret, off-the-record meeting. Some participants signed into Zoom with pseudonyms or only their first names, but a considerable number of others provided their full names or identified themselves as federal employees. Several were current or former USAID employees. One of the participants recorded the whole event and sent it to a pro-Trump blogger, who subsequently posted it on the internet.

At the beginning of the Zoom meeting, the organizers gave a tutorial on undermining Trump's policies and reelection campaign. Several speakers, including two government lawyers, offered the federal employees tips for thwarting Trump appointees, such as concocting excuses for procedural delays, demanding protracted legal reviews, leaking information to sympathetic journalists, and bringing complaints to the inspector general. A PowerPoint slide advised attendees to claim that their actions amounted to "protecting democracy," in order to spare themselves from prosecution under the Hatch Act, which prohibited federal employees from engaging in partisan activities. "Protecting democracy is non-partisan," the slide explained.

Of especial note was a slide headed "We Have Power + Responsibility." In bullet point format, it laid out the aims and methods of administrative state subterfuge with a remarkable bluntness. The federal civilian workforce of over four million members, the first bullet stated, was "touching every segment of [the] US economy with essential/important resources." The second bullet explained that federal bureaucrats were not merely implementers of policies and followers of rules conceived by elected officials, but had authority to make rules themselves: "We are in roles of power, setting and enforcing rules, holding people accountable to social norms." The third bullet stressed the bureaucracy's power of selective enforcement. "Rules have meaning because we *decide* they do," it asserted. These statements were all too true—bureaucrats had demonstrated the ability to create rules and punish violations by rivals and enemies while disregarding violations by allies and friends.

The fourth bullet spotlighted the bureaucracy's ability to sway public opinion. "The rest of the country," it stated, "looks to us about what is normal and allowable—we can help shape opinion on what is right." Here was another claim whose truth pained me and others who cared about representative governance. Kansas cattle ranchers or Pennsylvania welders might not look to federal bureaucrats for guidance on political norms, but New York journalists, Maryland lobbyists, and California executives definitely did.

The USAID employee who starred in the video was Josh Machleder, a civil servant assigned to the agency's Center for Democracy, Human Rights, and Governance. I had come across Machleder during my time as CMC Director, through my work on the agency's messaging activities. As one of the only people in the agency who possessed expertise in countering disinformation, Machleder enjoyed access to some of the most sensitive national security information in the agency's possession.

Near the hour mark, Machleder posted a question on the Zoom chat board under the pseudonym Komrade Lokh. Anticipating that Joe Biden would win the election the following week and create a presidential transition team, Komrade Loch asked, "If a transition team comes in next week, is there a way to work with them that would slow roll the damage that this administration will do in the last few months?"

Twenty-two minutes later, Machleder unmuted his microphone and began speaking. To sabotage the Trump administration, he explained, he had been leaking internal agency information to the media, and he urged his fellow bureaucrats to get in on the act. "I would recommend that everyone in the federal government, if you read the mainstream press, [determine] who is covering your agency, who is working for *ProPublica*, who is working for *Politico*," Machleder counseled. "They all have Signal accounts." Signal, an encrypted messaging application, would ensure that no law enforcement agencies or other outside parties could read the communications. Once the appropriate reporters were identified, Machleder said, "Text them, leak everything you can. Save your emails, record. I record these meetings. I send it over." He added, "I've been doing this for months."

Several minutes later, after other federal employees had talked about the value of government lawyers in foiling the efforts of political appointees, Machleder chimed in to reinforce the message. The lawyers at the USAID Office of General Counsel, he said, "have been my best friends in slowing things down for weeks, sometimes months." The Office of General Counsel was the office where Jack Ohlweiler worked.

Machleder tacitly acknowledged awareness that his words could get him fired should they get out. When questioned by the moderator about the risks government employees took in leaking to the press, Machleder said with a nervous giggle, "I don't anticipate keeping my job for too long. I'm just taking a risk and I just believe in it and I don't really care about the job anymore, which is terrible, because I don't know what I'm going to do without it, but I just figure I'll get another job."

The video appeared on the internet the next day. Soon thereafter, it was viewed by a senior USAID political appointee who knew Machleder. The words he heard coming from Machleder's mouth shocked and disgusted him. As he saw it, any government employee who had willfully subverted the White House in concert with the Office of General Counsel, leaked profusely to the press, and encouraged other federal employees to follow his lead had no business holding a security clearance or working in the federal government. The guidelines for security clearance adjudication listed as potentially disqualifying "an effort" to "prevent Federal, state, or local government personnel from performing their official duties." Another potentially disqualifying factor was "deliberate or negligent disclosure of protected information to unauthorized persons, including, but not limited to, personal or business contacts, the media, or persons present at seminars, meetings or conferences."

The senior official promptly forwarded the video to John Voorhees. His Office of Security, which had suspended my clearance based on an unsubstantiated allegation, took no action against Machleder despite the video's incontestable proof of egregious offenses. As weeks passed and Machleder kept reporting for work as if nothing had happened, a number of USAID officials became worried that Machleder might escape punishment. Eventually one of them went to Voorhees and asked what his office was doing about Machleder's statements on the video. "It's none of your business," Voorhees replied brusquely. When I found out about the whole episode, nearly six months later, Machleder was still working at USAID.

At this same point in time, my search for permanent employment came to an end with a job offer from Hillsdale College. As one of the few bastions of Western Civilization left in American academia, it stood at the center of the ongoing struggle for America's soul between conservatives and classical liberals, on the one hand, who wanted to preserve the core elements of Western Civilization, and leftists and modern liberals, on the other, who wanted to purge Western Civilization and replace it with secularism, multiculturalism, and socialism. The college required all students to take courses on the history, literature, philosophy, religion, and politics of the United States and Europe so that, unlike their counterparts at other colleges, Hillsdale students understood the strengths of Western Civilization before reading Marx and Foucault and others who sought to tear it down.

The Left's systematic exclusion of conservatives from the mainstream of higher education had built up the interest of conservative donors in right-leaning academic institutions, and under the leadership of President Larry Arnn, Hillsdale had become the most prominent and affluent of them. Arnn had made some favorable remarks about Trump, and significant numbers of Hillsdale graduates had gone into the Trump administration, both of which attracted the attention of the national media. "Trump University never died," proclaimed a 2018 *Politico* article, in ironic reference to the defunct educational institution Trump had once owned. "It's located in the middle of bucolic southern Michigan."

To characterize Hillsdale as a pro-Trump institution was to capture only part of the truth. Hillsdale, it was true, showed a more positive disposition toward Trump than nearly all other colleges and universities. Hillsdale was one of the very few academic institutions that invited Trump administration officials to speak on campus, and one of even fewer that greeted the speakers with courtesy and applause rather than curses and boos. Relatively few of the college's students and faculty, however, were die-hard Trumpians. During the Republican primary, Trump had been considerably less popular with the Hillsdale community than with the Republican Party as a whole. A straw poll taken of Hillsdale students in March 2016 had found support for Marco Rubio at 43 percent, Ben Carson at 30 percent, Ted Cruz at 19 percent, and Trump at just 6 percent. Many Hillsdale students, faculty, and administrators ended up supporting Trump for the same reason I had—they believed he was better politically, and no worse morally, than Hillary Clinton.

As the experience of the Trump administration demonstrated, the Republican Party's mounting suspicion of the Ivy League and other elite universities meant that it was increasingly reliant on students from other institutions to govern, and Hillsdale topped the list of those institutions. Numerous Hillsdale graduates were going on to important positions in politics, policy, law, and journalism, where, equipped only with their wits and their Hillsdale educations, they did battle for the survival of Western Civilization. Were I to join Hillsdale, I could help prepare them for the war.

Moving to Hillsdale would take our family away from the networks of friends and professional acquaintances we'd built in the Washington, D.C., area over nearly two decades. Washington was the epicenter of national and international power, a place where you could rub elbows with congressmen and pitch policy ideas to the world's most powerful leaders. Yet Washington was also a transient place, its suburban sprawl continuously drifting closer to statism and multiculturalism as the federal government and its appendages grew ever larger. For Ohio natives like Kelli and me, Michigan was closer culturally than the Washington area, and it was closer physically to our parents in Cleveland, who were now in their eighties.

I also was gaining a new appreciation for the belief of the founders that Washington should be a temporary destination for American citizens, a place where they served in politics for a few years before returning to the states where the vast majority of Americans lived and worked and produced. I frequently thought back to what a congressman had told me on this subject not long after I had moved to the nation's capital. Many of the Americans who came to Washington to hold political offices, he had explained, were initially eager to engage in swamp draining. If they stayed too long, however, the swamp was liable to exhaust their patience and their political capital, and might even turn them into swamp creatures.

The battering I had received from the swamp ensured I would never become one of its zombies. It had also depleted my political capital, and with it my prospects for positive achievement. I knew of a few people who had managed to hang on to their integrity and their political capital after decades in the swamp—Senator Grassley was a notable example—but they typically did so by building or reinforcing institutional fortresses that protected them from Washington's toxic sludge. I had no such fortress.

Entering the political circles of Washington, I had come to believe, was like moving into a gold rush town run by a mayor known for sleaze and gluttony. If you intended to maintain a life of integrity and civic responsibility, you had better arrive with a swift horse and an exit plan. When you learned that the mayor was extorting silver dollars from the saloon and the bank and the general store, you wouldn't want to inform the sheriff unless you knew you could get out of town fast should the sheriff declare you the villain.

Adding to the repulsiveness of Washington was the nasty internecine warfare among Republicans over Trump, the 2020 election, and the Capitol riot. Never Trumpers and others from the establishment wing claimed that the Republican Party would never win another presidential election unless it renounced Trump and apologized to the American people for his bad behavior. Trump supporters fired back that establishment Republicans were so out of touch with the American people that the party could never regain the White House under their leadership. This debate, which drew in friends and acquaintances of mine on both sides, seemed to accomplish little except to weaken the Republican Party, maintain employment for anti-Trump Republicans at mainstream media outlets, and distract Republicans from the more pressing task of resisting the Biden administration's ambitious left-wing agenda.

I asked President Arnn if I could spend the first year at the Kirby Center, Hillsdale's satellite campus in Washington, D.C., so that I wouldn't have to relocate while Trent was still undergoing chemotherapy. He graciously agreed. That settled it. After talking it over with Kelli one more time, I agreed to take the job.

Chapter 26

To the Pentagon

On April 13, Senator Grassley launched the first public salvo at the Department of Defense. In a letter addressed to Secretary of Defense Lloyd Austin, Grassley stated that his office had sent the Pentagon "repeated requests for information" concerning "DoD's potential involvement in the revocation of Dr. Mark Moyar's security clearance." The Defense Department "has made repeated promises to be responsive to my staff's requests, but continues to fail to deliver on those promises." Grassley informed Austin that he wanted answers to his questions within the next eight days.

"Did any individual from USAID ever advise or instruct the Department of Defense, the Washington Headquarters Service, or the Department of Defense Consolidated Adjudications Facility that Dr. Moyar's security clearance should be revoked?" The senator inquired of the Secretary of Defense. "Is it DoD's official position that Dr. Moyar's security clearance was reinstated 'in error'? If so, who made this error to reinstate Dr. Moyar's security clearance? And based on what information, or lack thereof, was this error made?"

Within hours of receiving this letter, the Pentagon responded to a letter it had received from Grassley's staff three months earlier, which contained some of the same questions. This response didn't address all of the senator's questions, but it did disclose a crucial chain of events. In August 2020, it divulged, USAID had contacted the Defense Department to question the decision to reinstate my clearance the previous month. The Defense Department had then decided in October 2020 to reconsider the reinstatement—a decision that appeared to have been driven by the meddling of USAID, given that no new evidence against me had emerged. Another two months then went by before the department issued the revocation notice.

When I conferred with McClanahan, he was exuberant over the new holes this revelation had opened in USAID's defenses. "Why was USAID second-guessing DoD after they spent a year saying they couldn't possibly second-guess DoD?" he commented. "If it was so urgent for USAID to suspend your clearance because you were such a threat to national security, why did DoD take two months to even think about it?" He shared my view that the motive behind this meddling must have been fear that reinstatement of my clearance would invite further questioning of the original assertion by Voorhees and Ohlweiler that I would lose my clearance if the agency leadership didn't fire me.

The next significant turn took place at the end of April with the confirmation of Colin Kahl as undersecretary of defense for policy. A hyper-partisan veteran of the Obama administration, Kahl had tweeted in 2019 that Republicans "debase themselves at the alter [sic] of Trump." (The Biden administration clearly hadn't bought into the idea that Pentagon appointees should be "apolitical.")

Among the objections Republicans had raised in their bid to block Kahl's confirmation was Kahl's alleged publication of classified information on Twitter. Several of Kahl's tweets from 2017 had come much closer to breaching non-disclosure rules and damaging U.S. national security than the book that had cost me my job and my security clearance. Kahl had never submitted his material to the Defense Office of Prepublication and Security Review as I had done, let alone given the government an entire year to raise objections. Unlike my book, Kahl's tweets concerned policy controversies that were playing out at the very moment he published them.

According to a report in *Politico*, Kahl defended himself to the leadership of the Senate Armed Services Committee by asserting that "the information in his tweets was widely available in the public domain." That assertion was true for the most part, though he did tweet that he had confirmed certain information with inside sources, which could have been interpreted as using information that had been outside the public domain. The fifty Democratic senators and Vice President Kamala Harris didn't hold it against him; they all voted for him in the end, ensuring his confirmation. Equal in their lenience were the adjudicators at the Defense Consolidated Adjudications Facility, the same outfit that had revoked my clearance just before my return to the Trump administration. They granted Kahl the security clearance that permitted him to begin work at the Pentagon on April 28, 2021. Once again, career bureaucrats had demonstrated their partisan bias through selective enforcement of rules and laws.

Another Biden appointee, Jake Sullivan, escaped punishment in 2021 for security incidents of a much more serious nature. During the FBI investigation into Hillary Clinton's illicit use of a private email server, the bureau had learned that Sullivan, while working for Clinton, had used unclassified email systems to send Clinton at least seven emails containing Special Access Program information, among the most highly compartmentalized of all classified information. The repeated and willful transmission of highly classified material through unclassified email to evade governmental scrutiny was a security violation of a very high order. It was the type of action that ordinarily would have caused a federal employee to lose his security clearance for life. When the details of Sullivan's complicity in the email scandal first surfaced in 2016, even Clinton-friendly media published stories asserting that Sullivan and the other Clinton aides involved would be unlikely to receive security clearances ever again.

Curiously, the mainstream media did not revisit the issue when, shortly after the 2020 presidential election, Biden picked Sullivan for the job of National Security Adviser—a position requiring the highest of security clearances. One suspected

that if a Trump appointee had committed comparable security violations, the media would have reprised its treatment of
Sullivan's Trump-era counterpart, Lt. General Michael Flynn,
mass-producing derogatory articles based on slanted leaks from
hostile officials. And the FBI would have pursued a criminal
prosecution, as it had done against Flynn for alleged offenses
that had been less serious than Sullivan's actual offenses. The
FBI didn't touch Sullivan, and neither did the security clearance
bureaucrats. On the first day of the Biden administration, Sullivan showed up to work with a freshly granted clearance.

The month of May was a quiet one. It was so quiet, in fact,
that I did something I hadn't done in a long while, scour the
internet for information that might have a bearing on my case.
I didn't expect to find much, and at first I didn't. But then, suddenly, there emerged from the dark ether a gleaming stone.

It appeared on the website of a conference hosted in December 2020 by the Global SOF Foundation. One of the speakers
listed on the program was Angela Greenewald, and a link to
her bio was included. This bio revealed that in 2018, just before coming to USAID, she had "served as the Director of the
Commander's Initiatives Group in the John F. Kennedy Special
Warfare Center and School working on specializing in projects
supporting the Commanding General as well as serving as the
interim Executive Officer to the Commanding General."

Although I'd known that Greenewald had come to USAID
straight from the world of special operations, I hadn't known
that she'd worked at the Kennedy Special Warfare Center and
School, or that she had worked directly for its commander. The
Kennedy Special Warfare Center and School was in Fort Bragg.
And its commander was a two-star general.

In 2018, that commander had been Major General Kurt
Sonntag. I'd heard of Sonntag before. His name was on the list
I'd compiled of two-star generals who had been in Fort Bragg in
the spring of 2019, when the accusation against me had traveled
from Fort Bragg to Tampa. Until now, however, I had seen no
direct link between him and anyone at USAID.

Even earlier, during the fall of 2017, I'd come across his name in a series of widely circulated news articles. Shortly after Sonntag's assumption of command at the Kennedy Special Warfare Center and School, instructors at the Special Forces Qualification Course began complaining that he had lowered the physical, mental, and ethical standards for Special Forces candidates. When instructors attempted to hold candidates to standards that had been in place for decades, it was alleged, Sonntag and his inner circle countermanded the instructors and, in some cases, rebuked or punished them. According to Kristina Wong of *Breitbart*, who wrote some of the most informative stories on the brouhaha, Sonntag responded to the complaints by asserting that the standards had to be enforced less stringently because higher authorities had ordered him to produce more Special Forces.

In November 2017, one instructor became so fed up with Sonntag's conduct and his deafness to subordinates that he emailed an anonymous denunciation to thousands of special operations personnel. "The recent systematic dismissal of course standards and continuous violation of regulations at the Training Group and [Special Warfare Center and School] echelons makes student failure nigh impossible," the email stated. The inferior graduates coming out of the course, claimed the author, left the Special Forces "less capable than ever before."

The author believed that Sonntag and another senior officer had made the course easier in order to catapult themselves into the upper ranks of the Army's general officers. "They pursued this," he wrote, "by, first, ensuring that the Q-course graduation rate was raised so they could lay claim to making the Q course more efficient and, second, ensuring that the standards were lowered so as to make certain that the first women able to pass selection would have the best possible chance of making it through the grueling 14 month (at its quickest) pipeline practically unimpeded. Being able to say they graduated the first female Green Beret is a milestone no officer (devoid of principles, that is) can possibly pass up."

The email rocketed across the defense community in a matter of hours. Whether service members and civilians were sympathetic toward the author's views or not, the biting candor was an exciting change from the dullness and obfuscation of everyday bureaucratic prose. A variety of media outlets scarfed up the email and amplified it, and military-oriented blogs and comment boards filled with supportive remarks from current and former military personnel. The author's account appeared to confirm what many in the military had long predicted—that President Obama's decision to open combat positions to women near the end of his presidency would result in a lowering of standards for combat troops, and hence of the effectiveness of the nation's combat forces.

Sonntag went to the press to deny he'd sold out the Special Forces to radical feminists and their sympathizers inside the government. "No fundamental standard for assessing future Green Berets has been removed or adjusted," he told Richard Lardner of the Associated Press. That answer may have been technically correct, but it was as misleading as announcing that a high school hadn't changed its official graduation requirements without mentioning that it had inflated grades to increase the percentage of students who met the graduation requirements.

Sonntag acknowledged to Lardner that some issues identified in the email "warrant further evaluation." In the days and weeks ahead, however, he didn't investigate or address those issues. He chose, instead, to embark on a quest to find and punish the author of the email.

A few days after the anonymous jeremiad had flooded the Defense Department's inboxes, Sonntag brought all of his instructors together. As recounted by Wong, who spoke with multiple witnesses, Sonntag pulled off the top of his Army combat uniform and challenged anyone who disagreed with his managerial decisions to step forward and fight him. When no one came forward, Sonntag declared that the production of the email could be punishable "by death."

Sonntag then ordered an official investigation into the origins of the email. After forensic examination of all the computer drives in the headquarters building failed to identify the culprit, the investigators fixed their attention on seven individuals whom Sonntag thought most likely to have authored the email. In January 2018, these individuals were removed from duty and their security clearances were suspended pending further investigation.

Over the next six months, Sonntag narrowed the number of suspects to three. In July, he issued administrative, non-judicial punishments to all three of them. At this juncture, one of the three confessed to writing the email, apparently to spare the other two. He was kicked out of the Special Forces and sent back into the regular Army.

Although the other two soldiers, Sergeant First Class Micah J. Robertson and Sergeant First Class Michael Squires, were not implicated in the production of the email, Sonntag refused to rescind their punishments. The type of punishment he'd chosen deprived Robertson and Squires of the opportunity to defend themselves, unless they exercised their right to a court-martial, which could result in the harshest of punishments should they be found guilty. Robertson and Squires were sufficiently convinced of their innocence that they nonetheless decided to exercise this right.

When Sonntag learned that the two soldiers wanted to contest the charges before a court-martial, he came up with another way to punish them that would snatch away the court-martial option and the due process rights that went with it. Withdrawing the original disciplinary actions, Sonntag issued each soldier a General Officer Memorandum of Reprimand (GOMOR), another of the administrative actions that Army leaders were increasingly abusing to minimize the rights of the accused and absolve the accuser of the need to provide corroborating evidence. The General Officer Memoranda of Reprimand allowed the Army to terminate both men after more than ten years of service without any severance compensation or other assistance.

Robertson and Squires filed complaints with the Army inspector general. It would have been difficult to perform an investigation as biased and superficial as the first investigation the USAID inspector general had performed in my case, but the Army inspector general proved equal to the task. The investigators assigned to the cases did not even bother to interview Robertson and Squires before deciding their complaints lacked merit.

Sonntag also issued administrative punishments to several other individuals who had not been complicit in producing the email but were suspected of sympathizing with its content or otherwise undermining Sonntag's authority. He fired the officer who had commanded the email writer's company, and then blacklisted him to prevent him from getting another job at Fort Bragg, unconcerned that the officer's four-year-old daughter was undergoing specialized medical treatment that would be disrupted by a relocation. The officer was compelled to take a job in Tampa at MacDill Air Force Base, where his family was placed in a housing unit that contained toxic mold. The officer filed a complaint with the Army inspector general, which led nowhere.

An instructor who was able to evade career destruction told Kristina Wong that Sonntag was "one of the most toxic commanders I've ever had. He keeps order by threats. He's a hundred percent toxic. He leads by threats and intimidation. He's ruining people's careers because he can." Another Green Beret attested that everyone at the Kennedy Special Warfare Center and School was "horrified by that man. They don't want to talk, they don't want to say anything because they feel like he's going to destroy their careers."

The accumulation of negative press reports about Sonntag eventually compelled the Army to convene a board of inquiry. As reported by Lolita Baldor of the Associated Press, the board decided to take no action against Sonntag for wrecking so many lives, on the grounds that Sonntag had ostensibly based most of his punitive measures on alleged infractions unrelated to the inflammatory email. The board members somehow disregarded the highly suspicious fact that Sonntag had not been handing out career-destroying punishments evenly across his command throughout his tenure, but instead had concentrated them on the one small part of his command where he believed the email author resided and had done so only during his hunt for the email writer. They likewise paid no heed to Sonntag's underhanded efforts to prevent defendants from exercising due process rights.

The Army did decide, however, that Sonntag would not receive a new assignment or a promotion, effectively forcing him into retirement. Senior Army officials told Baldor that "there were lingering concerns about Sonntag fostering a toxic command climate and failing to communicate well enough with the troops about the changes in the course." No doubt there were also lingering concerns about the bad publicity Sonntag was bringing upon the Army. Upon his retirement in August 2019, Sonntag walked away with a pension and lifetime healthcare, unlike many of the people whose careers he had ruined.

As I read the news accounts of Sonntag, I was stunned by the similarities between the weapons and tactics he'd used to destroy his perceived enemies and the ones that had been used to destroy me. Suspension of security clearances based on unsubstantiated accusations. The crafting and recrafting of punishments to deprive the accused of due process rights. The prompt termination of employment without severance.

Sonntag's compulsory retirement was first mentioned in the press on May 3, 2019. That was just eighteen days before SOCOM launched the allegation against me. At the time of launch, therefore, Sonntag had already received the most serious of the punishments that senior officers generally received for major offenses like facilitating a retaliatory scheme. So unlike just about every other two-star general in the Army, he had nothing to lose by recklessly hurling career-threatening accusations or inserting himself into matters of prepublication review that lay entirely outside his job responsibilities and expertise.

Was Sonntag, in fact, the two-star general who had fed me to the security lions? Given that only a handful of two-star generals called Fort Bragg home, the odds couldn't have been very high that two of them were maliciously ruining people's careers at precisely the same time. Nevertheless, I didn't have evidence proving definitively that Sonntag was the guy. I forwarded the new information to Brady and McClanahan so that they could probe further.

Chapter 27

Star Power

Although the Defense Department's revocation of my security clearance had exposed the Pentagon to charges of whistleblower retaliation, the complicity of USAID in that action meant that my most promising route to justice still went through USAID and its administrator. The office of the USAID administrator had a new occupant now. Joe Biden had nominated Samantha Power for the position in January, and after a lengthy confirmation process she was sworn in on May 3.

A former journalist and author who had won the Pulitzer Prize for her book *A Problem from Hell: America and the Age of Genocide*, Power had served in Barack Obama's National Security Council and then had become his Ambassador to the United Nations. In early 2011, Power joined with Hillary Clinton and Susan Rice in convincing Obama to intervene in the Libyan civil war. Both the Right and the Left would castigate Power for the calamitous outcome.

In an article published in *Foreign Affairs* at the end of 2020, Power had advocated "a high-profile fight against corruption at home and abroad," and urged Biden to "clean up after the most corrupt and self-dealing presidency in U.S. history." I hoped that Power would clean up one of the most corrupt and self-dealing agencies in U.S. history. I was worried, though, that the allure of diplomatic events, international conferences, and congressional klatches would keep her from paying attention to the agency's inner workings and problems, for she seemed more interested in big ideas and public relations than management.

Power had a history of adversarial relations with my most powerful ally, Senator Grassley. Their mutual antagonism had arisen from a 2017 Republican investigation into the surveillance of Trump associates at the end of the Obama administration. Grassley had led the investigatory charge, and Power had become one of the main Republican targets after it was revealed that she, along with Joe Biden and Susan Rice, had repeatedly sought to "unmask" Michael Flynn and other people close to Trump.

"Unmasking" referred to revealing the names of U.S. citizens that had been redacted from intelligence reports, typically reports derived from surveillance of foreigners. It was supposed to be used sparingly because of its infringement on privacy and civil liberties. Democrats had skewered John Bolton in 2005 after learning he had requested unmasking on ten occasions over a four-year period. The unmasking during the 2016 presidential campaign was much greater in magnitude, the requests numbering in the hundreds over a period of a few months. News outlets reported in September 2017 that Power, while serving as Obama's Ambassador to the United Nations, had requested the "unmasking" of American citizens more than any other official. Republicans and some Democratic civil libertarians were shocked by the revelation and demanded to know why the Ambassador to the United Nations had compelled the intelligence community to identify so many Americans. Summoned to testify before the House Permanent Select Committee on Intelligence on October 13, 2017, Power said that people on her staff must have made some of the requests "without my knowledge." Republicans doubted that such a sensitive matter would have evaded her attention.

On July 1, USAID communicated with Senator Grassley about my case for the first time in the Power era. The communication, a three-paragraph letter, provided no answers to the questions the senator had posed in his letter of March 19. The USAID Office of Inspector General, the agency stated, had already "reviewed this matter" and concluded that the "suspension of Dr. Moyar's security clearance was predicated solely upon receipt of information from SOCOM concerning Moyar's unauthorized disclosure of classified information." The letter ended with the customary lip service: "The Biden-Harris Administration takes all whistle-blower complaints seriously and is committed to due process."

The document had been signed by a deputy assistant administrator, Diala Jadallah-Redding, so we couldn't know for certain whether Power had influenced or approved its content. It seemed highly unlikely, however, that the agency would have sent such a dismissive letter to a senior U.S. senator without the concurrence of the agency's head. Why Power would snub Grassley again, over a matter that predated her arrival, was another mystery. Her contentious relationship with Grassley might have been the cause, but it could have been that Jenkins, Ohlweiler, and Voorhees had already worked their voodoo on her.

Grassley returned fire on August 27. In a public letter, he notified Power of his "extraordinary disappointment" in the agency's response to his March letter. "Your response was sent to my office on July 1, 2021, nearly three months after the requested deadline for the information, and answered none of my questions," Grassley wrote. "Further, your response was a mere six sentences in length, meaning that your department drafted, on average, two sentences per month, in response to my oversight inquiry, which by itself is disturbingly slow. This is a wildly unacceptable response from an administration that has claimed that it would be the most transparent administration in American history."

Grassley noted that "since Dr. Moyar contacted my office, nearly a dozen new whistleblowers have come forward with similar allegations of wrongdoing." Singling out Rob Jenkins by name, he stated that "Jenkins has been mentioned on several occasions by whistleblowers as having created a toxic work environment, retaliating against those he deems disloyal to him, and in Dr. Moyar's case, working in concert with other USAID officials to get Dr. Moyar's security clearance suspended." The senator noted that "USAID's position since the onset of my investigation has been that once DoD made the decision to suspend Dr. Moyar's security clearance, USAID was in no position to question the suspension," yet "once DoD reinstated Dr. Moyar's security clearance, USAID took it upon itself to, for unknown reasons, ask DoD why it reinstated Dr. Moyar's security clearance."

To promote public transparency and shed light on the agency's excuses for ignoring his questions, Grassley continued, he was going to publish the entire Office of Inspector General investigation of April 2020. That office, he noted, "did not investigate Dr. Moyar's underlying claims of whistleblower reprisal," but only the agency's immediate reaction to "the unfounded claims that Dr. Moyar leaked classified information in a book published years before DoD's allegations."

Senator Grassley also published two responses he'd received recently from the Department of Defense, both pertaining to the granting of my clearance in July 2020 and the revocation in December 2020. Both had been written by Deputy Assistant Secretary of Defense for Legislative Affairs Matthew Williams. I'd never heard of Williams before, but a quick internet search revealed that he'd moved to the Pentagon in January 2021 from the office of Kamala Harris, Joe Biden's vice president.

In one of the documents, Williams stated that USAID had informed the Defense Department in June 2020 of a "special investigation" report stemming from my clearance suspension the previous year. But, according to Williams, the Defense Consolidated Adjudications Facility hadn't taken that report into consideration when it had granted the clearance the next month. Williams made no attempt to explain how the Department had failed to consider a freshly arrived report that it subsequently claimed was so radioactive as to warrant revoking my security clearance.

In August 2020, the narrative continued, USAID "queried" the Defense Department about the granting of the clearance. On September 10, USAID and Defense Department officials met to discuss the case. Williams didn't mention which officials attended this meeting, what they discussed, or why they needed to meet at all if the only object of USAID was to ask Defense officials to consider the "special investigation" report. After the meeting, Williams stated, the Defense Department decided to begin "the process of revoking Dr. Moyar's security clearance eligibility."

McClanahan already possessed evidence supporting the conclusion that the Defense Department, in fact, had considered the "special investigation" report during the July 2020 adjudication. If that conclusion was accurate, then Williams, or another Defense Department employee involved in producing the response, had lied to the senator. Why would someone take on the risks of lying to a senator on such a matter? Probably because the stakes had become very high. Truthful acknowledgment that the information had been considered in July would have confirmed that Defense officials overturned their own decision based on opinions and exhortations from USAID, rather than any new facts. That confirmation would have laid bare several truths of an even more incriminating nature: that the Defense adjudicators had reviewed the charges the first time and found them unconvincing; that USAID officials had gone out of their way to meddle in a decision that had exposed them to charges of fraud for previous actions; and that Defense officials had acquiesced to the meddling.

Samantha Power's next thumbing of her nose at Senator Grassley came the following Monday, August 30. In a notice sent across the agency, Power announced that she was appointing Rob Jenkins to the position of assistant to the administrator for the CPS Bureau. It was the prize he had craved from the very beginning, and the one that had made me his mortal enemy.

"I know Rob will continue to help the Agency address some of the toughest and most complex challenges in the world, as he has done for more than two decades," Power stated in the announcement, "while representing the values of the Biden-Harris administration." At a swearing-in ceremony the very next day, Power remarked, "The reason why Rob has risen [in] the ranks as an indispensable leader at USAID is because he cares deeply about people, about their dignity, and their well-being." I doubted Power had any idea what Rob Jenkins really cared about.

Power was handing a crown jewel to someone whom Grassley had accused of whistleblower retaliation just three days earlier. Was she tone-deaf and ignorant of the power of Congress? Or was she purposefully slashing back at Grassley in the belief that not even a U.S. senator could mess with Samantha Power? We would have to wait and see.

In the August 27 letter, Grassley had asked Power to turn over information on my case by September 10. That day came and went without any response from her. As the senator soon learned, moreover, the frontal silence of USAID was accompanied by a surreptitious USAID end run, aimed at thwarting publication of the inspector general report. Just after the senator's letter landed in Power's inbox, someone from the agency asked Democrats on the Senate Finance Committee to prohibit release of the report until the current committee chair approved redactions. Grassley, like every other Republican committee chair, had been compelled to surrender his committee chairmanship to a Democratic counterpart after the unlikely victories of Democrats in the Georgia Senate runoff election of January 2021. The new Finance Committee Chair was Ron Wyden, Democrat of Oregon.

Like every other senator in the minority party, Grassley didn't buy the argument that the chairman who had originally requested the documents needed release approval from the current chairman, but the Democrats in the Senate Finance Committee bought it. They compelled Grassley's office to postpone publication of the report until the new chairman had given his consent. The only part of this arrangement that wasn't discouraging was the fact that Senator Wyden was co-chair of the Senate Whistleblower Caucus alongside Grassley. Brady and McClanahan foresaw approval coming in a matter of days or weeks.

The agency's obstructionism came at a moment of broader confrontation between the Biden administration and Congress over the sharing of executive branch information and the prosecution of corrupt officials. On September 15, the Senate Judiciary Committee held a hearing on the federal government's mishandling of sexual abuses committed by former USA Gymnastics physician Larry Nassar. National team gymnasts Simone Biles, McKayla Maroney, Aly Raisman, and Maggie Nichols appeared before the committee, ensuring that every major media outlet would cover the story.

Senator Grassley and his Democratic counterparts joined the gymnasts in chastising the FBI for its failure to respond to allegations against Nassar, its delays in answering congressional inquiries on the scandal, and its unwillingness to hold officials accountable. W. Jay Abbott, head of the office that had received the gymnasts' complaints about Nassar, had buried the allegations by purporting to refer them to another FBI office without actually referring anything. During the same period, Abbott had approached USA Gymnastics, which was trying to cover up Nasser's crimes, for assistance in a post-retirement job. Abbott had chosen to retire once these facts came to light, which spared him from internal FBI disciplinary measures and ensured he could keep his full federal retirement benefits.

At the hearing, FBI Director Christopher Wray offered apologies for his organization's failures, and acknowledged that the FBI's unresponsiveness to complaints had allowed Nassar to victimize additional girls for a period of more than one year. Democratic Senator Richard Blumenthal pressed Wray to explain why neither Abbott nor anyone else had been prosecuted for this gross violation of the public trust. "If I were in your shoes," Blumenthal said, "I would be walking across the street to the attorney general of the United States, and I would be saying, 'You need to prosecute.' Why aren't you doing that?"

"I don't want to get into my discussions with the attorney general," Wray answered. "I have a lot of respect for him and for the privacy of our conversations."

The senators of both parties came away from the hearing dissatisfied. "The Department of Justice, today, was a no show," Blumenthal steamed at a post-hearing press conference.

If the Democrats really were furious about the Biden administration's lack of transparency, perhaps they would be willing to support Grassley's quest for information on my case.

It would prove to be another misplaced hope. Senator Wyden's office failed to move on releasing the inspector general report on my case. Days and weeks would turn into months and years.

Chapter 28

Ignoring Orders and Breaking Rules

At the end of the summer, I began my Hillsdale teaching career at the college's Washington campus, an island of conservative education in a left-liberal sea. The demands of conducting new graduate seminars on U.S. foreign policy and the Vietnam War kept me from thinking too often about what developed into a season of unresponsiveness from government officials, lawyers, and journalists. No new information on my case surfaced until the middle of December.

The new information was mined by journalist James Rosen of the Sinclair Broadcast Group. A short time earlier, Rosen had begun working on a television news story about me for the show *Full Measure with Sharyl Attkisson*. Rosen had become intimately familiar with abusive national security officials from a personal ordeal that had started in 2009 when he'd upset the Obama administration by publishing sensitive information on North Korea from an anonymous American official. Although the Obama White House routinely leaked information to the press for its own benefit, it had zero tolerance for government employees who leaked information that could make the White House look bad.

Under previous administrations, the federal government had pursued suspected leakers with the tools of criminal investigation, but had kept their mitts off journalists like Rosen who received and published the leaks, because of the First Amendment's protection of the press. The Obama administration, darling of the media though it was, proved to be a pioneer when it came to violating media rights. Attorney General Eric Holder sought warrants for sweeping access to Rosen's private email records on the grounds he was involved in espionage. The first two judges to receive the request turned it down, but the Justice Department eventually found a receptive judge in Royce Lamberth of the D.C. District Court. Lamberth later had to issue an apology for the court's failure to unseal the warrants in the required time frame, which he blamed on "a series of administrative errors."

In May 2013, while explaining to Congress why the Justice Department had issued subpoenas for the phone records of Associated Press reporters, Holder remarked, "With regard to the potential prosecution of the press for the disclosure of material, that is not something I've ever been involved in, heard of or would think would be wise policy." At this point, someone informed the media of Holder's espionage accusation against Rosen and the warrants for his emails. Holder responded by saying he hadn't really intended to prosecute Rosen, but had only accused him of espionage as an "investigative step." That excuse satisfied no one. Even Erik Wemple, the media critic at the pro-Obama *Washington Post*, called it "weaselly garbage."

On December 15, 2021, as part of his research on my case, Rosen interviewed a spokesman at Special Operations Command. The discussion took place "on background," meaning that Rosen could attribute what was said to a government official, but not provide the individual's name. I expected SOCOM to give Rosen the usual bureaucratic reply—no one in our organization did anything wrong, we'll tell you a few things you already know, there is nothing to see here.

The spokesman did dish plenty of that slop to Rosen. But amid the banalities and restatements of established facts, one dazzling nugget of useful information emerged. The spokesman informed Rosen that SOCOM had not decided to revisit my book two years after publication on its own initiative, as we had been led to believe for the past two and a half years. Instead, the official divulged, the "post-publication review" had been conducted because "someone from USAID reported to us that someone there had published classified information."

McClanahan and I couldn't contain our glee. Concrete evidence of USAID complicity in the accusation would make it much easier to prove that whistleblower retaliation had taken place. The origination of the accusation at USAID, rather than the Defense Department, also destroyed the claim some officials had been making that the accusation had come from a distant authority with no knowledge of my activities at USAID.

The SOCOM spokesman apparently became scared when Rosen told him how important this new disclosure was. On the following Monday, December 20, the spokesman told Rosen that SOCOM had actually received the accusation from "another DoD organization." In February 2018, he said, the Defense Department's Unauthorized Disclosure Program Management Office had asked SOCOM to review *Oppose Any Foe* for possible unauthorized disclosures of classified information.

Rosen was unimpressed. The Defense Department's Unauthorized Disclosure Program Management Office didn't have a two-star general, so it couldn't have been the driving force behind the May 2019 accusation. If SOCOM had initially received a compelling accusation of unauthorized disclosure in February 2018, it was duty bound to take action in a matter of days, as opposed to spending fifteen months figuring out what to do. In the spring of 2017, a Defense Department allegation of unauthorized disclosure against contractor Reality Winner had prompted the FBI to open an investigation within two days, and two days thereafter the FBI had raided Winner's home and arrested her. Subsequently she was convicted of a felony offense and sentenced to five years in prison. The government had zipped into action with similar alacrity upon learning of the alleged classified information in the manuscripts of Anthony Shaffer and Matt Bissonnette.

James Rosen would leave the Sinclair Broadcast Group for a job at Newsmax before the segment could air on *Full Measure* or one of the network's other programs. As a result, the network decided not to air it on TV, but instead only posted it on the websites of its local TV stations. Because local TV station websites are one of the last places people look for news, the story received minimal attention, and thus its impact was nil.

On December 21, I heard at long last from the company that had requested a security clearance for me in February. They forwarded me an email from the Defense Counterintelligence and Security Agency, which contained a file entitled "MOYAR EYES ONLY PACKAGE." I opened the file to find a freshly issued Statement of Reasons. For the second year in a row, the government had sent me a ticking time bomb just before Christmas.

McClanahan and I had hoped that Defense Department officials had been taking so long to reconsider the prior Statement of Reasons because they had realized how ridiculous it was and were digging into the complaint's suspicious origins and the whistleblower retaliation claims. Now we learned that they had undertaken no further investigation, but had only edited and trimmed the original document. The changes they'd made over the past ten months could have been made in ten minutes. Their withholding of notification for ten months could only have been intended to string matters out, for the benefit of the bureaucrats who wanted to deny me rights of appeal and allow the matter to fade away.

Whoever had edited the Statement of Reasons had removed some of the most preposterous text. While the document repeated the allegation that I'd violated Defense Department policy by publishing the book without governmental approval, it had been stripped of the prior charge of violating a non-disclosure agreement. Perhaps someone had gotten around to reading the non-disclosure agreement and realized that it gave the government only thirty working days to review the manuscript. All references to the USAID Office of Security investigation were gone as well, suggesting that someone was trying to erase the link between USAID employees and the security clearance action.

One important part of the Statement of Reasons had been rewritten. Whereas the first version had announced a preliminary decision to revoke the clearance, this one stated the following: "Because this office is unable to find that it is clearly consistent with the national interest to grant you access to classified information, your case will be submitted to an Administrative Judge for a determination as to whether or not to grant, deny, or revoke your security clearance." Whether an administrative judge would be better than a security bureaucrat was impossible to know, though it would be hard to be worse than the security bureaucrats I'd encountered thus far.

The Statement of Reasons did have a silver lining—it afforded the recipient access to information. For targets of security clearance denials and revocations, Executive Order 12968 required the government to provide "any documents, records, and reports upon which a denial or revocation is based," as well as "the entire investigative file" within thirty days. McClanahan promptly contacted USAID and the Defense Department to request these materials.

On January 11, an employee at the USAID Freedom of Information Act Office informed McClanahan that she wanted to meet with McClanahan the next morning to talk about his new request. The agency evidently wanted to avoid a written record of the discussion.

McClanahan was having none of it. "I am willing to discuss any concerns or questions you might have, but only in writing," he wrote back. "We have had bad experiences with representatives from your agency telling us things on the telephone about Dr. Moyar's previous attempts to obtain information which later turned out to be blatantly false."

USAID then sent McClanahan the response to a Freedom of Information Act request he had submitted eighteen months earlier. In the cover letter, agency FOIA Chief Christopher Colbow stated that USAID "regrets the delay in responding to your Freedom of Information Act (FOIA) request" and is "very committed to providing responses to FOIA requests and remedying the FOIA backlog." According to the response, a "comprehensive search" of Office of Security records had yielded 182 pages. We were given a file containing 133 pages, which contained next to nothing that was new. The other 49 pages, we were told, had been referred to the Department of Defense. Those pages almost certainly contained what we really needed, like the identity of the two-star general, communications between USAID and the Defense Department, the evidence supporting the charge of unauthorized disclosure, and Justice Department analysis of the accusation.

On January 21, USAID sent McClanahan a letter explaining the agency's position on our Executive Order 12968 request. The letter stated that the provisions of the executive order didn't apply, because "your client resigned from USAID before a final determination was made regarding his access to classified information." It was signed by none other than Jack Ohlweiler.

I wasn't surprised to see Ohlweiler's name. I'd already guessed that he'd been pulling the strings once more. As the person who had orchestrated my "resignation," and who had then perpetrated additional acts of fraud that were likely contained in the records I was seeking, he should have recused himself from this matter, but by now no one should have been surprised that he would ignore a conflict of interest when it stood in his way.

Days and weeks and months went by without further information from USAID. There was no word on the forty-nine pages USAID had referred to the Defense Department.

On January 26, McClanahan sent emails to the Department of Defense asking why we hadn't received any documents concerning my case under the provisions of Executive Order 12968. They wanted us to respond to the Statement of Reasons in a twenty-day period, he noted, and yet the request had already been sitting with them for more than twenty days. The Pentagon extended the response period to the next month and said it would get back to us on the document request.

In the middle of February, the Defense Department sent McClanahan a response to our request under the executive order for the "documents, records, and reports upon which a denial or revocation is based." It contained 177 pages, none of them useful. The Department claimed that if records used in producing the Statement of Reasons had come from USAID, we could ask USAID to provide them through the Privacy Act. Yet we had already asked USAID for those documents through the Privacy Act, and had been told we couldn't receive the key documents because they belonged to the Defense Department.

To sum up, USAID refused to give us the key documents on the grounds that they contained information belonging to the Defense Department. The Defense Department refused to give us the same documents on the grounds that they were held by USAID. Both were flipping off the executive order that required them to turn everything over within thirty days.

McClanahan said we now had to sue the government to get the information. With my consent, he filed a lawsuit on February 23 with the federal district court of the District of Columbia. Although a private citizen was required to respond to this type of lawsuit within twenty-one days, a federal agency had sixty days to reply. It wasn't obvious why a bloated government bureaucracy with battalions of lawyers deserved more time than individual citizens who had to pay legal fees from their own pockets.

The government's sixty-day response period began on the date when they were served, which meant they had until May 9 to respond. On April 27, the Department of Justice attorney assigned to the case, Sian Jones, submitted a request for an extension of forty-five days beyond May 9. In her petition to the judge, she offered two explanations. First, she "took sick leave between April 18 and April 28, 2022, for, among other reasons, recovery from contracting Covid-19." (She didn't say what the "other reasons" were.) Second, she had "a robust caseload," and had been given "an emergency assignment on April 12, 2022, that required her attention for several days." If these excuses were valid, then a fifteen-day extension for the sick leave and emergency assignment might have been warranted. Jones didn't explain why she needed a forty-five-day extension. But the judge granted the extension.

During the spring, I learned of Katie Arrington. A former state representative in South Carolina and a Trump supporter, Arrington had been appointed to a career executive position at the Pentagon near the end of the Trump administration. On May 7, 2021, the Department of Defense had suspended her security clearance and put her on administrative leave, ostensibly because the National Security Agency had reported her for an unauthorized disclosure of classified information. On October 28, the Defense Department issued a notice of intent to revoke her clearance, but the accompanying Statement of Reasons provided no specifics concerning the alleged unauthorized disclosure. According to press reports, the Air Force Office of Special Investigations had reviewed the details of the incident and decided that it "could not identify any nefarious intent which would warrant a criminal or counterintelligence investigation at this time."

Arrington had been thrown into the same boat of government obfuscation as me. And, like me, she had decided to sue the government to get the supporting evidence. A judge ruled in her favor at the end of 2021, compelling the government to provide evidence and pay her legal fees.

Mysterious security clearance allegations had also tripped up another Trump supporter at the Defense Department in 2021. Michael Ellis, a former Trump appointee, had been selected for the career position of general counsel at the National Security Agency near the end of the Trump administration. Nancy Pelosi, Democratic activists, and some career bureaucrats objected to his hiring on the grounds that it was an effort to infiltrate a former political appointee into a career job. (These same people had raised no objections when Barack Obama had appointed his White House Staff Secretary, Rajesh De, to this very job in 2012.) Complaints to the Department of Defense inspector general resulted in an investigation, which found that the hiring process had been proper and fair. So then Ellis's enemies arranged for suspension of his security clearance on charges of mishandling classified information—the details of which the

Defense Department refused to provide. Ellis quit three months later after neither he, nor his lawyer, nor U.S. senators could get the Defense Department to turn over the information.

On June 23, 2022, the Department of Justice submitted its response to my lawsuit. The Department made a motion to dismiss the case, based on legal hocus-pocus and selective withholding of facts. They didn't defend the government's refusal to provide the information specified by the executive order, but said that the court didn't need to get involved because "other adequate remedies are available to [the plaintiff] via FOIA or the Privacy Act." The government had already met its obligations, they claimed, by answering requests made under the Freedom of Information Act and Privacy Act. They neglected to mention the government's egregious delays in responding. Just one day before the Justice Department's submission, in fact, we had received a response to a request that had been submitted more than two years earlier. The Justice Department also failed to mention USAID's withholding of forty-nine pages of the USAID investigative file that was cited by the government in justifying revocation of my clearance. Nor did it explain why the Defense Department was justified in withholding those documents or other documents that were clearly covered by Executive Order 12968.

In August 2022, I moved to the main campus of Hillsdale in bucolic southern Michigan. Kelli and Trent stayed in Virginia, where they were to remain until December while Trent underwent a new series of chemotherapy treatments. The fall semester flew by without any progress on the lawsuit or the publication of the inspector general report Senator Grassley had been urging Senator Wyden to release for more than one year. The failure of the Republicans to retake the Senate in the mid-term elections ensured that the federal agencies would continue to ignore his requests for information. As 2022 neared its end, I decided to submit this book to the Defense Department for prepublication review.

Chapter 29

Wheels of Justice

The Justice Department had until January 11, 2023, to submit its latest response to our lawsuit. It waited until that day, at which time it sent a rehash of its previous arguments as to why the court could not compel the government to adhere to its own due process requirements. Prominently featured was the argument that "adequate remedies" existed through the Freedom of Information Act and Privacy Act. That same day, in what could not have been a coincidence, USAID sent us a response to a Freedom of Information Act/Privacy Act request from July 2020—two and a half years earlier.

The response, signed by USAID Freedom of Information Act Chief Christopher Colbow, didn't even include the usual apology for failing to meet the required response time of twenty business days. Pulling yet another rabbit from the hat of bureaucratic chicanery, Colbow asserted that a clause in the Privacy Act exempted the Office of Security's documents from disclosure. In actuality, this clause could not have applied to the entirety of the materials I had requested, as it stated that investigatory material was exempt "only to the extent that the disclosure of such material would reveal the identity of a source who furnished information to the Government under an express promise that the identity of the source would be held in confidence."

The most revealing information in this batch of documents was a statement by Nick Gottlieb about the seizure of my computer in May 2019. Gottlieb said that he had initiated the investigation because he had "overheard an office rumor suggesting [Moyar] was using his government computer and while on duty time was writing a book unrelated to his duties."

Overheard an office rumor.

Searching and seizing is a topic of such importance that the founders dedicated an entire amendment to it: the Fourth Amendment. In general, the government must obtain a warrant, based on probable cause and witness statements, in order to search and seize. Rumor alone doesn't cut it. Federal employment puts some limits on Fourth Amendment rights, a matter of ongoing debate among lawyers and judges, though the debate usually concerns cases where a questionable search or seizure produced incriminating evidence. In my case, the questionable search and seizure produced no incriminating evidence, which at minimum should have raised questions about whomever had produced the false allegation.

On March 28, thirteen months after the filing of the lawsuit, Judge Timothy Kelly issued a decision. He rejected the Department of Justice's argument that the court lacked jurisdiction over the case, which was a win for us. But then he turned down my request for intervention on the grounds that the relevant executive order did not apply to a "preliminary" determination, only a "final" determination. A "final" determination was, in his view, a decision that came right before the final appeal. (He didn't clarify how a determination could be "final" if it could be overturned through a subsequent, and actually final, appeal). The executive order itself did not specify whether the determination needed to be preliminary or final, so the judge was speculating over semantics—and disregarding how everyone else had interpreted the order.

The government, as standard practice, had interpreted the executive order as granting rights to information to anyone responding to the Statement of Reasons—the document that the judge was calling a "preliminary" determination. The Defense Department, in its own policy documents and the two

Statements of Reasons issued to me, acknowledged that their preliminary determination about my clearance entitled me to request the investigative file. The defendant was supposed to have access to the records in responding to the Statement of Reasons, just as the defendant in a criminal trial had access to any potentially incriminating information before the start of the trial. By disregarding these realities, the judge had ordered the equivalent of denying due process to an accused murderer until a jury had convicted him and sent him to death row to await his final appeal, even though every prior accused murderer had received due process rights before the jury trial.

Moments like these reminded me that I had been right to avoid law school. They also caused me to wonder, not for the first time, how so many people were perpetrating outrages at my expense. Was I becoming paranoid?

McClanahan reassured me that I wasn't the crazy one, that the judge's decision was one of the craziest he'd ever seen.

A short time later, we received a new version of the USAID OIG report of 2020, which revealed several passages that had been blacked out in previous versions. The most important showed that Jenkins had told investigators he'd approached Ohlweiler in 2019 to ask about helping Crnkovich. Ohlweiler had replied that Crnkovich was under investigation "regarding a conflict of interest with Crnkovich being on the board of a company." Ohlweiler advised Jenkins to "talk to Crnkovich as a friend, but not as a colleague, and tell him he should start looking for a job outside of USAID sooner rather than later." Ohlweiler also urged Jenkins "not to disclose the investigation to Crnkovich," because "if Crnkovich was not told he was under investigation, he could truthfully respond to any employment questions which asked about ongoing investigations."

This paragraph gave us the first concrete evidence that Jenkins and Ohlweiler had been working together to help Crnkovich. It proved unequivocally that the lawyer who had orchestrated my termination was simultaneously assisting the leading perpetrator of the corruption I had reported.

Another newly unredacted section contained information about the alleged unauthorized disclosure of classified information. According to the report, the Naval Special Warfare Command had reviewed the manuscript in September 2016 and "identified three specific citations that involved classified material." It had "recommended revising these citations and offered alternative language in two of the three instances."

The inspector general had cited this section in claiming that the government had possessed valid grounds for suspending my security clearance. Yet the information raised new questions, questions the inspector general had ignored. Why had the Naval Special Warfare Command taken five months to review a manuscript by an employee whose non-disclosure agreement permitted only thirty working days for a review? Why were the findings of the Naval Special Warfare Command never communicated to the author during the seven months between completion of the review and publication of the book? Why was the government trying to punish an author for ignoring information that had never been forwarded to him? If an author really had committed an unauthorized disclosure of information, why hadn't the FBI raided his house and arrested him?

During the spring and early summer, I corresponded with the Department of Defense about the manuscript for this book. I was repeatedly told that the review would be completed by a date, and each time the deadline was missed. At the end of June, nearly seven months after I had submitted the manuscript, a Defense official responded to my latest inquiry by saying that SOCOM was busy and couldn't say when it would be done.

On July 15, McClanahan filed a lawsuit to compel the completion of the prepublication review. Two days later, an official from the prepublication office said he was informing Pentagon lawyers of the suit. Then, on July 19, the same official told us the government had actually approved publication on July 11. When pressed further, he stated that he and his colleagues hadn't had a chance to go on classified email to obtain the clearance until July 18.

It sounded like a way for the government to avoid getting pulled into a lawsuit it was sure to lose, and a way to avoid having to reimburse me for legal fees. The government did, indeed, use the claim to avoid any payment of legal fees.

The lawsuit did have one clear benefit. It placed two key documents—the Intelligence Community Inspector General complaint and the OIG investigation—on unrestricted websites, available for all to view.

With the government's prepublication review out of the way, we were back to waiting, for the next court decision and for an answer from the Inspector General of the Intelligence Community on our request for a new investigation. At this point, more than four years into the ordeal, this sort of case would probably have been destined for the cave where old whistleblower complaints go to die. The only reason it did not was that I had been blessed with the education, experience, and spirit to write a book.

At first, I'd hoped to put off publication until all the facts emerged and the government acknowledged the truth of my retaliation claims. The government's success in hiding so many facts for so long, however, eroded and eventually crushed my confidence in the feasibility of those outcomes. And so I decided, near the end of 2023, to move ahead with publication.

A happy ending, it is true, would have given me a better chance of selling the movie rights to the Hallmark Channel. But an ending near the cave of dead whistleblower complaints has its virtues. By bringing into starker relief the federal bureaucracy's willingness to destroy employees who report corruption, a bleak end scene may spur the legislative and executive branches to improve protections for the honest employees of the future.

Chapter 30

The Future

This book is intended to help Americans make better decisions for themselves and their government. The most important of these decisions, from the point of view of the American people, are those affecting the control of federal bureaucracies and the spending of taxpayer funds. The proliferation of power grabbing and corruption by the administrative state, in parallel with the growth of the federal government and the weakening of the national culture, ranks among the top reasons why so many Americans have lost confidence in their government.

The ethical problems of governance are as old as human nature. A just government hasn't changed since Plato described it more than two thousand years ago as one that serves the interests of the entire citizenry equally, without favoritism toward the personal interests of the governing class. Each era's struggle, nevertheless, has peculiar characteristics. In the Trump era, toxic polarization and Trump's persona caused partisans to rationalize the breaking of constitutional, legal, and ethical rules for the greater good of obstructing Trump and his political appointees, even if those appointees were combating corruption or engaging in other activities of indisputable public benefit. Anti-Trump crusaders in the Department of Justice, the Offices of Inspector General, and other federal agencies concealed information, slow-rolled bureaucratic processes, misused hiring authorities, weaponized the security clearance system, and tampered with investigations. (For additional evidence on this point, see David L. Bernhardt's 2023 book *You Report to Me: Accountability for the Failing Administrative State.*)

The crossing of these thresholds makes it more likely that others will cross them in the future. Just as Bill Clinton's philandering eroded Republican opposition to adulterous presidential candidates, so is the Left's reliance on illicit measures likely to encourage the Right to use illicit measures against Democratic officials. Safely navigating the country through this perilous time will require adherence to the nation's founding principles, particularly pluralism and constitutional constraints on executive power.

Governing

America's republican form of government has required both the Left and the Right to forge alliances between populist and elite elements. Certain segments of the Republican establishment depicted Trump's election as the end of the conservative elite, but what it really signified was the end of those establishment segments as influential voices in conservative politics. Although the elites of the Right have, in general, been less than enamored of Trump, the number of highly educated conservatives willing to serve in a Trump administration greatly exceeded the number required to fill the ranks of federal political appointees. Within the conservative elite, most were willing to serve because they recognized that the country was better off with a Republican government led by a populist than a Democratic government led by any of the various politicians who have ruled in recent decades.

The splintering of the Republican establishment by Trump's nomination did complicate Trump's efforts to fill the ranks of political appointees, but a much bigger problem was the administration's lack of preparedness for filling thousands of appointee positions. As the administration's first months flew by, many positions were filled with the wrong people for the wrong reasons, and many other positions remained vacant because the White House didn't recognize the importance of filling them. Future administrations should expect to encounter as much bureaucratic resistance and policy drift as the Trump administration if they don't produce thoroughly researched slates of appointees before election day, and if they don't take care to put the selection processes in the hands of people with the right skills and motives.

The next Republican administration needs to train and educate new political appointees before sending them out into the bureaucratic wild. New appointees should be taught, for instance, how authorities should be allocated to political appointees, what methods appointees can use to obtain information that careerists try to hide, and how appointees should defend themselves against bureaucratic smear campaigns. The absence of such preparation allowed the dark wizards of the administrative state to tie Trump's political appointees in knots.

Political appointees can keep the bureaucracy on the straight and narrow if they maintain a firm grip on the reins. The reins, though, are far from easy to hold and control. Political appointees can easily be bamboozled and manipulated by career staff who ply them with praise, favors, and promises of future rewards. For this reason, the White House must ensure that it appoints individuals of integrity and conviction. No political appointee will concur with the president on every issue, but political appointees do need to agree broadly with the administration's principles and objectives. Only a firm belief in principles will ensure that they see the president's policies through, no matter the resistance from the career bureaucracy's apparatchiks.

Another good way to rein in the bureaucracy is to shrink it. Government bureaucracies are like garden shrubs—they are genetically programmed for continuous growth. It takes vigilant leadership in the executive and legislative branches to keep them trimmed to the proper size. When federal agencies grow unchecked, they find new ways to overstep their authorities, misuse money, and impinge on the liberties of private citizens who can't afford lawyers to defend themselves against the government's vast armies of prosecutors, investigators, and regulators.

Since the rise of Progressivism in the early twentieth century, the U.S. Congress has usually acceded to White House requests for big-government solutions to the nation's problems. While the growth of federal power alleviated some of the problems it was designed to address, it created many new ones by eroding the central pillars of American civilization—family, religion, and the market economy. In making much of the country dependent on federal largesse, big government ensured that voters would perpetuate lavish spending on the federal shrubbery. Nevertheless, large-scale pruning is still possible, as was demonstrated by the Republicans who came to power in 1994 and 2010. The same type of determination, and the same indifference to the howls of the chattering classes, is required again today.

Educating

For the Trump administration, finding Republicans with the right motivation was considerably less difficult than finding Republicans with the right expertise. Individuals need to obtain expertise, through education and experience, before they assume senior appointee positions, because once they are caught up in the hectic churn of bureaucratic life they are too busy to acquire expertise quickly enough. Expertise is hardly a political panacea; presumptuous experts can often cause more harm than good, particularly when politicians put unlimited trust in them. Nonetheless, appointees need to know the subject matter at hand if they are to promote the causes of elected officials, rather than the causes of unelected bureaucrats. As the case of USAID demonstrated, political appointees who lack expertise are unable to tell when career staff are hoodwinking them, and unable to come up with viable policy ideas that differ from those of the bureaucracy.

The Republican Party is, in general, short on experts in a number of key fields. Republican administrations used to draw large numbers of conservative experts from college and university faculties, but rampant political discrimination in faculty hiring has turned those wells dry. In addition, the absence of conservative professors discourages conservative students from pursuing careers in numerous public policy fields.

The Left's success in excluding conservatives from the faculty has had one positive side effect: smart donors, parents, and students have stopped patronizing the colleges and universities of the academic Broadway and taken their money to off-Broadway institutions. They are aware that the glitz and cachet of the high-rent district confer important advantages on graduates, but they are increasingly willing to forego those advantages. As I often hear from people who have abandoned Broadway for Hillsdale and other off-Broadway institutions, the pros of the big-name schools are outweighed by the cons of radical faculty, anti-Western curricula, administrative bloat, and exorbitant tuition. These alternative institutions are worthy of further investment as preparatory schools for governance, given the improbability that the politicization of mainstream academia will be reversed in the next hundred years.

Prepublication Review

During the second half of the twentieth century, a handful of judicial rulings established reasonable parameters for the First Amendment rights of former federal employees who had signed non-disclosure agreements. Of special significance, for me and for many other authors, the courts held that former employees could publish information already in the public domain, and that the government had to exercise its censorship powers in a timely manner. At first, the executive branch accepted those provisions and abided by them. Over time, however, executive branch bureaucrats have encroached on those rulings to increase governmental control over prepublication review, at the expense of citizens' First Amendment rights. The government has been most inclined to abuse prepublication review on matters of potential embarrassment to the government—which are often the matters of greatest importance to the public. Authors are constrained by the reality that challenging the executive branch may require suing a federal government whose unlimited time and resources can exhaust the resources of a private citizen.

Most of the current prepublication frictions can be eliminated if Congress passes legislation compelling the executive branch to comply with existing directives and regulations. Legislation will eliminate most of the wiggle room that has allowed executive branch lawyers and bureaucrats to flout those directives and legislations. To remove the problems caused by inconsistencies from one agency to another, the Office of the Director of National Intelligence should publish a set of guidelines for current employees and another set for former employees, applicable to all branches and agencies. These guidelines should include most of the text already contained in the Justice Department's regulation 28 CFR 17.18.

Whistleblower Protection

Management constitutes the first and strongest line of defense for whistleblower protection. Employees brave enough to report misconduct by other employees almost always begin by notifying the organization's leaders, not law enforcement or the media. They are driven in this direction by respect for organizational leaders and organizational processes, and by awareness that organizations don't look kindly on employees who take problems outside the organizational family. It is thus crucial that leaders have the integrity and courage to act promptly and fairly on complaints of wrongdoing. Reports from whistleblowers repeatedly failed to dislodge serial criminals like Larry Nassar, Jerry Sandusky, Frank Tassone, and Leslie Wiggins from their jobs because top organizational leaders responded by punishing the accusers rather than the accused. Rob Jenkins was likewise able to survive at USAID by getting into the good graces of top leaders and convincing them that they needed to fire the whistleblower instead of the fraudster.

Leaders at higher levels must be attuned to the character of leaders at lower levels, and must promptly remove those who demonstrate a lack of sound moral judgment. They also bear responsibility for shaping organizational culture, through words and deeds. When leaders emphasize ethics in their messages to employees and handle complaints of misconduct properly, employees are encouraged to report additional problems. When leaders react to reports of waste, fraud, and abuse by destroying the reporter or allowing others to do so, dozens of other potential whistleblowers are scared into silence.

Political appointees can be particularly valuable in both protecting whistleblowers and serving as whistleblowers because the limited duration of their time in office limits their dependence on the federal government for future employment. Unfortunately, the Whistleblower Protection Act does not allow political appointees to seek help from the Office of Special Counsel as it allows other federal employees. The coverages provided by Whistleblower Protection Act and Office of Special Counsel need to be extended to political appointees to help protect them from nightmares like mine.

In the federal government, inspectors general serve as the second line of defense. Ostensibly independent and impartial overseers of federal agencies, inspectors general too often act as the protection detail for agencies and their leaders. The sordid performances of the USAID and Department of Defense inspectors general in my case demonstrated much of what is wrong with the inspector general system today. Separating the inspectors general from the agencies they oversee, physically as well as organizationally, would go a long way toward stopping the collusion between the watchers and the people they are supposed to watch.

The inspectors general also need to be separated from the body responsible for watching them, their so-called Integrity Committee. That committee has been so reluctant to investigate fellow members of the guild, and so sluggish in pursuing the few cases it is willing to consider, that it must be stripped of its self-policing function. That function should be vested in a body that is wholly independent of the inspector general community and the federal agencies it serves.

External pressure is a vital means of ensuring that federal agencies and their inspectors general protect whistleblowers. Whistleblower champions in Congress, especially Senator Grassley, have enjoyed some success in forcing agencies to give whistleblower complaints proper consideration. Someone else will need to take up the mantle when the elderly senator decides to retire—someone who, like him, cares deeply enough to toil relentlessly on a crucial issue that the nation insufficiently appreciates.

The media has a critical role to play in safeguarding whistleblowers. When press outlets broadcast accounts of retaliation against whistleblowers, they not only advance the causes of those whistleblowers, but also discourage future acts of retaliation. The publicity accorded the occasional high-profile case of whistleblower retaliation obscures the reality that most cases never gain media attention, even when the victims are more than willing to share their stories. Whistleblowers need journalists, and also lawyers and advocates, who can help package their stories in ways that appeal to the media and the public.

Security Clearances

Federal authorities enacted Presidential Personnel Directive 19 and 50 U.S.C. § 3341 to stop the use of security clearance actions as instruments of retaliation against whistleblowers, but federal agencies have repeatedly found ways to deprive individuals of their protections. Agencies have also refused to compensate victims even after retaliation has been proven. Congress needs to compel agencies to comply with the laws it has passed, and should also pass new legislation permitting whistleblowers to sue agencies for abuses of the security clearance system.

Among the worst features of the current clearance system is its concentration of power in the hands of a tiny few. Agencies are allowed to vest the authority to revoke a clearance, and thus to destroy a career, in the hands of a single person, who is usually a product of a bureaucratic class that has a long record of abusing authority. Arbiters of security clearances can and sometimes do revoke clearances for minor offenses as a means of retaliation, while condoning major offenses committed by employees who are on their good side.

USAID, like other agencies, permitted an appeal to a panel in the event that the primary arbiter revoked a clearance, but that arbiter cut me off from the appeal process by convincing the agency's leadership to fire me. For those who do find themselves appealing a revocation to a panel, the reality remains that some, if not all, of the panelists belong to the same agency. They may even have been involved in the original revocation decision. In such situations, senior agency officials are often inclined to close ranks around the agency, particularly if some of them owe favors to others, as was true in my case. In light of the foibles of the agencies, decisions on security clearance revocations should be taken away from the agencies and given to an external entity.

Finally, government leaders must take great care when giving any individual authority to deny or revoke security clearances. My case and many others have shown that the power to make these decisions has too often been granted to people willing to use it as a weapon of retaliation, whether for their own benefit or as a favor to someone else. The basket of security personnel contains more than a few bad apples, people who chose the line of work less for the power to do good than for the power itself. As a wise security official once put it to me, the government must avoid empowering security officials who get a thrill from punishing employees, and instead must empower those who strive to prevent employees from taking punishable actions.

Public Ethics

Within the federal government, corruption is disturbingly common among inspectors general, chiefs of security, ethics attorneys, investigators, and other officials who are supposed to enforce ethical and legal codes. That fact explains why toxic government employees are often able to thrive while conscientious employees are often ensnared in Kafkaesque nightmares. The corrupt also wield greater influence than most Americans know in the awarding of contracts, grants, jobs, and other items of value that are funded by the $5 trillion federal budget.

More numerous than the corrupt are the federal employees who do not perpetrate corrupt acts themselves but merely tolerate them, usually because they either fear the perpetrators or are beholden to them. At USAID, the corrupt ran free because they intimidated and co-opted employees up and down the organizational structure. Putting a stop to the corruption requires leaders whose moral convictions make them impervious to the blandishments and bribes of the corrupt, and who are willing to hold others accountable for their misdeeds.

For leaders to enforce the laws and rules against corruption, they must believe in their hearts that the good of government and society takes precedence over their own interests. A few people may derive this belief from the U.S. Constitution or a secular ideology, but such "minds of peculiar structure," as George Washington once termed them, appear to be as scarce today as they were 250 years ago. Religion and nationalism have been the most effective of the forces that instill such civic-mindedness, and they have been most potent when woven into a society's cultural fabric, for abstract principles carry little force when no one appears to believe in or live by them. Neither religion nor nationalism has made humans perfect, and neither has been immune from abuse, but both have made humans better.

Among individuals who have blown the whistle on waste, fraud, and abuse, the influences of religion and nationalism have been particularly strong. Journalist Eamon Javers, in the course of producing a CNBC series on corporate whistleblowers, learned that a disproportionately large share of these whistleblowers were people of faith. "Religious people have an anchor to their personal identity that isn't caught up in their place in the corporate ladder," he was told by expert lawyers. For other corporate whistleblowers, national identity served as that anchor. The same has held true in the public sector—a large fraction of those willing to bear the risks of crying foul have been guided by the conviction that the demands of God and country supersede the interests of government bureaucracies.

God began falling out of fashion with large segments of the American intelligentsia during the nineteenth century, and country underwent a similar decline in the twentieth. Modernists and postmodernists have attempted to fill the void with ideologies, institutions, and enlightened experts, yet they have only made the problem worse, by replacing the authority of an immaculate God with the authority of flawed humans. The more sensible of American liberals now try to sew the country back together by replacing the threads of religion and nationalism with threads of justice, equality, and civil rights, while the more extreme press upon America's educational institutions the doctrine that our entire civilization should be transformed for the purpose of redistributing wealth and privilege from purported oppressor groups to purported victim groups. None of their nostrums have resonated with the mass of American society. Instead, the liberal elites have merely widened the cultural gulf separating them from the rest of America, the gulf that facilitated the rise of Trump.

As American secularists pushed God and religion out of the public sphere, liberals stopped speaking of faith in public settings. This silence, though, often resulted from fear of condemnation by militant secularists, rather than from a personal contempt for the divine. According to the Pew Research Center, close to 80 percent of American liberals still believe in God. Americans shouldn't allow themselves to be bullied by a small minority of atheists and agnostics.

America's founding fathers, and many Americans after them, believed religion to be the core of America's culture and the essential precondition for its virtuous government and society. "Of all the dispositions and habits which lead to political prosperity, religion and morality are indispensable supports," George Washington declared in his farewell address. "Reason and experience both forbid us to expect that national morality can prevail in exclusion of religious principle."

When the Frenchman Alexis de Tocqueville visited the United States in the 1830s, he observed that religion was the wellspring of American vitality, its principles guiding all facets of American life. "There is almost no human action," he wrote, "that does not arise from a very general idea that men have conceived of God, of his relations with the human race, of the nature of their souls, and of their duties toward those like them." In Tocqueville's view, religious belief was the key to moral behavior, which in turn was the key to the American preservation of freedom through limited government. Religion also imparted the intellectual humility that promoted openness to the ideas of others and wariness of concentrated power. "Only God can be all-powerful without danger, because his wisdom and justice are always equal to his power," asserted Tocqueville. "Thus there is no authority on earth so inherently worthy of respect, or invested with a right so sacred, that I would want to let it act without oversight or rule without impediment."

Well into the twentieth century, Americans of all political persuasions acknowledged the centrality of religion. "We have a profound religious faith," announced President Harry S. Truman, a liberal, in a 1949 radio address to the nation. "The basic source of our strength as a nation is spiritual. We believe in the dignity of man. We believe that he is created in the image of God, who is the Father of us all. It is this faith that makes us determined that every citizen in our own land shall have an equal right and an equal opportunity to grow in wisdom and in stature, and to play his part in the affairs of our Nation."

Leading the nation's elites away from baleful secular ideologies and back toward God and country requires focusing on the original source of the problem—higher education. The liberals and leftists responsible for purging God and country and Western Civilization from American higher education defended themselves by claiming that college wasn't a place for imbuing students with values. That argument repudiated centuries of American tradition, beginning in the colonial period, when the first colleges had been created to provide Christian education to clergy and laymen. With the formation of the United States, most American colleges and universities assumed the additional responsibility of promoting the principles of the republic and the nation, in recognition of Aristotle's dictum that what "most contributes to the permanence of constitutions is the adaptation of education to the form of government," because "the best laws, though sanctioned by every citizen of the state, will be of no avail unless the young are trained by habit and education in the spirit of the constitution." For most of the nation's history, it was common for college presidents to teach a course to all seniors on moral philosophy, centered on God, country, and Western Civilization.

As the professors of the mid-twentieth century swung their pickaxes into the traditional moral bedrocks, they didn't heed their own bromides about value-free education, but instead imposed new values, including secularism, multiculturalism, and socialism. They promoted the theory that American history was little more than the oppression of minorities, women, and the poor, and cited the need to halt the oppression as justification for enlarging the resources and authorities of the state. Disinterested in the founding of the United States, they ignored the dangers of unchecked governmental power that had led to the U.S. Constitution. They dismissed the foundational American tenet that a healthy society requires the free exchange of ideas, preferring instead to suppress voices that articulated viewpoints different from their own.

The off-Broadway colleges and universities are not in the business of teaching rightist ideology, as liberal critics often assume, but in the business that occupied mainstream institutions until the latter part of the twentieth century—teaching Western Civilization and its American branch. Rather than promoting the values of a particular ideology or political movement, they promote the values of a civilization whose belief in human fallibility cautions against the concentration of political, cultural, and intellectual power in a single political faction.

Elected officials can and should require all publicly funded colleges and universities to teach American history and civics courses to all students, as is presently done only in a small minority of colleges and universities. These courses should emphasize the strengths that give value to the nation and its government and bind the citizens together, from the separation of powers and the protection of civil liberties to the culture of pluralism and the spirit of philanthropy. Students need to understand people and events that embody these strengths. They also need to learn about American failures to live up to national ideals, not for the purpose of instilling guilt or justifying favoritism toward particular groups, but for the purpose of showing that the well-being of the United States depends upon moral reasoning and culture as well as political principles and institutions.

People sometimes ask me if my experience at USAID and the subsequent fallout caused me to lose faith in the American people or the American government. The first question is easier to answer than the second. I have spent enough time living distant from Washington, D.C., to know that the bulk of the American people retain the virtues that made the country into the most powerful in the world—patriotism, faith, self-reliance, generosity, industry, and thrift.

Only inside the federal government and academia have I found people who so adore big government and their own privileges that they will try to destroy people who get in their way. The actions of these people disappointed me, but they didn't destroy my confidence in America or its government. As a conservative, I didn't have especially high expectations, and as a historian, I knew that toxic people have always gravitated to government because it is the easiest place for them to function and thrive. The prevalence of toxicity in government serves as another reminder that our founders were wise to impose checks and balances on the government and to allow the replacement of officials through elections.

Even with those protections, however, the government needs virtuous people if it is to prevent the squandering of taxpayer dollars and the violation of the citizenry's rights by overreaching bureaucrats. No system of government can succeed if the government's people and its culture are corrupt to the core. When, in moments of deep despair, I have been tempted to write off the U.S. government and devote my remaining time on earth solely to friends and family, I have reminded myself that the freedom to live virtuously and prosperously depends on a national culture that prizes civic duty. Friends and family rank among God's most wonderful gifts, but like most gifts they can be spoiled by distortion and excess, as demonstrated by the many societies where the powerful have used the state to advance the interests of friends and relatives without concern for community or nation.

Plenty of Americans in both political parties have the mental fortitude to handle government's most frustrating aspects and the moral courage to stand up to its corruption. Some of them currently work for the federal government. Conscientious public servants will act as good stewards of governmental power if they have leaders who are committed to good stewardship, and who will protect them from the malignant forces that forever lurk in the human heart.

Acknowledgments

One of my few regrets in writing this book is that I could not name most of the individuals who came to my assistance. I had to leave out their identities to avoid exposing them to retaliation by those who had retaliated against me, most of whom have managed to stay in the federal government despite all the evidence of their complicity in criminal activities. The names of those who came in my hour of need will always occupy a special place in my heart.

Circumstances do permit me to thank a few people by name. Senator Charles Grassley, as an early champion of my cause, compelled an inspector general to redo a shoddy investigation and forced two federal agencies to answer critical questions they would have preferred not to answer. Kel McClanahan agreed to serve as my lawyer on gracious terms in spite of our different political persuasions, and he has been relentless in fighting government bureaucrats and lawyers on my behalf. At Encounter Books, Roger Kimball saw promise in this book from the start and moved it forward with the wonderful verve for which he is renowned.

The events described in this book imposed enormous stress on my family, and the pressure increased exponentially in the middle as the result of the diagnosis of my son Trent with cancer. Through mutual support and love, we have been able to persevere through the darkest of hours. We are especially grateful to all of the friends, relatives, and medical professionals who have carried burdens when we could not carry them all ourselves.

Index